The Jewish Derrida

The Library of Jewish Philosophy

The Jewish
Derrida

Gideon Ofrat

Translated from the Hebrew by **Peretz Kidron**

 Syracuse University Press

Copyright © 2001 by Syracuse University Press
Syracuse, New York 13244-5160

All Rights Reserved

First Edition 2001

01 02 03 04 05 06 07   7 6 5 4 3 2 1

Originally published in 1998 by Ha-academia, Jerusalem, as *Derrida Ha-Yehudi*.

The paper used in this publication meets the minimum requirements of American National Standard for
Information Sciences—Permanence of Paper for Printed Library Materials, ANSI Z39.48-1984.

Library of Congress Cataloging-in-Publication Data

Ofrat, Gideon.
     [Deridah ha-Yehudi. English]
     The Jewish Derrida / Gideon Ofrat ; translated from the Hebrew by Peretz Kidron.
         p. cm. — (The library of Jewish philosophy)
     Includes bibliographical references and index.
     ISBN 0-8156-2885-4 (cloth : alk. paper)
     1. Derrida, Jacques—Criticism and interpretation. 2. Philosophy. 3. Philosophy, Jewish.
    I. Title. II. Series.
    B2430.D484 O3713 2001
    194—dc21

                                            00-046202

Manufactured in the United States of America

Genealogy cannot commence with the father.
. . . I commence with love.
—Jacques Derrida, *Glas*

Name of father: Aimé (beloved)

Gideon Ofrat has written extensively on philosophy, postmodernism, and Israeli art and culture and is author of more than thirty books in Hebrew and English, including *Triple Darkness: Plato, Kant, and Kierkegaard, One Hundred Years of Art in Israel,* and *Yonder: Theology of the Obscure.* He has published numerous articles and essays on art and philosophy and has compiled or written more than fifty catalogues for Israeli artists and group exhibitions.

Contents

The Jewish Derrida

Pre-face

Taking aim at Derrida's philosophy from its Jewish dimension may look like a mis-take. "It's way off center!" pronounces the run-of-the-mill Derridean, pointing out that, of the torrent of books on Derrida's philosophy, not one has hitherto been written on "Derrida the Jew." Even at the more modest level of articles, chapters, or secondary topics of research, the Jewish aspect of his thought has caught the notice of a mere handful of philosophers and literary critics. It must also be conceded that, beyond a few fitful glimmers, the decisive sway Derrida's philosophy has exercised over Western creativity and critical ideas these past twenty years, called for no illumination of its Jewish aspect.[1]

It could thus be argued that "the Jewish Derrida" is a mere whimsy of mine, a topic that, albeit intriguing, remains marginal; a possible (and not uncommon) branch of Jewish studies—of Jewish history, Jewish mysticism, Jewish literature. Nevertheless, if only by virtue of the Derridean deduction regarding "the margins of philosophy" (as he named a work published in 1972) that are its core, I have granted myself the license to argue that Derrida cannot be thoroughly understood without elucidating the Jewish current running through his philosophy, right down to the scar of his circumcision.

Is that possible? There are entire books by Derrida ostensibly without so much as a hint of Jewish reference (Jewish authors, Jewish concepts, Jewish issues): *L'archéologie du frivole* (The archaeology of the frivolous) (1976); *Memoires: Pour Paul de Man* (Memoirs for Paul de Man) (1988a); *La verité en peinture* (The truth in painting) (1978b); *Du droit à la philosophie* (From right to philosophy) (1990a); *Apories* (1996a); *Khôra* (1993a), and so on. Indeed, many of Derrida's most important works seem indifferent to our topic, while others linger on it lightly (*De la grammatologie* [On grammatology] [1967a]; *La dissémination* [Dissemination] [1972a]; etc.). A few books are partially candid on the issue (various chapters of *L'écriture et la différence* [Writing and difference] [1967b]). More recent

1

volumes, written as Derrida was increasingly attracted by the ideas of Sigmund Freud or (especially) of Emanuel Lévinas, give the subject a marked degree of attention. I refer to works such as: *Mal d'archive* (Archive fever) (1995a), *Le monolinguisme de l'autre* (The monolingualism of the other) (1996c), or *Adieu* (1997a). Indeed, his work of recent years seems to have confirmed the eddies of a certain Jewish undercurrent (strictly limited, as we shall note) in Derrida's consciousness and his philosophy.

All the same, and without detracting from Derrida's relatively extensive discussion of Jewish thinkers (Emanuel Lévinas, Walter Benjamin, Franz Rosenzweig, Karl Marx, Sigmund Freud, Hannah Arendt, etc.) and modern Jewish writers (Paul Celan, Edmond Jabès, Franz Kafka, etc.), one must conclude that overtly Jewish themes in his writings represent quite a meager "ratio." This impression is reinforced by the fact that Martin Heidegger—the philosopher most widely present and influential in Derrida's thinking—does not concern himself with Judaism or its component elements.

This is all quite true. Nevertheless, Judaism does lurk beneath the surface. Is this Judeo-centrism? Is Judaism there as essence, logocentric substance, primary source of truth in Derrida's philosophy?

Ostensibly, such an assumption would seem anti-Derridean. For in his heroic battle with Western metaphysics, Derrida sets his sights on demolishing an idea pursued ever since Plato: the notion of an essential center, of light, of transcendental subjectivity or objectivity. Derrida's philosophy unmasks the various metaphorical aspects of a traditional metaphysical center (in itself innocent of any structuralism, and therefore eluding all structures)—sun, idea, god, soul, archetype, phallus, and so on—as an embellishment concealing nothingness, or imperial regalia within which there is no emperor. The muted logos (speech) is the silenced deity, the absent phallus, and so forth; it is a black sun (as in the chapter "Ellipsis" in *L'écriture et la différence*. See below p. 000). Now, we add "Judeo-centrism" to this list as though Judaism likewise is doomed to nothingness and obscurity. Yes, indeed, it belongs there, insofar as Judaism is endowed with centrality and profundity, in consciousness and culture alike, as it was so endowed in the culture (society, family, childhood) in which Derrida was brought up, and from which he broke away. After all, was it not he who taught us that taking leave of something is a precondition for recognizing its significance? Was it not he who impressed upon us that significance rests upon exile from a primary truth that turns away from us? Here we have the basic Derridean paradox: the practical yearning for primary truth is a condition for forfeit of primary truth and its exchange for fragments of the secondary substitute. This is "the originality of the secondary," to use Derrida's term. Is that the story of Derrida's relationship with his Jewishness?

We ponder: does Derrida's work not stem from the question of the possibility (impossibility) of evoking and revealing the Jewish identity, its elevation from obscurity to the light of day? Is this not the "ultimate," the "source" (essence, *eidos, logos*) of Derrida's writings? These are highly heretical questions in relation to this book's hero and his philosophy. Nevertheless, what could easily be taken for ethnocentric coercion, if not to say narrow-minded nationalism, will seek, by means of this modest work, to establish itself as the philosopher's stone, even if it drags the writer down into the ocean depths.

What does Jewishness mean to the seventy-one-year-old French-Algerian Jew going by the name of Jacques Derrida? One possible answer is: childhood memories, the homes of his parents and grandparents, transcendentally castrating fatherhood, the tension between Exile and spatial center (Jerusalem, the Temple), the Promise of Redemption (Messiah), belonging to the immutable, and a link to the absolute (the Torah as God's Word). Conversely, there is Derrida's biography: orphanhood, cultural estrangement, lingual estrangement, divorce from tradition, a grueling peregrination between texts and countries (universities). Within these contexts, it makes sense to ask: is Judaism an essence from which Derrida was exiled? Is his writing perforce philosophical therapy, conveying the message that there is no cure? In other words: isn't Derrida's philosophy the philosophical corroboration of the fragments of Jewish identity from which it grew?

Once its center had been uprooted and it had been derailed along the return route to its concealed starting point, the Derridean identity no longer advanced in circular motion: never again would the spirit return after emerging from itself, never again would it revert from its otherness to itself, charged with a heightened awareness of itself. The Hegelian circle had collapsed, to be breached from every quarter. That which emerges from itself to its otherness has been condemned to otherness and perdition. And he who wishes to return to his own past, to tell his life's story, to rummage there after his lost fleece—what is to become of him? In other words, what is the destiny of a man like Jacques Derrida, in quest of the "ashes," the embers, the remnants of the fire, the relics of a general holocaust—of intellect overall and of his own intellect in particular (the intellect that illuminates and scorches its bearers)? The pages to come will testify that he was condemned to ashes, to absence, to memory, to mourning, to death, without any Hegelian phoenix of intellect to rise reborn from its debris. The destiny of Jesus of Nazareth, restored to life to ascend from his sepulcher to the heavens, is not imprinted upon the philosophical consciousness of Derrida, the Jew whose crucifixion is relentless and lifelong. His torment does not entail a redemptive intellectual elevation. Derrida, who seeks to redeem memory, past, ashes, is thus utterly distinct from the futuristic redemption offered by Christian salvation and its philosophical adherents.

Derrida reverts repeatedly to the past. The annals of philosophy are his paths in the wilderness, often his odyssey to his autobiographical past. In works like *Circonfession* (1991a), *La carte postale* (Postcard) (1980) and *Le monolinguisme de l'autre* (Monolingualism of the other) (1996c) (and, we would add, at the source of his self-torment) the philosopher is stuck midway between the objective destination of absolute reason and the particularist uniqueness of an autobiography soaring to its climax at the subjective event of the nonrepeatable circumcision. At the autobiographical level, Derrida seems to be in quest of his identity in a regressive odyssey doomed to failure, of the type inevitable in any psychoanalysis (the inviolable, impenetrable place, *Résistances de la psychanalyse* [Resistance to psychoanalysis] [1996e]. His odyssey across the ocean of writing signs—between St. Augustine's *Confessions*, an untiring correspondence with a secret beloved (*La carte postale* [1980]), texts of other philosophers, and so on—must inevitably reach its destination at the Isle of the Dead. Since embarking on his hermeneutic course (his works of 1967: *L'écriture et la différence, De la grammatologie*) Derrida has consistently sought to convince us that—owing to the superficiality, the artificiality, and the repetition of the writing signs, each sign being a trace of speech (logos) that is absent—writing is the death principle of being; that all writing is a court sentence of remoteness, of grave, of exile, of destruction, and of otherness. As primary speech is antecedent to writing (Derrida deals incessantly with the mythical and theological aspects of a hoary contention argued all the way from Plato and Aristotle to de Saussure) the writing signs mislead, precluding any return to the origin. In the course of his monumental writing, Derrida therefore is unable to pinpoint his sources (his primary-unifying identity). This merely blows him further off course of the return of his spirit to itself. He who is identical with himself is shown up again and again as other than himself. The sun does not reveal its light, God does not show benevolence, Judaism remains inaccessible. The philosopher's lot is nothing but darkness and ashes.

Derrida won't give up. His books are nothing if not reiterated attempts to cling to the altar of philosophical generality (in effect, to come to grief there). His multitude of books are a multiplicity of ashes. Regard the pages of Geoffrey Bennington's *Derrida* (1991a): in the upper portion, the principle of general reason—objective, absolute, universal; Otherness in the form of Bennington analyzing Derrida's writings. In the lower portion of each page (the "Derridabase," to adopt Bennington's term) the principle of the subjective individual, Derrida's autobiographical confessions. No, we shall not be led astray: there is no Hegelian dialectic between upper and lower portion, between genealogy and reason, between biology and logic, and so on; accordingly, there is no Hegelian (or Christian) levitation (*Aufhebung*) toward one form or other of transcendental absolute. Not at all, for the private confession has no substance outside of its narrative existence, and the story is doomed to fragmentation and death.[2] The absolutely spiritual, in the sense of origin and objective, is condemned to deconstructive collapse into chance the moment it is formulated as story. "The autobiography of 'Jacques Derrida'," writes Robert Smith, "takes place within this institution or ritual. It could be described as the institution of the ongoing death of chance that keeps alive in its energy for further adventure."[3] Indeed, from the moment of its conception as autobiography, the story of Derrida's past (i.e., his identity) is doomed to fracturing and internal antagonisms. It is not fortuitous that he seizes upon the texts of "others" (it is beyond Derrida to tell his own story without resort to reading and interpretation of philosophical and literary texts). His clutch at the text of the Other leaves him in a state of inextricable division between the personal and particular on the one hand, and on the Other, a content not entirely his own.

The confessions in his autobiographical books, commencing with his "circonfession," hinge upon the technique of stressing and intensifying that which is unrepeatable and personal, while losing it. As I already noted, shaping the confession in the literal—in the language of signs, in writing—does not permit the absolute to reveal itself. Thus, he who renders up his confession is separated from himself forever. Henceforth, he exists in his own self-vivisection, constituting himself by violent separation from himself. The confessor-author resembles God: dividing himself from himself, exiled from self (*L'écriture et la différence*). In other words, each confession is an adventure seeking redemption from fracturing in the unified; from the doubtful in certainty; from literature in scripture. But at the climax of his expression of the rift as confession-story-history, out come the constraints of literature: the expanse of differential signs, scattering abysses of nothingness between one sign and the next. The absolute is above and beyond.

The tranquil, concentrated absoluteness of the identity, whether Jewish or otherwise, cannot therefore be pinpointed in a lurch into the past. He who is identical with himself will be shattered to smithereens by the other-than-himself. Here is a paradox: identity is that which is reiterated, whereas writing prevents it precisely because of the reiteration (sign). That which is reiterated will not be reiterated. Even if it is, it will find itself smashed, defective, disfigured, robbed of foreskin; truly, a blow below the belt.

We are at a starting point. We stand before an open gate, venturing within and proceeding along our way even though we shall never reach our destination. We meander in the tracks of a Jewish wanderer, tracing his footsteps, which are not easy to identify. The way is bumpy, replete with chasms and fissures, and the wanderer is crippled and wounded. He is a different Jew, bearing the bundle of a different Judaism. Is it the personal tale of an other? The emasculating path a traditional Algerian Jew treads toward a secular Franco-European culture? The son's path to an impossible encounter with an absent father? Accordingly, we shall ask: Are we encountering Judaism as theological generalization of the individual's distress? Expanding the personal rift into the infinite dimensions of metaphysical rift? Is Jacques Derrida sucked into the mortal abyss of modernism, there to excavate his own abysslike pit of postmodernism?

Derrida is not the first to blaze this trail: the *via dolorosa* is a well-beaten track. God's remoteness and man's alienation have been etched into the tablets of culture for hundreds of years. Suffice it if we recall Giambattista Vico and the dramatic distinction he drew (*The New Science*, 1725) between "the world of nature" (eternity, truth, God) and "the world of nations" (culture, language, history, relativity); the dismissal of the human consciousness from "the thing into itself" (Kant, *Critique of Pure Reason* 1781); our banishment from innocence and unity to remoteness and alienation (Schiller, *Naïve and Sentimental Poetry*, 1795); the virtually impassable chasm of consciousness that Schelling (*System of Transcendental Idealism*, 1880) uncovered between subject (consciousness, freedom) and object (nature, necessity); Nietzsche's Dionysian darkness; Heidegger's recalcitrance of a hidden truth of being; Sartre, Camus, and others and alienation, exile, absurdity, darkness. The reader could justly say: model way stations on the nocturnal path of absence, refusal, and nothingness, scattered along the course of Western thought, from its origins with Plato (the human knowledge that is neither perfect nor attainable) and Aristotle (who cast the absent into the physically existent) right up to the present day.[4]

Cannot it be justly claimed as well that rupture, the absence of God, the rift—are among the basic experiences of Judaism, whether ancient or modern? "Rabbi Shimeon Bar Yochai teaches that the Holy Name and all His appellations are contained in a cabinet, Rabbi Hona said and taught that the tablets and fragments of tablets are contained within the Holy Ark of the Torah."[5] The segment is not separate from the whole, nor the Torah from its fragments; the divine message is dumb and incomprehensible: "Who is like unto Thee among the gods, oh Lord, who is like unto Thee among the dumb, oh Lord."[6] Judaism of exiled man, exiled God, Judaism of inflamed and divisive contradictions, Judaism of intimacy along with remoteness and darkness: "What is it we refer to when we speak of the eclipse of the Divine light, that is in effect at this time?" demands Martin Buber, adding: "On this question, we make the significant assumption that we can lift to God our 'spiritual eye', or should we say: our essential eye, as we can lift to the sun our 'corporal eye'; and that something is liable to intervene between our own being and his being, as between earth and heaven."[7]

All this holds true, without ever mentioning the Kabbalah, with its mystery of reduction, fragmentation, the sparks and the averted countenance of God, or the tales of the Hassidim, with their experiences of death, unattainable metaphysical yearning, and existential orphanhood.

Multitudinous are the footsteps along the *via dolorosa* toward truth, god, and death—in Western thought, in Judaism, and in other cultures. Derrida is but one more "secular pilgrim" on the winding path up to the empty Holy of Holies. For his writings are a series of interpretative encounters with antecedent philosophers, or evocations of spirits from the domains of death in the Western cultural memory. After all, what is Derridean philosophy if not an exposure of the transcendental wound, bloody and festering in the corpus of Western thought from its very outset?

That being so, the reader may wonder what all the fuss is about? What are the tidings that Derrida bears? Wherein lies his uniqueness? Possibly, it lies in the radical reraking of truth, justice, God, and death in the single fell swoop of his undertaking; possibly, in the great avalanche that demolishes all fences between the disciplines of truth and language (philosophy, poetry, law, prayer, etc.) in the abyss-of-nothingness that constitutes the truth and language? But—dare we forget—Derrida's uniqueness stems also from his clarity of expression and tragic puissance, which remove the human tongue from the certainty of representation of truth, applying the selfsame removal to all claims to truth. Above all, his uniqueness lies in his exposure of the death lurking within the constructions of culture. Is it not conceivable that the fundamental Derridean experience is "the dance of death": the dance of the spirits at nightfall?

We face a different encounter with the tomb devils of Expressionism, with romantic devils, with the medieval *danse macabre*. In this, Derrida is different, and his encounter (if at all feasible?) is different. For we find in his writings no hope of the authentic, spontaneous Buberian encounter between man and God. The salvation of Judgment Day is likewise absent from his writings. The fissure is opened in the divine existence itself, while messianism is the impossible visitation of a ghost. Just as he disputes Plato's metaphysical sun, so likewise does he decline the optimism accompanying the Enlightenment, or the faith in reason after the manner of Kant (the

Kantian "moral imperative," for example, bearing within its utopian reach the seed of its own downfall and defeat by violence, and so on). Derrida's writings thus recall the others: his writing is linked to others and is deeply indebted to others. But the "together" explains the "separate," the link elucidates the remoteness. That is the experience of the Derridean odyssey: bringing near and farther, joining and separating, reviving and killing.

1

The Last Jew

I am the end of Judaism," wrote Derrida in 1991 in *Circonfession;* "[the end] of a certain type of Judaism," he added; and elsewhere: "I am the last Jew; I merely demolish the world on the pretext of creating truth." (178) The latter comment further points up the intellectual provocation of "the last Jew" claim, confronting the reader with a unique challenge: to regard Derrida's "destructiveness" (whose pretext is the creation of truth) as interpretation of his statement "I am the last Jew." To put it simply (although simplicity and Derrida are mutually exclusive), we face an equation between Jewish identity of a certain type and deconstruction (which is nothing if not "creation of truth").

"I am the last Jew" is a statement typically Derridean in its susceptibility to conflicting interpretations: (*A*) I am the last Jew, for Judaism is at an end and I am its last remnant; accordingly, I may be the only one capable of bearing witness to it and perhaps, offering it salvation, or (*B*) I am the last Jew, that is, the last person one could call a Jew. In other words, I am entirely remote from Judaism. How is one to unravel this knot? It can't be done. One is left entangled, perhaps even trussed up as sacrificial victim, in what Derrida terms (in English) a "double bind." The more you unravel one knot, the more you are ensnarled in the other. And indeed, in an interview on the subject of [his] Judaism, Derrida referred to the dilemma, declaring " 'I am the last Jew' can be understood—and in any case I understand it in numerous ways: simultaneously 'I am a bad Jew . . . but also 'I am the end of Judaism,' that is, the death of Judaism, but also its only chance of survival, I am the last who can say it, the others don't even deserve to say it, they've forfeited the right, because to say 'I am a Jew' one should perhaps say how hard it is to say 'I am a Jew'."[1]

He cannot help being aware of being provocative when he proclaims "I am the last Jew." (Some would say he has a knack for intellectual provocation, a bent Geoffrey Bennington identifies as his philosophical desire to quit philosophy—"*désir de sortir de la philosophie*" [G. Bennington, *Jacques*

Derrida (Paris: 1991), 22.].) Indeed, Derrida concedes outright that "there is a kind of hubris in that sentence." (Weber, 101). Perhaps only a man like Jesus was entitled to utter such words, Derrida explained, for "Jesus was 'the last Jew'" (ibid.). Derrida does not elucidate his meaning, but his large preoccupation with Hegel and the dialectic evolvement (*Aufhebung*—elevation) of Christianity out of Judaism (*Glas*, 1974a) may reasonably be taken to explain the claim that he refuses not so much to the death of Judaism, as to the incessant evolution of the human spirit. This view perceives Judaism as a dynamic idea, and Derrida proffers his own consciousness and identity as the beginning and end of variable concepts whose variability is facilitated exclusively by virtue of the contradiction at work within and outside them; in other words: Judaism is perceived in the light of its Christian other (its negation, its end—"Jesus was the last Jew"). The substance is denied, the one expelled from the system is therefore the one who safeguards its identity. Hence, we have the issue of Judaism "versus" Western culture.

Indeed, in response to the suggestion from his interviewer, Elisabeth Weber, that Judaism be regarded as the obscure, repressed condition, the "crypt" for the feasibility of the Western system of thought (i.e., as Otherness) Derrida replied: "Yes."[2] All the same, we should not forget that Derrida is no Hegelian. Derrida is a Derridean. The human spirit has neither beginning nor end. The spirit has its fissures, graves, ruins, and chasms. Accordingly, in relation to his statement "I am the last Jew" Derrida regaled his interviewer with what may be considered a key declaration for comprehension of deconstruction: "There is no 'last.' Just as there is no 'first,' no origin" (90).

How can one confirm Judaism (even if it is "different") without acknowledging its source (the authority of the Torah, of divine law) or "end" ("Judgment Day")? It is possible, even if the concepts of Judaism are condemned to a degree of "denting." "I regularly express the concepts of Judaism in an oblique way," Derrida admitted to me.[3] All the same, he is condemned to relentless preoccupation with the concepts of Judaism and the issue of Jewishness, being aware that the question will never be resolved and the concepts will never be defined finally or unequivocally. Thus, on a pseudo-Hegelian circular course (the circle of the spirit emerging from itself to its contradiction, so as to return to itself), which we shall come to know as the foreskin route, Derrida circles around his different Judaism, a Judaism unresolved and incapable of resolution: "the compulsion to 'circle around' is also the experience of the impossible circle, or turning: the impossibility of closing the circle. One turns about because one is unable to stop the circle. It can't return to itself. The impossibility of returning to self . . . but also in the sense of awareness" (Weber, *Questions au judaïsme*, 81).

The circular movement of the consciousness, the circular movement of life, the movement of history, whether individual or collective.

Derrida's Jewishness intersected (like a cross!) in several instances with his biography, particularly the Algerian chapter (1930–49) which was, of course, crucial in shaping his identity (his powerful links with the Algerian period of his life are illustrated in the term he coined: "nostalgeria").[4] Right from the outset indeed, Derrida's life was a mixture of tradition and secularism, Jewish and non-Jewish (Algerian, French, European, Western) identity. He retains fleeting memories of Hebrew, or, as he testifies: "It turns out that I don't know Hebrew, or very little, I have a very poor knowledge of Jewish history or the texts of Jewish culture. This ignorance requires me . . . to shift to the metaphorical, rhetorical, allegorical dimension of Judaism. Circumcision, for example."[5] Recollections of his father officiating at Jewish funerals, or hoisting the sacrificial chicken aloft, various festivals, the *shofar* (a ritually sounded ram's horn) blown at festivals, a circumcision, the Torah "finger," and various other flashes of memory of traditions mingle with the modern and secular lifestyle of a bourgeois Algerian family, following the patterns of French culture in virtually all its respects. These glimpses of reminiscence surface repeatedly throughout the numerous ramifications of Derrida's philosophy; unconsciously functioning as quasi spirits coming to press their demands of the "son." Characteristic and significant is Derrida's testimony that, while studying an album of photographs of Heidegger, the philosopher's features suddenly seemed to him to resemble the head of an aging Algerian Jew (*La carte postale*, [1980], 204).

Although born into a family that observed Jewish tradition, at the age of five he was sent to a secular Jewish elementary school at El-Biar. Promptly upon the rise of the Vichy regime in France in 1940, Algerian Jews were stripped of their French citizenship. Like other institutions in Algeria, often far more blatantly than in France itself, the El-Biar school underwent a rapid process of Petainization whose anti-Semitic offshoots were plain to see (inter alia, educational and judicial institutions were purged of Jews). In 1942—a year after entering secondary school at Ben Aknoun near El-Biar—Derrida was expelled when the Jewish *numerus clausus* was slashed from 14 percent to 7 percent. "French culture was not created for *petits Juifs* (little Jews)!"—that sentence would long reverberate in Derrida's ears. The anti-Semitic climate obliged him to stay away in hiding for close on a year, forcing him to wait eleven months until he could re-register at the Émile Maupas school. Recalling these events later, he would write a sentence whose form and substance could be linked with many of his ideas: "Isn't this the reason that I always adopted a stance to provoke them and give them the greatest desire, always on the verge, to expel me again?" (*La carte postale* [1980], 97).

The traumatic events depicted here (and mentioned repeatedly in *La carte postale*, *Circonfession*, etc.) left painful scars on his soul—it was no mere chance that he would associate Judaism with injury[6]—and endowed him with a particular sensitivity towards any Otherness per se. Those scars may explain his refusal—within the family unit at least—to accept the uniqueness of Judaism.[7] "Not just in the texts you mention, but in everything I may do or say, there is a 'Of course, I'm a Jew!' or 'Of course, I'm not a Jew' . . . and a way of living simultaneously slightly maladroit and ironical, the condition of the Jew."[8]

As a philosopher who writes copiously on theological topics, can his perception of God be defined as "God of the Jews"? Again we have the inevitable dual answer: Yes (see below in the chapter "Countenance Averted") and No. His mother's query as to whether he believed in God elicited the reply that his God has other appellations, an entirely private God, not a superior voice addressing him, or Holy Ghost, and so forth; rather, his God is a well-guarded secret that would never be revealed to him, a secret from whose solution he had been banished (*Circonfession*, 1991a, 146–47). Elsewhere, he has written of the atheist God, the other ego dwelling within him, "infinitely smaller than me and infinitely larger than me" (201).

That being so, one lives in duality; in other words, in a rupture:

"I am a kind of Marrano [Spanish Jews who kept their faith behind a sham conversion to Christianity. Trans.] of French Catholic culture, and I also have my Christian body, inherited from St. Augustine. . . . I am one of those Marranos who, even in the intimacy of their own hearts, do not admit to being Jewish . . . because I doubt it" (160).

But again—he does not doubt altogether: on Yom Kippur in New York, Derrida stalks out of a restaurant near the Museum of Modern Art, to make for a Reform synagogue. As part of his link with death and the dead (a motif that will likewise reappear in the chapters to come) Derrida prefers to speak of the Judaism of relics, or the relics of Judaism. Accordingly, his own Judaism can be understood as the Judaism of the dead, or dead Judaism, or in fact, both: "*Ich bleibe also jude* [German: "So, I remain a Jew"] that is to say nowadays, whatever remains of Judaism in this world, Europe and elsewhere, and in this remnant I am just someone to whom so little remains that he is, fundamentally, dead . . . I await Elijah and the resurrection of the dead" (279).

The experience of the living dead; the experience of the absent, present merely as witness; the testimony of the blind, whose eyes are unfit to see, merely to shed tears; the experience of destruction and expectation; a "Western Wall" internalized to the personal, existential level: Derrida repeatedly underwent this experience whenever he paced the streets of a city he loved, weeping at its walls. Thus, returning from a visit to London, he took the Metro, getting off at the St. Michel station to pick up his car, walking along rue de l'Abbé-de-l'epée. The street name, honoring the founder of the school for the deaf-and-dumb located there, made Derrida ponder on the deafness and dumbness of man and God, as well as on the metaphysics of human infirmity: "One thinks of what could be the prayer of the deaf-and-dumb, and those who only have eyes to weep with. . . . Therefore, it's a kind of a Wailing Wall."[9]

Are these relics of Judaism? Of a dead Judaism? Or perhaps, of a different Judaism, a living Judaism founded upon a new and different interpretation of Judaism, a Judaism arising out of its nothingness, out of remoteness from it? The chapters ahead will indeed deal with this other Judaism, the Judaism of injury, fissure, and the grave. In other words: Derrida's Jewishness cannot be gauged by the degree of his immersion in the written sources of Judaism, certainly not by his adherence to *halacha* (law; the rules that govern Jewish life); rather, it is gauged precisely by the transcendence of the dark chasm that he identifies, lying between himself and his Judaism. Thus, an astonishing intimacy with Jewish sources emerges in domains where it is questionable whether he had a profound acquaintance with Jewish texts. In discussing Edmond Jabès's *Book of Questions,* Derrida drew a connection between the author's theological reflections and elements of the Kabbalah: "Negativity in God, exile as writing, the life of the letter, are all already in the Kabbalah. . . . And Jabès is conscious of the Kabbalistic resonances of his book" (*Writing and Difference* ["L'écriture et la différence"] [Chicago: Univ. of Chicago Press, 1978, 74). Likewise, Derrida's ceremonial leavetaking of his dying mother is accompanied by the singing of the four Jewish sages of ancient times who "entered the 'fruit grove'" of mysticism (*Circonfession* [1991a], 220) [The Hebrew *pardess,* "fruit grove," is simultaneously an acronym representing the four vital elements of mystic interpretation of Scripture. Trans.] Furthermore, in the early 1980s Derrida wrote: "I discover the four-sided model of the paradisaical discourse of Jewish rationalism . . . even if the *pardess* of that partition . . . [is] in my blood" (106). And accordingly, the concept of "the secret," which we will get to know extensively as a key concept in Derridean hermeneutics and theology, is understood by Derrida as a "Kabbalist" term (ibid). Similarly, he transmutes the apples from this "grove" into the apple trademark on the Macintosh computer into which he types his books. Thus, evidence from Jewish sources is harbored alongside critiques that refuse to acknowledge Derrida's philosophy as Jewish thought.[10] Studying Derrida's *La dissémination* (1972a), Jerusalem Kabbalah scholar Moshe Idel detected an undeclared mention of the notions of the prophetic Kabbalist mystic Rabbi Avraham Abulafia that appear to have come to Derrida's attention by way of a book by Gershom Scholem.[11] Idel claims that, in order to decipher the Torah's coded message, Abulafia's prophetic "Kabbalah" relies upon "a higher inner rationale," which resorts to letters and their permutations in place of concepts. This is therefore restoration of the text to the primary condition of separate letters that are perceived as divine appellations. And Idel adds: "In this context, it should be added that Derrida blended Abulafia's logical outlook with Stephane Mallarmé's definition of the tasks of poetry. In his *Dissémination* he writes in relation to the Kabbalah: 'The science of the combination of letters is the higher science of inner logic, and it combines into an Orphic elucidation of the world.'"[12]

Conversely, a Jewish philosophical publication—*Network (Journal of the Postmodern Jewish Philosophy)*, no. 4 (1996), published on the Internet at Drew University, Madison, New Jersey—included a critical text disputing the identification of deconstruction with the spirit of Judaism. According to this argument, the participation of humanity overall in the macrocosmic spirit (the Kabbalist notion of partnership of spirits in the spirit of primeval Adam, and the inclusion in every soul of a spark of the original spirit) entails proof of the Jewish faith by the possibility of recognizing "the light," and of course, by the possibility of grasping the original meaning of holy Scripture. We have here therefore a depiction of Judaism (we should add: Judaism in an Orthodox rendering, sealed and petrified) contradicting the Derridean position, which postulates the impossibility of reverting to primal speech.

One way or another, Derrida's text itself is like a field of signifiers open to a variety of interpretations, it being questionable whether these signifiers have it within their power to confirm "the real Derrida" and his Judaism.

2

The Mono-identity of the Other

Derrida's *Le monolinguisme de l'autre* (published in Paris in September 1996 [1996c]) bears an inner "infirmity" soon revealed in the sub-title: *ou la prothèse d'origine* (or, the artificial limb of origin). Readers who had come to know Derrida as an "injured" man whose injury will never heal, were now presented with a wooden leg. It is no trivial matter to make your way among fragments, abysses, and ruins while injured and dragging an artificial limb (a deformed leg like that of Oedipus?).

Derrida's readers find themselves in the throes of an anti-Derridean experience, as they confirm a reflective relationship between a man's history and his thoughts. Along came this book and set the analogies vigorously: a French Algerian, tattered of identity and rootless, neither here nor there, within the culture and beyond it, within his Judaism and without it, formulates his dissociation, cultural and autobiographical, as universal truth of culture and language. Although most of Derrida's books translate the death of his own father into the overall postmetaphysical experience of the eternal disappearance of the heavenly father (God, *logos*), this work extends the dumbness of his mother, dying in Nice in the early 1990s, into the overall universal lingual experience of the "dumbness" of the mother-tongue.

Readers who had plowed their way through works like *Circonfession* and *Khôra* had already encountered the theological and ontological metaphorization of the mother. Derrida's theme now is a man's relationship with his "mother" tongue, and his forcible "exile" from his language, even when it is his "mother-tongue." Derrida's orphanhood from father and mother condemns him to solitude, which envelops this book in an extraordinary existential melancholy. Readers discover a tragic philosopher, "the Franco-Maghrebian martyr who, ever since birth . . . has chosen nothing, and understood nothing . . . and who still suffers and bears witness" (*Le mono-linguisme de l'autre*, pp. 39–40). The fundamental claim "I have but one language, and it isn't mine"(15) is rooted in a profound sense of dislocation that also affects Derrida's experience of the abyss separating him from his

15

Jewish culture. No, it isn't exactly an abyss: rather, a link and a remoteness, unity and division, a philosophical contradiction clinging to the philosopher's thinking, just like the contradiction expressed in the words "I have but one language and it isn't mine." An "is" that is not, an "is not" that is. The monolinguism of a speaker whose language is not his own matches the mono-identity of a man whose identity is not his own, instead belonging to the "other."

Le monolinguisme de l'autre originated in a symposium held in Louisiana, USA, in 1992, attended by Francophiles, some of North African origin (such as Abdelkebir Khatibi, and Derrida). Inevitably, the topic of the cultural and lingual identity of the "Franco-Maghrebi" came up. "Our question," Derrida pointed out "is forever identity" (*Le mondinguisme de l'autre*, 31), resting content with an understanding of "identity" to denote nationality, while simultaneously uniting identity-by-citizenship with lingual identity (35). Abruptly, the 1940 trauma of being stripped of his citizenship resurfaced. A social entity whose civil identity is arbitrarily taken or restored by the dominant society remains condemned to eternal exile from its identity, and therefore, too, from its language. The language is no longer the natural possession of its speaker; the language will never be "his," argued Derrida; it is forever "conquered" or "conqueror" in a quasi-colonial process (45). Your language is the Other's language of which you have taken possession as your own ("possession" to a limited degree, that will never attain to the "natural" unity between an individual and his or her language). It [taking possession of the Other's language] is an underlying colonialism of culture (47, 68). His language, our language, is always the language of the Other, and hence, the substantive alienation (48).

Such alienation and estrangement do not make for harmony between the individual and his identity. At most, they generate yearnings for identification with the language—conqueror and conquered—that will never be yours. This experience of "colonialist" estrangement (at the autobiographical level, signifying the ban on studying Arabic, or Hebrew; or the Berber tongue) also leaves the French language as an alien and remote objective (*Le monolinguisme de l'autre*, p. 57). Thus, what appeared to be the French "mother tongue" of Algerian Jews (and of Derrida) turned out to be a "forbidden" language: "For I could never call French, this language I'm speaking with you, 'my mother tongue'" (61) The mother tongue is a borrowed language, quoted and appropriated. In contrast with Abdelkebir Khatibi, who speaks of the loss of his mother tongue (64–65) Derrida argues the absence of a mother tongue, the dumbness of the mother (65). The mother has become an alien entity, domineering, obsessive, and forever remote: "The metropolis, the Capital-City-Mother-Motherland, the city of the mother tongue, here we have a location appearing, without being, a distant land, near yet far" (73). Thus, mother tongue is transformed into substitute-mother-tongue, the language of the Other. Between the language studied at school and the mother tongue lies an abyss Derrida would never bridge, even when, at nineteen, he crossed the sea separating Algeria from France. His awareness of his Franco-Algerian accent is the other aspect of his ambition to acquire a pure and perfect French, better than that spoken by the Frenchmen "over there" (81).

That which holds true for Derrida's lingual identity probably applies equally to his Jewish identity. The hyperbole of duality involved in: "remote from . . . and yearning for . . . ," Derrida would write, is also the duality of "a little French Jew from Algeria . . . more *and* less French . . . but also more *and* less Jewish than all the French, all the Jews, and all the Jews of France" (*Le monolinguisme de l'autre*, 83). "A little French Jew from Algeria," he was equally remote and alienated from "his own" Jewish culture: "Strangers to Jewish culture: alienation of the spirit, a boundless estrangement . . . Such in any case was the radically uncultured state from which, without doubt, I have never emerged" (88). At the same time, in referring to the Arabic and Berber languages he was barred from learning, he would appear to be writing about Hebrew: "I sometimes wonder whether that unknown language is not my language of choice. . . . I like to hear it principally outside of any 'communication', in the poetic solemnity of song or prayer" (71).

Indeed, the assimilation of Algerian Jews, as Derrida testifies, condemns Judaism to a state of virtual death, respiratory arrest. "I bear, in negative fashion if I may put it so, the heritage of that amnesia which I have never had the courage, the strength, the means to resist" (*Le monolinguisme de l'autre*, p. 89). Accordingly, he adds: "I think I had dealings with a Judaism of 'external signifiers'" (ibid.). Furthermore, just as French was internalized as the language of the Other, the Jewish religion, too, was internalized as the religion of the Other, being imbued with Christian characteristics, internal and external (copying the church): the *bar mitzvah* ceremony is called "communion"; the rabbi's robes resemble those of the priest; circumcision is "baptism," and so on. And all this had to be borne without recourse to refuge in the identity of a "Jewish" language, neither Yiddish nor Ladino being current in the North African Jewish communities, and Hebrew not studied ("I don't recall anyone ever learning Hebrew at the *lycée*" [59]

Derrida identifies this consciousness of estrangement from roots and tradition, of amnesia, with deconstruction. The eternal estrangement between writing and origin is a person's sentence of estrangement between his culture and its sources. In the chapters to come, we shall again note how the hermeneutic outlook, which deals in lingual interpretation, lingual truth, lingual source, translation, and so forth, bears with it a theological and cultural outlook that condemns Jacques Derrida's Jewish identity as artificial limb and injury.[1]

3

Shibboleth of Evil

Before we ever get around to Derrida's theological autobiography *Circonfession* (1991a), the flashes of autobiographical confession that are a regular feature of his multitudinous books reveal that his middle name is Elie (Elijah) (*Ulysse gramophone* [1987d]; that his father's name was Haim-Aimé (*Mal d'archive* [1995a]); that his mother's middle name was Esther (*La carte postale* [1980]) and that his Algerian grandfathers were Moïse and Abraham (*Circonfession* [1991]). His *Memoires d'aveugle* also disclose that his father enjoyed officiating at funeral ceremonies of the Algierian Jewish community.

In 1996, Derrida dedicated his annual seminar at the *École des hautes études* to the concept of "hospitality"—opening up your home to the other. The key figure here was another Jew, Sigmund Freud, and his *"Das Unheimliche,"* (On the uncanny), an article dating from 1914 to 1919 whose subject is a certain form of anxiety; Derrida picked out the "no home" in *un-heim*. But we shall return to Freud. On Wednesdays between 5:00 P.M. and 7:00 P.M., multitudes of students, philosophers, and guests packed the central auditorium, where Derrida pursued his acrobatic juggling act, interlingual (making regular use of French-German-English-Latin-Greek) and multitextual (Heidegger, Lévinas, Freud, Nietzsche, *Oedipus Rex, Hamlet, Ulysses, Don Juan,* etc.) as he deciphered-dismantled-dismembered and reassembled the concept of "hospitality." Throughout, the air was heavy with thoughts about the ethos of the attitude toward foreigners—Derrida preferred to say "Others"—and the question of granting them political asylum (a hot issue in a France with a resurgent right wing). The listeners in the auditorium could not help thinking of the elegant, gray-haired Algerian Jew, born in El-Biar in 1930 and enjoying French hospitality since 1950. Nor could they help pondering on the talmudic mind of this tireless interpreter of texts, whose thoughts often verge upon traditional Jewish *midrash* interpretation, and whose course entails a constant crossing of borders of languages and texts. In other words, they pondered a Jew.

Indeed, Derrida himself (in his discussion of Edmond Jabès's *Book of Questions* (Paris: Gallimard, 1963), in his *L'écriture et la différence*, 1967b) pointed to the substantive link between Judaism and interpretation. Small wonder that "crossing a border" (we shall come later to his *Schibboleth*, 1986c) is among the most outstanding concepts in Derrida's philosophy. Small wonder that the "invisible" (a Lévinasian concept, with philosophical rights also accruing to Maurice Merleau-Ponty and his *The Visible and the Invisible* [Paris: Gallimard, 1964]) became a fundamental term in interpretation of art drawings (in the late 1990 Louvre exhibit "Memoirs of a Blind Man," of which Derrida was curator), particularly when Derrida elevated the "invisible" to representation of "the transcendental Other" in drawing. Did this mean the invisible as God? The God of Judaism? The French Jewish philosopher Emanuel Lévinas, whose concept of "Other" had a less-than-marginal influence on Derrida (see below in the chapter "Facing Lévinas") would have answered an unhesitating Yes. Was the layout Derrida designed for his *Glas* (1974)—two parallel texts (on Hegel and Genet) side by side, almost along the lines of a page of the Talmud—another indirect Yes?

In one of these lectures, Derrida spoke of the prophet Elijah, who, he claimed, represents unconditional "total hospitality": the expectation and willingness to extend hospitality at all times, awaiting the arrival of the unknown Other without any prior assignation of the time of meeting; keeping the Elijah chair forever vacant as an ever-open "here-and-now," in expectation of the advent of the Messiah— in Elijah's case, expectation of the Messiah's herald. Instantly, Elijah was transformed into one of the heroes of the course. When Derrida mentioned Elijah's presence in a brothel in James Joyce's *Ulysses*,[1] prostitution promptly became the archetype of hospitality (the prostitute as "hostess" and the brothel as a house where the borders of the ethos are crossed).

Elijah is crowned as hero of a different type in *Ulysse gramophone* (1987d), Derrida's work on Joyce's *Ulysses*. In a book replete with references to the Bible (the Tower of Babel), the Passover seder, the *Shma Yisrael* prayer (the Fundamental prayer of Judaism) (Derrida associates the cry *"Shma!"*—*"Hear!"*—with the *"Hello!"* of a telephone conversation) and other elements of Jewish tradition, all relating to the much-publicized Jewishness of Bloom, Joyce's anti-hero—we again encounter the prophet Elijah. It is characteristic of Derrida, who has a fine ear attuned to the syllables constituting words, that he should pick out of the name "Elijah" the *"ja"* of affirmation, which he attributes to various affirmations constituting *Ulysses*. But he is principally interested in "the second coming of Elijah," to use Joyce's term: his appearance as Jesuit, which Derrida analyzes as though it were broadcast by gramophone, telephone, or other means of communication. He dwells on a sentence Molly utters in relation to Elijah: "Book through eternity junction" to link "book" as verb (denoting "seat reservation") with "book" as noun ("eternity junction"). What is (or is not) booked at that "eternity junction" of the book? In this fashion, the prophet Elijah becomes the superimage of multimedia communication. From here it is a short leap to a portrayal of the prophet Elijah—hailed in Jewish tradition for his ability to decipher obscure texts—as superinterpreter of the book, of the Joycean narrative, as superexpert on *Ulysses* (107). Presenting this view at a Joyce convention held in Frankfurt in 1984, with the participation of many of the world's experts on the works of the Irish writer, Derrida set the prophet Elijah over them as supreme arbiter.

But Derrida is not the man to let too many texts pass through his hands without pinpointing the circumcision syndrome. The act of excising the foreskin, the ceremony Freud perceived as symbolic castration of sons by their fathers, gives him no rest. *Ulysse gramophone* quotes a passage from *Ulysses* about a collector of foreskins named, apparently, Moses. But Derrida is particular to remind his readers that the prophet Elijah attends every circumcision ceremony, of which he is the patron. "Elijah's chair" [where the one who holds the infant during the *bris* sits] is a further reminder, but it also offered a fine pretext for further teasing the Joyce experts seated in the hall: Derrida told them that anyone holding a "chair" (a university appointment) deserves the title of *mohel* (one who performs the act of circumcision).

Derrida settles accounts over his own circumcision in other books, such as *Circonfession* (a boldly revelatory work, in which he takes his leave of his dying mother, simultaneously examining his own life by way of his circumcision, his eternal Yom Kippur, spelling it *coupure*—"the day of the cut"), or *Glas,* where he deals at length with Hegel's perception of the Jewish God as castrating deity. But Derrida readers encounter the zenith in *Mal d'archive,* where they discover the complexity of his Jewishness.

In Derrida's habitual mode of interpretation, that is, by way of text on text, he casts his own book in the mold of *Freud's Moses* (New Haven: Yale Univ. Press, 1991) by the great Jewish historian resident in New York, Yossef Haim Yerushalmi, likewise a book about a book (Freud, *Moses and Monotheism*) in its turn again a book about a book (in this instance, the Bible). Yerushalmi's important work receives a warm, pungent embrace from Derrida (a contemporary of Yerushalmi), who made it the focus of his long lecture at the conference on "Memory: The Question of Archives" held in London in 1994. Yerushalmi's book analyzes Freud's reading of the birth of Judaism out of the Oedipal murder of Moses, a non-Jewish prince who adopted Akhenaton's monotheism. Furthermore, Yerushalmi's book (whose climax "Monologue with Freud" is an intimate address the writer delivers in Freud's ear) hinges upon the attempt to solve the riddle: Is psychoanalysis a Jewish science? Thus, the reader gains the growing sensation that the material he is perusing is less a study (fascinating in itself) of philo-Semitic and anti-Semitic documents relating to the psychoanalytical circle in Vienna than Yerushalmi's incisive confrontation with the issue of his Jewish identity. Indeed, Derrida's analysis preoccupies itself less with Freud's perception than with Yerushalmi's existential and phenomenological stand in relation to the "archive"—whether the topic is the science of history, or cultural memory, or a history of Freud and psychoanalysis, or psychoanalysis itself as "archival" discipline (a discipline accumulating memory).[2] Derrida seeks Yerushalmi within *Freud's Moses:* "The Freud of *Freud's Moses* is none other than Yerushalmi's Moses" (108): Is he not also seeking himself?

Is it a surprise that, just into *Mal d'archive,* Derrida detects, in the act of circumcision, the onset of archiving (cataloguing, naming, categorizing) in a Jew's life, a kind of "imprinting" of identity upon the skin of the newborn (39–52). Not fortuitously, Derrida dwells at length upon the inscription Freud's father wrote on the leather binding (skin!) of a Bible, to impress upon his son the obligation of preserving his Jewish identity. Yerushalmi performs a circumcision on Freud, says Derrida (68). Indeed, his book (by means of words, book, documents, archive) introduces Freud and Freudianism into the Covenant of Judaism. Furthermore, Yerushalmi's monologue to the absent, dead Freud reminds Derrida of Hamlet conversing with his father's ghost.[3] Let us emphasize: the man-and-phantom, or man-and-death, relationship is among the most conspicuous motifs in Derrida's works, being linked to Lévinas's concept of "the ultimate otherness"; to the dread of ghosts as depicted by Freud (*Das Unheimlichkeit*); and of course, to the existence-death relationship in Heidegger and hence, to the relationship between existence and nothingness in Sartre's writings (although Sartre is startlingly absent from most of the Derridean discourse. Is this another parricide?)

That being so, from where does the "evil" or the "pain" pervading the archive come? From where the "mal d'archive"? Derrida identifies this evil-pain with the Freudian death wish, revealed in the technique of printing, the regularly reiterated pattern, which is a way of retarding life and preserving the past. He recalls clearly that Yerushalmi wrote the equally important *Zakhor* (remember), a book about Jewish history and Jewish memory, where he attributed to the Jewish people the precept of remembrance as absolute and unique ordinance. As though appealing the commitment, Derrida hastens to comment: "I ask myself, trembling, if there is any justice in the sentences that reserve to Israel, and the future, and past, as they are, and hope . . . and the obligation of remembrance . . . uniquely assigned to the people of Israel" (122) Seven pages after posing that question, Derrida answers it in terms of archive and death wish:

> [T]here will be no future without repetition. Thus, Freud would say (this would be his argument) that there is no future without the specter of Oedipal violence repressed in the *arkhonic*[4] institution of the archive, in the one and only position, in the *arche*-nomology and in the death urge. Without this evil (sickness), which is also the archive sickness (evil), the desire and the disaster of the archive, there will be neither assignation nor consignment (*consignation*). (128)

Does Derrida identify the death wish in the murky depths of a Jewish culture essentially archival? Or does he refer to culture in general, the archival syndrome as such? His *Schibboleth* (1986c), echoing the tale of the massacre of the tribe of Ephraim [when victims were singled out by their unique dialect that pronounced "Shibboleth" as "Sibboleth." Trans.] is dedicated to interpretation of Paul Celan, the great German Jewish poet whose main work was overshadowed by the impending Holocaust. But anyone expecting a study of Holocaust concepts very soon discovers that the book's principal topic is circumcision. The very first sentence sets the theme: "Once only: circumcision occurred once only." Circumcision is here as "shibboleth"—the code word for transition from life to death, like the foreskin whereby the covenant is struck (12). Incidentally, the prophet Elijah again puts in an appearance, this time as patron of the circumcised (103).

Derrida displays an enormous interest in dates and dating, taking care to stress the precise date of composition of each of his books. "The date is the seal of our location in the here-and-now," he specified in one of his seminar lectures. "Dating is signing," he wrote in his *Otobiographies* (1984b, 53) adding: "And dating also means indicating the place of the signing." *Schibboleth* keeps track of the dates set out in Celan's poetry. Derrida reads: "Call him, Shibboleth,/ the stranger in an alien land;/ February. *No pasaran* [passage forbidden]." There is a connection between Shibboleth and being an alien, away from one's own country. "Alien, the alienness from being at home, your being outside home" (*Schibboleth*, 58).[5] The time of Shibboleth, the date of Shibboleth, is February. Thus, in Celan's 1955 poem "Schibboleth," Derrida found the key word of the stranger's transition or nontransition from one place to another. "Shibboleth" is also the imprinting of your alienness into your body by means of circumcision. And Derrida reads on in Celan's poem: "Rabbi, . . . circumcise the word [*beschneid das Wort*]." Circumcision, *brith-milah,* is covenant of circumcision and of word.

Derrida is aware of the dual meaning of the Hebrew *milah*—word/circumcision; he inscribed the word in Hebrew in 1976 on the cover of the notebook where he began writing "the book of Eli," which he would later integrate into *Circonfession:* the rite of passage that attaches the Jew to his community is a signature in blood, writing in blood, says Derrida (97).

Circumcision is thus the Covenant of the body, the injury, the incision inscription, writing steeped in blood. That being so, the Jew is poet (writing with his own blood, from his own wound). All the circumcised are poets. Furthermore: "All the poets are Jews" (98), for all write in their own blood. Plain and simple. If we connect this with something Derrida wrote in 1964 (in his study of the work of Edmond Jabès) about Jews being condemned to poetry, like their condemnation to "writing" (*L'écriture et la différence* [Chicago: Univ. of Chicago Press, 1978], 65), we can establish with certainty that this is not a novel motif in Derrida's writings.

No, Derrida doesn't pull his punches. His acrobatics recall a conjurer hauling rabbits out of a hat. Even if his words do not sink in right away at the commonsense level, they take you by storm at the level of the open border (yet again, the "open border") between philosophy, poetry, and psychoanalysis—in fact, between anything and everything. Be that as it may, Derrida reads Celan's rabbi (the rabbi of Prague) as *mohel.* And when Celan writes: "EINEM, DER VOR DER TÜR / STAND, eines / Abends: / ihm / tat ich mein Wort auf . . ." ("TO ONE WHO STOOD BEFORE THE DOOR one evening, to him did I open up my word . . ."), Derrida knows that opening the gate is launching into speech, before morning, at dawn, at the beginning, in the act of circumcision. (The gate of language is a major theme in Derrida's interpretation of Kafka's "Before the Gate of the Law"; see Derrida's "Prejugés" in Lyotard's anthology *Faculté de juger,* 1985b.) Opening the gate is nothing if not affirmation of the right of passage for the stranger who bears the code of Shibboleth, whose body bears the disfigurement (Shibboleth in place of Sibboleth) the physical cut, the circumcision. "I have never spoken of anything but [circumcision]" (*Circonfession,* 70). As every Derridean knows, subtraction and absence constitute the secret of Derrida's philosophy.

Hence, too, we see the significance of the date. For circumcision, the Covenant of adherence to the "Shibboleth" camp, is also the membership card of the pariahs, the Others, the outcasts, the strangers, those annihilated in the death camps; on a given date. Derrida only plucks up the courage to say so at the end of his book about Celan (111), on the penultimate page. Some twenty pages earlier, when dealing with the subject of the repeated date (in the context of the occupation of Austria or the defeat of the anti-Franco fighters), he puts it plainly to his readers, enfolding it in an image of igniting the flame of the date (fire, conflagration, ashes):

> May I be forgiven if I here refer to the *holocaust,* that is to say, literally, as I have liked to call it elsewhere, the *burn-all,* only to say the following: there is certainly at present the date of this holocaust, the inferno we recall; but there is a holocaust for every date, and in some part of the world at every hour. Each hour counts its holocaust. Each hour is unique, albeit recurrent, and this is the wheel that turns by itself, even if, lately, all that returns is . . . its other returnee. (*Schibboleth,* 83)

This intellectual universalization of the Holocaust (on which we will expand further in the chapter "Fire") may outrage some, while others would applaud Derrida's high-minded, moral-existential sensitivity. Be that as it may, the Holocaust—historical and onto-theological—is a recurrent motif in the writings of the philosopher whose Jewish origins got him expelled from school at the age of eleven.[6] That trauma gives him no rest.

On his third visit to Jerusalem, Derrida gave a lecture at the Hebrew University. It was 1988, the period of the Palestinian *intifada,* when universities in the occupied territories were closed down, a fact that Derrida did not omit to mention in the text of his lecture, ninety closely typed pages entitled "Kant, the Jew, the German."[7] It is interesting that, when addressing members of his own people (although Palestinian intellectuals were also present) Derrida dispensed with his acrobatic style, making his lecture simple and clear. Ostensibly, its heroes were Hermann Cohen and Franz Rosenzweig—"Neither the one nor the other was a Zionist, and Rosenzweig was, so it would appear, overtly hostile to the project of an Israeli state" ("Kant, the Jew, the German," 1990d, 214)[8]

Derrida's study hinged on "Deutschtum und Judentum" (Germanism and Judaism), the essay Hermann Cohen wrote in 1915, at the height of the First World War. His choice of this particular article is especially interesting, for the patriotic chauvinism Cohen exhibited here vis à vis Germany, brought it condemnation in Zionist circles (notably from M. Buber and G. Scholem) as an "ill-fated" essay ("Kant, the Jew, the German," 224). Did Derrida set up a provocation for his listeners (even if, in conversation with me, he utterly denied doing so)? It is a further hunch of mine that Derrida regards Hermann Cohen ("this great figure of rationalist German Judaism, liberal and non-Zionist, if not assimilationist, this thinker, Jew *and* German" [218]) as an occasion for self-scrutiny and self-examination. (Now translate that last quote, with some minor corrections, substituting "French" for "German," and "phenomenalism" for "rationalism.") What we discover is something resembling the "mirror effect" he found in Yosef Haim Yerushalmi, especially as Derrida did not identify with Cohen.

Derrida's point of departure is the eulogy that Franz Rosenzweig composed for Cohen on his idol's death in 1918. It hinged upon the phrase "Jew *and* German." "*And* German" Derrida stressed: the two terms are not identical; there is no total synthesis; there is "*and*." (Incidentally, Rosenzweig identified Cohen's Jewishness in the blend of cool rationalist thinking with the stormy pathos of his speech. It should be pointed out in this context that Derrida's own delivery is equable, restrained, and lacking any pathos, albeit taking delight in lingual frills. He remains seated, sticking fairly closely to the written text he has brought from home.) But the main subject is Cohen's "Germanism and Judaism" (and the question the reader must pose, just like the writer, is: How is one to resolve the issue of "Frenchness and Jewishness"?).

Cohen's essay exhibits the spirit of Judaism as genetic (and genealogical) ally of the German spirit that reached its zenith with idealism and Kant. According to Cohen, the cultural trinity—Judaism, Hellenism, and Christianity—processed Western civilization as an idealistic culture founded upon Judaism. By the term "Hellenism" Cohen meant Platonism, and "Christianity" referred to Protestantism and the Lutheran revolution (according to Cohen, the Rambam—Rabbi Moses Maimonides—was the forerunner of Protestantism). The figure of Philo of Alexandria towers powerfully as herald of the merger of Judaism and Platonism, and forerunner of Christianity and the idealist revolution, that is, the German spirit. Accordingly, as Derrida put it without pulling his punches, "Whether they know it or not, whether they want it or not, the Germans are Jews" ("Kant, the Jew, the German," 227). The German spirit exists, it unfolds in the course of history between pivotal events, each turning point casting the contribution of the Jewish genius into a key role. So claimed Cohen. This led to the Judaization of Immanuel Kant as pinnacle of the aforementioned Jewish-Platonic-Protestant genealogy. "Who is Kant? The Holy of Holies of the German spirit . . . but also the man who represents the closest affinity (*die innerste Verwandschaft*) with Judaism" (259)

Cohen's total Jewish identification with Germany spurred him to ardent support for the German war effort and the German army. In his view, the campaign against the czar would bear with it Kantian universal peace, enthroning the spirit of idealism (and equally, the emancipation of the Jews of Russia and Germany) as well as attaining the utopia of international socialism. In other words, German nationalism and militarism would achieve their culmination in the supranationalism of confederation and the abolition of the army. In the same context, Derrida was careful to emphasize, Cohen's essay also called on U.S. Jews to exert pressure on their government to dissuade it from fighting against Germany (for it would be a "fraternal war" between two Judeo-Protestant nations).

But it did not seem that Derrida had come to Jerusalem to deliver a lecture on Hermann Cohen. And if he reflected on a united Europe as the implementation of Cohen's vision (*L'autre cap* [1991c], his book on European unity, proposed to define the European identity as sensitivity to non-Europism) or on the Nazi Holocaust as the utter annihilation of the Judeo-German alliance—he offered no hint thereof. As I have suggested, I doubt whether Derrida came to Jerusalem for any purpose other than to lecture on Jacques Derrida, Israel, and Judaism. Accordingly, insofar as it related to himself, he found it necessary, in his interpretative discussion of Cohen, to drag in repeatedly the name of the successor to Cohen's chair at Marburg University, Heidegger (who was to Derrida, if one may put it in such terms, as Kant was to Cohen). Derrida's aim, I believe, was obvious: to release and liberate Heidegger (i.e., Derrida) from the Jewish connection.

Heidegger and Husserl (his teacher) evolved phenomenology as against the Kantian tradition that H. Cohen renewed, Derrida stresses (215), adding that Heidegger marked the end of the German spiritual connection with Hellenism (Platonic Hellenism we hasten to specify) (215); further, it does not seem that Heidegger took an interest in this point of view in Protestantism, any more than in some Judeo-German affinity around the Principle of Reason" (241).

Thus, when Derrida comes to Cohen's interpretation of God's self-definition as "I am that I am" (Exod. 3:14), he exposes to its full extent the philosophical chasm between Heidegger (i.e., Derrida) and Cohen: for Cohen translated the sentence in Platonic terms: "God is the primary experience" (and all the rest are external phenomena); whereas Derrida stresses the future tense of the sentence "I shall be whatsoever I shall be": experience + future, the essence of the Heideggerian philosophy. Derrida freed himself from the shackles of Cohen's Jewish hypothesis.

A covert satirical thread runs throughout Derrida's lengthy lecture-essay: Judaization of German philosophy, Judaization of Kant, Cohen's militarist nationalism. The deconstruction of all these reflects Derrida, as well as his listeners in the Jerusalem lecture hall. For in the Jerusalem context of the *intifada* period, his critique of nationalism and militarism comes across as a critique of Zionism (Derrida launched his lecture with a reference to the violence in the occupied territories, a declaration of solidarity with the Palestinian people and its national rights, and a call for an Israeli withdrawal [210–11]). Derrida seems to suggest that an overintimate, one-way alliance (under a hallmark of similarity) between Judaism, philosophy, and nationalism is liable to yield bitter fruit. In other words, Derrida releases his great moral mentor Heidegger from Cohen's Jewish context (which did not hinder Derrida in pointing a vitriolic pen at the nationalist Heidegger of the Nazi era in his *De l'esprit, Heidegger, et la question*, 1987a). In this manner, Derrida secured an open route (open borders) through the various options. What could be more Jewish?

Is there anyone nowadays who does not hasten to brandish quotes from Derrida's philosophy as transit permit (Shibboleth) granting safe passage to the "in" of "intellectualism"? The term "deconstruction" (in itself a kind of anarchist syndrome worthy of the kind of Jewish mind rapidly falling extinct, to my regret) became bon ton, to the chagrin of Derrida, who found himself helpless against its misrepresentation. It is not my intent to contribute further to the mutilation of Derrida (as I have observed, his circumcision itself is enough of a burden to bear). The writings of "the Jewish Derrida" should not be permitted to overshadow the fact that we are considering a philosopher who, albeit influenced by Lévinas, and despite a love-hate relationship with Freud verging on obsession, nevertheless followed closely in the footsteps of the non-Jew Martin Heidegger.

Let us again make it plain: Derrida's writings include books on Marx (*Spectres de Marx* [1993d]); Walter Benjamin (such as "Des Tours de Babel" 1987e); and of course, important texts about Kafka and his story "Before the Gate of the Law"; but as I specified in the introduction, many of his most important works do not deal with Jewish thinkers or motifs. Thus, for example, one of his later books, *Apories* (1996a), focuses mainly on the Heideggerian concept of death, albeit hinging upon concepts like "shibboleth" and "crossing borders" (see below, the chapter on "Judaism and Death"). Likewise his *Sauf le nom* (1993c) deals with the concept of God, without direct reference to Jewish sources (in spite of the apparent reference of *le nom* of the title to "The Name"—the Jewish appellation for God). In another work, composed in 1983 on the subject of the Christian apocalypse (*D'un ton apocalyptique adopté naguère en philosophie* [1984a]), Derrida delves copiously into the New Testament, even if he is particular to establish the etymological link between the Greek "apocalypse" and the Hebrew *hazon* (vision). Likewise in *Memoires d'aveugle* (1990e) (a foray toward the blind of Western culture, and a veritable delight for any aficionado of profound artistic thought) Derrida combines a study of the sightless in the Jewish Old Testament (Jacob, Isaac, Eli, Samson, et al.) with a discussion of their counterparts in Greek mythology and the New Testament.

Derrida thus appears as both Jew and supra-Jew, Jew and philosopher;

in other words, Jew as well as philosopher; possibly, as philosopher perforce a Jew through the seal of physical mutilation, the "shibboleth" of circumcision. Otherwise, why—at the height of his discussion of the artist's blind regard, and within the context of his claim that any testimony comprises blindness (by replacing the regard with the verbal testimony)—should he unexpectedly refer to the witnesses of the extermination camps, affirming: "No authentication is able to show, presently, that which is observed by the most reliable witness, or that which he has seen and preserves in his memory, if it has not been removed by the fire (and as for the witnesses of Auschwitz, or the other extermination camps, there we have an abominable resource for "revisionist" deniers)" (*Memoires d'aveugle*, 106).

4

L'autre Kippa

In 1990, Derrida took part in a symposium in Turin, Italy, on the theme of "European Cultural Identity." Having imbibed into his very being the European culture in which he had been raised, the Algerian Jew now set about defining "Europeanism" by reference to the horrors of World War II and Nazism, and to a survey of the present day, with its "crimes of xenophobia, racism, anti-Semitism, religious or national fanaticism" (*L'autre cap* [1991c] 13). It was probably this "archive" that prompted Derrida to come up with his somewhat paradoxical definition of European cultural identity: "The characteristic of a culture is not to be identical with itself" (16); in other words, one's cultural identity lies in separation from oneself. Moreover, a knowledge of your own cultural identity is contingent upon knowledge of the culture of the Other; hence the title of his lecture, and his book: *L'autre cap* (the other head: "cap" denotes, inter alia, "hat"; in this chapter, we replace the "cap" with the Jewish skullcap or yarmulkeh to speak of Derrida's "other *kippa*" [the Hebrew equivalent of the Yiddish "yarmulke"). The philosopher plunged into detail, elaborating on the links between "cap," "capital," "captain," and so on, to discuss Europe's leading role as capital, simultaneously proposing a fundamental alteration in thinking about Europe, in terms of non-European Otherness. Europe will know itself as Europe if it advances toward that which it is not, toward "the other head"; donning "the other hat" to achieve "the experience of the impossible" (47)—Heidegger's definition of death, repeatedly adopted by Derrida.

Thus, your identity lies in your own self-denial, in your death (in identity). Moreover, Derrida points out a basic contradiction between the pursuit of universality by European culture, and, by implication, the sense of exemplariness: an individual national arrogance, setting itself apart from the rest of the world (71–72). It is the contradiction between the message of values designated for the whole world, and one society's claim to a monopoly of that gospel. Derrida puts forward a different concept: opening up Europe to Otherness, to the Other, the aliens, as recognition of the Other culture and its adoption into society overall—possibly, a proposal for the deconstruction of Europe (76), that is, a study of the Other root of the European essence, and its substitution by a pluralism of heterogeneity.[1]

Was Derrida extending his divided personal identity to the all-European identity? Was this non-European-*cum*-European, belonging yet alien, calling upon Europe to be itself and unlike itself, alien to itself? As we proceed, we shall seek to answer these questions in the affirmative. We shall see how the logical step of affirming identity while denying it could serve as model for the philosopher's other stabs into the domain of defining identity, and his gift for illuminating a certain principle of contradiction with which he lived: belonging through nonbelonging, affirming identity through alienation, and, at the metaphorical level, affirming your city through being in the desert.[2]

Those two latter metaphors foreshadow our next step in tracing the paradoxical course toward knowing the philosopher's identity: his interpretation of Edmond Jabès's "*Book of Questions.*"

The study—one of Derrida's earlier projects (1967)—exhibits a trailblazing effort to illuminate some links between his philosophical reflections and Judaism in the broadest sense. Many of the assumptions that Derrida attributes to Jabès appear to be oblique declarations touching upon his own identity as Jew. ("I always express Jewish concepts in an oblique manner," Derrida said in conversation with me 17 May 1996). It is a dialectical identity, simultaneously affirming affinity and remoteness. Indeed, the following lines, cited by Derrida from Jabès's work, could serve as overall motto for our book: "Addressing themselves to me, my blood brothers said: 'You are not Jewish. You do not come to the synagogue.' . . . 'You are Jewish for the others and so little Jewish for us.' . . . 'Drawing no distinction between a Jew and him who is not Jewish, is this not already to cease being a Jew?'" (*Writing and Difference,* 75).

And indeed, how does Jacques Derrida—a French intellectual with nothing Jewish in his external appearance, a man who neither observes religious precepts nor worships at the synagogue nor has his sons circumcised, and so on—affirm his "other" Judaism as it persistently emerges from his numerous writings, casting a giant shadow over his thought in form and content? First, he affirms it in a certain duality that he attributes to Jabès and that coincidentally summarizes his own spiritual bent: a quest for the root and recognition of the wound (see the discussion of circumcision in the chapter: "Derrida's Yom Coupure"): "A powerful and ancient root is exhumed, and on it is laid bare an ageless wound (for what Jabès teaches us is that roots speak, that words want to grow, and that poetic discourse *takes root* in a wound)" *Writing and Difference,* [1978], 64).

Indeed, as we probe Derrida's discourse on the roots of his Jewish identity, we uncover the size of the wound, the extent of the philosopher's remoteness from the "ethnological root." The answers with regard to his Jewish identity are dual in aspect and embrace contradictions. Bearing in mind the pivotal role Derrida attaches to the concept of "writing" (whereby he forever affirms our banishment to the exile of "writing" and all it entails), we must conclude that his remarks about the alliance between a certain Judaism and "writing"—"a certain Judaism as the birth and passion of writing" (*Writing and Differences,* 64)—apply equally to his own Jewish identity. Thus, his study of Jabès's *Book of Questions* increasingly takes on the aspect of a Derrida self-portrait: "The difficulty of being a Jew, which coincides with the difficulty of writing; for Judaism and writing are but the same waiting, the same hope, the same depletion" (65). Derrida refers to the hopes of unveiling the divine *logos* upon which all writing rests and that all writing impedes.

The people condemned to writing is the people condemned to the book, to interpretation. And yet the reader wonders: Is Derrida writing about Jabès or about himself? With his teachings consisting in the most part of an interpretative study of the texts of philosophers, authors, poets, and so forth—is Derrida condemned to interpretation and the book, that is, is he the Jew, and is this his Jewishness? Repeatedly finding his interpretations floundering in the contradiction between the quest for the primal source (the root) and the eternal rebuff from it (the wound), he defines Judaism in terms of that duality: "Between the fragments of the broken Tables the poem grows and the right to speech takes root" (*Writing and Difference,* 67).[3]

This duality combines the adventure of treating the text as sanctified and as encompassed by its interpreters. Interpretation is treated as exile from the source: "The necessity of commentary, like poetic necessity, is the very form of exiled speech. In the beginning is hermeneutics" (*Writing and Difference,* 67) But Derrida is careful to draw a distinction between the interpretation of a rabbi, or an observant Jew—and that of a poet (or interpreter of poetry, like himself): the distance between them is enormous, the rabbi being imbued with messianic faith in restoration to the original voice, at the termination of the Exile, whereas the poet and his interpreter believe only in interpretative writing and eternal exile. The latter also identify the shattered Tablets of the Law with the metaphysical fracture between divine speech and writing. Derrida's response to the question of his identity is therefore a response embracing rift, wound, and division.

In 1994, the *Jüdischer Verlag* of Frankfurt, Germany, published an anthology of interviews with seven philosophers on *Questions au judaïsme.*

Issued in French two years subsequently, the book was edited by Elisabeth Weber, who included an interview with Derrida alongside those with Lévinas, Lyotard, and others. Derrida the Deconstructivist, a dualist of recollection and destruction, speaks there of Judaism in terms of obsession and wound (the latter represented by the "wound" of circumcision). A few lines on, he points to the fundamental paradox in Judaism, vividly recalling the paradox he pinpointed on the issue of European identity. In relation to the notion of "chosen people," Derrida argues: "'We are the chosen people' signifies: we are, indisputably and demonstrably, the witnesses of what a people can be. . . . We are . . . the witnesses of God" (*Questions au judaïsme* [Paris: Desclée de Brouwer, 1996], 76). The contention did not rate too highly with the philosopher ("this logic of exemplarity [is rendered] slightly crazy . . ." ibid.) but that did not hinder him in adopting the selfsame logic and expanding it to the overall issue of Jewish identity: "the moment the identity of the Jew, or of Judaism, consists of this exemplarity, that is, of a certain nonidentity with oneself, 'I am thus' implying 'I am thus and universal' . . . the more one says 'My identity consists of not being identical with myself, of being alien, noncongruent with myself,' etc., the more Jewish one is!" (ibid.). Derrida goes even further, to draw his conclusion: "That argument . . . makes it possible to say . . . the less one is a Jew, the more one is a Jew" (ibid.); accordingly, "those Jews who proclaim an actual circumcision, a Jewish name, Jewish descent, Jewish soil, Jewish sun etc., are not by definition better placed than others to speak on behalf of Judaism. . . . There is 'Of course I am a Jew' and 'Of course, I am not a Jew' . . . both together, that is the condition of the Jew" (77)

Similarly, relating to the subject of memory in his *Mal d'archive*, he wrote:

> I would like to spend hours, an eternity in fact, in a trembling meditation of the following sentence [of Y. H. Yerushlami. Au.]: "Only in Israel and nowhere else is the injunction to remember felt as a religious imperative to an entire people." How can one refrain from trembling before that sentence? I wonder whether it is appropriate . . . I ask myself, trembling, if they are appropriate, those sentences that reserve for Israel past and present as such, hope . . . "the injunction to remember" . . . as assignment reserved exclusively for the people of Israel." (121–22).

Here we have the paradox: a definition of Jewish identity in terms of non-Jewishness (just as the European identity was defined in terms of the non-European). Have we discovered the key to Derrida's philosophical connection with Judaism and Israel, perhaps even—with his own father? The connection arises from its absence. Derrida the "non-Jew," the man "alien to his Judaism," affirms an absence of Judaism, without which Judaism is incomplete. The yearning from within the rift, the obsessivity from within the wound, the quest for the root from within the acknowledgment of the eternal banishment therefrom. Deconstruction. Accordingly, Derrida proves his Jewish identity neither by laying teffilin (phylacteries) nor by fasting on Yom Kippur, nor by having his sons circumcised; rather, he proves it by the experience of absence, by the experience of the Jewish abyss, by the death of his Jewishness, by its nullification.

Of course, this necessarily dictates a certain perception of religion overall, one resting upon its "death." In *La religion* (1996b), Derrida discusses the place of the religious experience, identifying that place with three main locations: (*a*) the island, (*b*) the promised land, (*c*) the desert. He is not referring to the desert of divine revelation, in the manner experienced by Moses and Elijah; rather, to a "desert within a desert," the experience of a total nothingness, the utter realization of total abstraction, constituting transcendental Otherness. Moreover, desert within desert, says Derrida, is that which allows, opens up, and infinitely deepens the Other (26). However, coincidentally, the "desert" abstraction is capable of serving as location for everything it omits and nullifies. Hence, he arrives at the dual aspect of religion, as abstraction of something (God) and his omission. Derrida offers two concepts to characterize this duality: the "messianic" and "*khôra*." The messianic is horizonless exposure to the future, that enfolds the advent of the Other as embodiment of justice. The messianic is the promise: "Without the desert within the desert, there will be neither act of faith, nor promise, nor future, nor unanticipated anticipation of the death of the other, nor relation toward the singularity of the other" (29). "*Khôra*"(the mysterious Platonic concept from *Timaeus* to which Derrida dedicated an entire book in 1993) denotes an unspecified place lacking any characterization, an utterly metaphysical vessel enfolding all the contradictions, but absolutely inaccessible: "*khôra* is neither Being, nor Good, nor God, nor Man, nor History. It will always resist all these; it will always have . . . the location even of an infinitely insurmountable resistance: a faceless total other" (31).

Thus, we have a contradiction: the promise of the infinite revelation, and the infinite refusal of any revelation. One cannot but recall the duality of Heidegger's "earth" and "world" in the origin of artistic creation (1935): the work of art as something enigmatic, rejecting any deciphering, and the work of art as revelation of truth.

Close to the end of his *De l'esprit, Heidegger, et la question* (1987a), Derrida contrived an imaginary conversation between Heidegger and a number of theologians. The yearning to return to the land of origin reverberates in the words of each of the participants (each theologian claiming to return to a source even more ancient than the once claimed by his predecessor), all three unanimous in glorifying this Otherness of the promise recalled. There is no distinction between this yearning and Derridean *différance* and the double bind it engenders, as the philosopher explained in an interview:

> That is the paradox of the *"différance."* On the one hand, the "différance" is motivated by desire, movement, an inclination toward an incessantly retarded source, toward future or past . . . but simultaneously, the *"différance"* is that which somehow blocks the source . . . the source is separated from itself . . . the nonoriginality of the origin. (Weber, *Questions au judaïsme* [Paris: Desclée de Brouwer, 1996], 98–99)

You will never reach the promised land, in other words: you will wander throughout eternity. As for the experience of "I am" (Heidegger's *Dasein*) that is time (the incessant movement between my future, my death, and my past and present—see Heidegger's essay "The Concept of Time" [1929]), roaming (wandering) is the foundation of human existence. Thus, "place" is forever promise, Derrida points out, never empirical location (*Writing and Difference* [Chicago: Univ. of Chicago Press, 1978], 145), adding: "For Heidegger, as for the Jew and the Poet."

Heideggerian earth and world have become wilderness.[4] In 1967, Derrida was already tracing the footsteps of Jabès (*Book of Questions*). The desert is viewed as alternative to the Garden of Eden, that is, desert as banishment from God, an ousting from voice (speech) to writing. Condemnation to the desert is condemnation to writing, to separation from the source. Derrida mentions the Pharisees, whose Hebrew title denotes "those who have *taken leave* of" (*Writing and Difference* [Chicago: Univ. of Chicago Press, 1978], 68). It is doubtful whether he knew that the name can also be taken to mean "interpreters" (which of course supports his contention). Being in the desert entails no longer being in direct discourse with the divine presence: "God no longer speaks to us; he has interrupted himself: we must take words upon ourselves" (ibid.). When Derrida sets Jabès's thought at some nowhere between city and desert (where the root of course has no prospect of growth) and adds: "city and desert which are neither countries, nor villages, nor parks," it is evident that we are dealing with Derrida's no-place that enfolds the desert within. Jabès's city was Cairo (69). Is Derrida's city Jerusalem?

Derrida refuses the philosophical distinction between religion and reason (intelligence, consciousness, science). "Religion and intelligence evolve together," he writes (*La religion* 41). On this point, he takes issue with

Heidegger, who called for a separation between philosophy and theology (78). All the same, Derrida recognizes a religious dimension in Heidegger's philosophy, "a dimension of testimonial sanctity." This dimension is identified with the attestation of responsibility, or of primordial guilt, and a vigorous determination—all at a transcendental level (80). In other words, according to Derrida, Heidegger affirms religiosity while yet rejecting faith (81). Derrida, having earlier drawn a line between the experience of sanctity and the experience of faith (46) on the argument that it is possible to sanctify without believing (faith: the testimony to the absolute Other), identifies Heidegger's thinking with sanctification while withdrawing it from faith.

Derrida charts his own course on issues of religion, faith, and sanctity by means of the dual-aspect relationship between the experience of faith and the social experience. It could be argued that he defines faith in terms of social values, that is, morality. Within faith, he claims, there exist social bonds and, simultaneously, severance of the social bond. In faith, there is no contradiction between social links and antisociality. For in faith, the link to the Other is opened up as the secret of the experience of faithful testimony (let us recall: faith is the testimony to the absolute Other). As Derrida says, "If faith is the Other of the address and relationship to any entirely different Other [*tout autre*], it even lies within the experience of an absence of relationship, or its absolute interruption" (*La religion*, 84–85).

Derrida sets the religious experience at the apex of contradiction: sanctification of the disconnection verges upon desecration or secularization, even upon a certain atheism. Be that as it may, it touches upon the extreme experience of the means of negative theology (*La religion*, 85) And he adds: "It will be necessary here to separate—by means of a different lexicon, Hebrew, for example (the sanctity of the *Kiddush* [blessing said over wine])—the consecrated from the hallowed." The philosopher now falls back upon Judaism's rejection of "saints," as against its upholding of the saintly (as he had earlier fallen back upon Heidegger's distinction between faith and religion).

This is how the secular philosopher traced the course of his religiosity: an infinite affinity toward the other, coinciding with an infinite remoteness from him. This is the desert (in "*khôra*"and in "*messianity*") that engenders the sanctity of the Other, and whose profound moral aspects correspond with its transcendental aspects. Derrida's "religiosity" is moral to an extent that vividly recalls the alliance between morality and religion in Kant's *Critique of Practical Reason*.[5] Thus, we are not surprised to find Derrida pointing to Kant's distinction between the religion of prayer for help and salvation, and religion as moral imperative. The latter, the religion of pure reason, is liberated of divine manifestation and affirms God as the general and absolute good underlying man's self-imposed moral imperative (by his free reason).

Derrida did not put God to death, taking no share in Freudian-Nietzschean deicide. On the contrary, he stresses the uniqueness of Judaism (and Islam) in refusing the death of God: "Judaism and Islam may perhaps be the two last monotheistic religions that continue to rebel against anything, in the Christianization of our world, that signifies the death of God, death in God . . . two monotheistic religions still sufficiently alien to the heart of Greek-Christian, pagan-Christian Europe, sufficiently alien to a Europe that signifies the death of God . . ." (*La religion*, 21).

Derrida's duality merely conceals God, leaving him as utter secret shrouded in the veils of "writing," beyond "the white metaphor" (*Margins of Philosophy* 1972b). Unlike the promises of the neo-Platonic and romantic traditions, Derrida does not believe in the feasibility of unveiling, merely in veil-weaving continued to infinity. The more you seek after the meaning of God, the more you continue to weave, that is, to conceal and distance ("whiten") God (see the chapter "Father's *Talith*"). Fulfillment of this duality is fulfillment of one's identity. In terms of Derrida's reading of Jabès, the more you interpret the "Book," the further away you get from the divine speech; but in the course of your interpretations, you fulfill your identity as Jew. This is what we are told by the man many would consider the greatest contemporary interpreter of Western philosophy.

But what is the fate of your identity in a storehouse of "textiles" (an assortment of woven interpretations, extending beyond the sole religious interpretation to other religious interpretations), all concealing and seeking their gods? Derrida directs the question to the culture of the "global village," or, in his term, "*mondialisation*." He poses the question as against the trend to globalization (the worldwide homogenization that blurs cultural distinguishing marks) that queries the concept of the Other, Otherness, and everything derived therefrom in relation to morality, religion, identity, and so on. Without answering the question, he writes:

> *The Jewish question* [Derrida's emphasis. Au.] still remains quite a good example . . . for elaboration of what is to come in that demographic-religious problem. . . . There is more than one way of interpreting the unheard-of survival of the tiny "Jewish people" and the worldwide radiation of its religion, unique source of the three monotheistic religions that share a certain domination of the world and which it equals at least in dignity. One can interpret in a thousand ways the resistance [of the Jewish people] to efforts to exterminate it, under conditions of demographic imbalance of which no other example is known. But what will become of that

survival the day (already come, perhaps) *mondialisation* reaches saturation point? That "globalization," as you say in American, may no longer permit the surface of the human earth to be carved up into these microclimes, these historical, political and cultural microzones, little Europe and the Middle East, where the "Jewish people" has already had plenty of trouble surviving and attesting to its faith. "I understand Judaism as the possibility of granting the Bible a context, of keeping that book legible," said Lévinas. Does not the *mondialisation* of reality and of demographic calculations render the probability of that "context" weaker than ever and as menacing for survival as the worst radical evil of the "final solution"? "God is the future," Lévinas added—whereas Heidegger saw the "last god" proclaim himself precisely in the very absence of a future. . . . That question may be more grave and urgent for the state of Israel and its peoples. (*La religion*, 73)

Derrida pursued the relationship between Judaism and the future (and past) in *Mal d'archive* (1995a), a study of Y. H. Yerushalmi's *Freud's Moses*, where Derrida discovered three doors opening up to the future and simultaneously shutting it out. One door is set in the book's final sentence: a door promising to protect the well-guarded secret (Yerushalmi's pledge to Freud that he [Yerushalmi] will be the only one to whom he [Freud] reveals his secret: whether he regards psychoanalysis as a Jewish science). Derrida comments: he pledges secrecy to a ghost; how does he dare present himself as a historian? The historian deals in the past; the archive does not house the future (111–12).

The second door opens up to two future definitions, of Judaism and of science. Both definitions are relegated to an unknown, uncertain future, an "abysmal" future. Each of the two definitions imposes a greater measure of uncertainty upon the other. The odds are that these definitions will never be formulated (*Mal d'archive*, 113) which, Derrida writes, casts a shadow over the theoretical value of Yerushalmi's book (114). The philosopher relates to a special category of "futurism" that he identifies with the concept "messianic" (not to be understood in the conventional meaning of the term). A condition for the coming of the expected is that it be unknown, and even unrecognizable. At that level, it rules out the future possibility of unification between Judaism and science (the essence of the latter being, of course, knowledge and recognition).

The third door has to do with the eternality of Oedipality, the eternality of the patterned "Jewish" repetition (*Mal d'archive*, 115). According to Yerushalmi, Derrida claims, Judaism has, in its past, an original, Oedipal essence. In that sense, Judaism is directed, not to the future, but to the past. Throughout Yerushalmi's book, Derrida observes the troubled father-son relationship between God and the people of Israel. He also finds there a prophetic vision for resolving Oedipal relations: "And he shall turn the heart of the fathers to the children, and the heart of the children to their fathers." (Mal. 4:6). Judaism here turns its face to the future. According to Yerushalmi, Freud's want of faith in the future is a mark of the non-Jewishness of his book (*Moses and Monotheism*). "Being open to the future, that is being a Jew" (118).

Derrida sees double: the door opening is the door shutting. For the look to the future rests upon the past principle of the Jewish archive (memory). Condemnation to expectation (of the future) is condemnation to commemoration, condemnation to the future is condemnation to the past (after all, Yerushalmi's book *Zakhor*—"Remember"—identified Judaism with commemoration). Judaism thus has two conflicting avocations: hope for the future and memory of the past. One rests upon the other (*Mal d'archive*, 121).

Derrida wrote,

> I would like to spend hours, an eternity in fact, in trembling meditation on this sentence [of Yerushalmi. Au.]: "Only in Israel and nowhere else is the injunction to remember felt as a religious imperative to an entire people." How is one not to tremble before that sentence? I wonder whether it is true. . . . I wonder, trembling, whether they are correct, those sentences that reserve for Israel the future and past as such, and hope . . . the duty of remembrance . . . an assignment reserved solely for the people of Israel . . ." (122)

Yet again, Derrida wishes to remind us that archival memory is not confined to one people; that it is worth recalling the Others, those who are different, and that *tout autre est tout autre* (the selfsame sentence we shall encounter in the chapter "Derrida's Sacrificial Offering" puts in an appearance here, *Mal d'archive*, 123). The imperative of archival memory swearing fealty to a supreme "justice" is liable to guarantee injustice when it removes the Other from its domain. Injustice will be perpetrated in the name of justice, if and when justice is not based upon the principle of Otherness. Derrida recoils from singularity select and arrogant, of the kind in that definition of Judaism which appropriates demands of past-and-future. Wound, violence, those are his terms for a singularity that forgets the Other and whose archives do not include the Other. That is an archive (memory) that contradicts itself, for it enfolds forgetfulness. That is an evil archive, the archive of the death instinct, the urge toward patterned repetition of both memory and forgetfulness (126).

> There will be no future without repetition. Accordingly, Freud would perhaps say . . . there is no future without the specter of Oedipal violence inscribed . . . in the archival institution of the archive . . . in posting oneself as the One and Only, in the archenomological. The death impulse. Without that evil, that is also the archival evil . . . there will be neither assignment nor consignment. (128)

Those, virtually the book's final words, close a great cycle commencing in the early section of this chapter. The Judaism of "the chosen people" guarantees violence. The Judaism of opening up to the Other guarantees the moral imperative (identified, we recall, with the religious experience). This will be Judaism transcending itself, denying itself, putting itself to death. The Judaism of *l'autre kippa*.

The concept of desert also serves Derrida in his nontheological studies, such as his reading of Marx (*Spectres de Marx* [1993d]). Here he seizes upon the image of the specter(s) he identified in the *Communist Manifesto,* deducing therefrom a certain messianic expectation of the return of the spirit at any moment, as purpose (*telos*) of history (specters of Marx [New York: Routledge, 1994], 37). A kind of messianism promising the advent of justice. The concept of justice (of the socialist-communist variety, inter alia) rests upon recognition of the uniqueness (*singularité)* of the Other, of giving to the Other and his absolute priority, arising from the assumption that his existence precedes mine. Derrida sets out this expectation of the advent of the messiah, as fulfillment of this concept of justice, in the "desert" terms familiar to us from his theological discussion:

> of this desert-like messianism (without content and without identifiable messiah), of this also *abysmal* desert, "desert in the desert" . . . one desert signaling toward the other, abyssal and *chaotic* desert . . . the gaping hole of the open mouth—in the waiting or calling for what we have nicknamed here without knowing the messianic: the coming of the other, the absolute and unpredictable singularity of the *arrivant as justice*. We believe that this messianic remains an *ineffaceable* mark—a mark one neither can nor should efface—of Marx's legacy, and doubtless of *inheriting,* of the experience of inheriting in general.(*Specters of Marx* [New York: Routledge, 1998], 28)

Subsequently, in the course of his consideration of the Marxist concept of fetishism and its connection with religion (and still according to the rites of exorcising the ghosts that he identifies as the cornerstone of the Marxist texts), Derrida reverts to the messianic context of Marxist utopianism, connecting it with the concept of Jerusalem as promise. His purpose appears to be to purge messianic expectation of its mythological and nationalist constraints ("the Abrahamic figures") but simultaneously, to present it as the foundation of any religious messianism whatsoever—Jewish, Christian or Moslem. This unversalism of messianism (of Jerusalem, of the desert, etc.) also establishes a convoluted connection with the great dialogue Derrida conducts with death, a kind of expectation of a Resurrection of another kind:

> At stake first of all is that which takes the original form of a return of the religious, whether fundamentalist or not . . . everything that concentrates its habitat in the at least symptomatic figure of Jerusalem, here and there. . . . How to relate, but also how to dissociate the two messianic spaces we are talking about here under the same name? If the messianic appeal belongs properly to a universal structure, to that irreducible movement of the historical opening to the future, therefore to experience itself and to its language . . . how is one to think it with the figures of Abrahamic messianism? Does it figure abstract desertification or originary condition? Was not Abrahamic messianism but an exemplary precondition, the name (*prénom*) given against the background of the possibility that we are attempting to name here? But then why keep the name, or at least the adjective (we prefer to say *messianic* rather than *messianism,* so as to designate a structure of experience rather than a religion), there where no figure of the *arrivant,* even as he or she is heralded, should be pre-determined, prefigured, or even pre-named? Of these two deserts, which one, first of all, will have signaled toward the other? Can one conceive an a-theological heritage of the messianic? . . . A heritage is never natural, one may inherit more than once, in different places and at different times . . . and sign thus more than one import. . . . Ascesis strips the messianic hope of all biblical forms, and even all determinable figures of the wait or expectation, it thus denuded itself in view of responding to that which must be absolute hospitality, the "yes" to the *arrivant(e),* the "come" to the future that cannot be anticipated. . . . Open, waiting for the event as justice, this hospitality is absolute only if it keeps watch over its own universality. This messianic, including its revolutionary forms (and the messianic is always revolutionary, it has to be) would be urgency, imminence but, irreducible paradox, a waiting without horizon of expectation. One may always take the quasi-atheistic dryness of the messianic to be the condition of the religions of the Book, a desert that was not even theirs (but the earth is always borrowed, on loan from God, it is never possessed by the occupier, says precisely [*justement*] the Old Testament whose injunction one would also have to hear); one may always recognize there the arid soil in which grew, and passed away, the living figures of all the messiahs, whether they were announced, recognized, or still awaited. One may also consider this compulsive growth . . . to be the only events on the basis of which we approach and first of all name the messianic in general, that other ghost which we cannot and ought not do without.

One may deem strange, strangely familiar and inhospitable at the same time (*unheimlich*, uncanny) this figure of absolute hospitality whose promise one would choose to entrust to an experience that is so impossible . . . so anxious, fragile, and impoverished . . . a quasi-transcendent "messianism" that also has such an obstinate interest in a materialism without substance; a materialism of the *khôra*. . . . But without this latter despair . . . hope would be but the calculation of a program. One would have the prospect but one would not longer wait for anything or anyone. Law without justice. One would no longer invite, either body or soul, no longer receive any visits, no longer even think to see. To see coming. Some, and I do not exclude myself, will find this despairing "messianism" has a curious taste, a taste of death. (ibid., 167–69)[6]

5

Derrida's "Yom Coupure"

If "writing" is rupture, destruction, and injury, any one of Jacques Derrida's numerous books is a scab upon the circumcision wound, his and ours, as Jews and human beings. But his *Circonfession* [1991] is the great operating table upon which he performed his autosurgery, harsh and incisive, on the subject of circumcision.

Circonfession (1991a) was written as three-hundred-page footnote to Geoffrey Bennington's *Jacques Derrida*. It is like a personal clocking in on Bennington's back, confounding the answer to the question: Who is writing whom (like that other blessed confusion in Derrida's other book, *La carte postale* [1980], featuring the unresolved mutuality between Socrates and Plato.)? *Circonfession* is thus a kind of drab subtext at the foot of the pages, a phantom text representing Derrida as "Other." Other than whom? Other than the Other who writes of him (as Other) and other than himself. For this philosophical autobiography is a bold experiment in self-awareness by means of an encounter with his Otherness, in this case—Derrida's mother; her death; and his death; and through her to the infinite Other, father and God.

Circonfession is a book of confessions (the title suggests "confession truncated," circon(cision)fession, truncated circumcision, a joining-together of truncated entities, of fragments set against the death agonies of the philosopher's sick mother. "One always confesses the other, I confess means I confess my mother" (*Circonfession,* 139). The book consists of fifty-nine ruptures, fifty-nine short chapters marking the author's fifty-nine years (he wrote the book in 1989–90) as he eulogizes himself no less than he eulogizes his mother in an abbreviated confession-eulogy—a book that is the book of life and the book of the dead, the injury: an incurable injury, the injury of circumcision; *Circonfession*: confession and circumcision, a duality that is one.

Derrida reverts repeatedly to his own circumcision as though recalling the trauma of his lifetime. He remembers the Hebrew *milah* (*Circonfession,*

p. 71) even though, as noted, Algerian Jews preferred the term "baptism" (72). Over and again he turns and re-turns the ring of his foreskin, an interminable repetition transformed into his psychic-existential time, just as it becomes the principal philosophical lever of his work. Thus, *Circonfession* becomes a book that associates—to an embarrassing degree—rarefied pinnacles of philosophy with narcissism. Derrida is aware thereof: "'my' circumcision, enormous narcissist monument . . ."(197).

Derrida is closely attentive to the *Confessions* of St. Augustine, another figure with whom he senses an affinity. Augustine likewise lived and worked in North Africa (Hippo), and he too composed his "Confessions" (his discourse with God) shortly after the death of his mother, St. Monica. But whereas Augustine wrote his theological reflections after his mother's demise, Derrida typed his own personal-theological reflections (in Santa Monica, California!) against the background of the grave illness of his mother, Georgette-Sultana-Esther Safar Derrida, still alive in Nice, albeit in a coma that rendered her unable to see or speak: like God, who neither speaks nor returns a regard. "I address her," wrote Derrida, "as [I address] my God, to confess" (*Circonfession*, 57). From this point on, Derrida's confessions are interwoven—intimately yet remotely—with those of Augustine, and with a third text: "The Book of Élie [Elijah]" that Derrida wrote between the years 1976 and 1981 but did not publish. This latter work focuses on the torments of Derrida's circumcision as existential-metaphysical crucifixion. It should again be noted that Derrida inscribed the Hebrew word *milah* on the cover of the notebook in which he wrote "The Book of Élie."

Death reigns in *Circonfession*: thoughts of suicide; the death of his year-old brother Paul-Moïse (a year before the birth of Jacques); the death of another brother, Norbert-Pinhas at the age of two (when Jacques was ten); a partial paralysis that affected Derrida's face in June 1989 (possibly, he explains, in retribution for his entry into forbidden places [118]); the death throes of his mother. Starting out with blood, he clings to that motif throughout the book. However, the dread of blood he recalls from his childhood experiences in Algeria, linking it with injuries, blood tests, a menstrual pad, and so on, makes way for the book's blood-fear: the blood of "the unforgettable circumcision" (16) that his father inflicted upon his physical body, as also the symbolical circumcision that Geoffrey Bennington inflicted upon his writings (30).

Taking this book as authority, we can affirm with certainty that circumcision is Jacques Derrida's most basic philosophical experience: the enforced incision (in substance as in form: for example, see the divided structure of this very book) the separation, the castration the father perpetrated upon his son; in theological rendition: the distance the divine father imposes upon the devotee-son; in hermeneutic rendition: the incision, the separation, the fissure, that "speech" inflicted upon "writing." As Derrida puts it: "Circumcision—I have never spoken of anything but that, consider the discourse on the limit, the margins, marks, marches, etc., the fence, the ring (Covenant and gift) the sacrifice, the bodily inscription, the *pharmakos*" [the "healer" in "Plato's Pharmacy," *Dissémination*. Au.] (*Circonfession*, 70).

Elsewhere he writes: "The limit is the circumcision, the thing, the word, the book" (*Circonfession*, 76) Further, "the desire for literature is the circumcision" (77). That being the case, Derrida embarks on a voyage to the absent phallus, an expedition to his Otherness (if not his subconscious): "In my grain store I accumulate my 'sublime' documents . . . about circumcisions in the world, and the Jewish one, and the Arab one, and the others . . . from the viewpoint of my sole circumcision, the circumcision of myself, the one and only one, the one I know well to have taken place, one single time, I have been told of it and I see it" (59–60).

What prompts an elderly philosopher to preoccupy himself so obsessively with a ritual act performed upon his sex organ when he was a mere eight days old? The answer should apparently be sought in Derrida's adherence to the doctrine of Jacques Lacan, which had a considerable influence upon his views (and with which Derrida preoccupied himself directly and frequently, as in "For the Love of Lacan," a chapter in his *Résistances de la psychanalyse* [1996e]). Lacan was renowned for his enormous interest in the Freudian theory of castration and the signifying preeminence he attributed to the phallus in his renowned essay "Significance of the Phallus" (1958). This preeminence is linked to the ego-molding theory, which draws a distinction between the "mirror stage" (the ego's narcissistic identification with the similar, the mother) and the "symbol stage," the stage of standing versus the Other, versus the father, in a system of signifiers.

According to this theory, the presence of the "symbolical" is contingent upon the absence of the symbolized (according to Lacan, absence has a symbolic potency equal to that of completeness). The "symbolical" is the heterogeneous, fractured domain, the domain of the disjointed ego. As the symbol is in effect the "murder" of the thing (and concomitantly the birth of the insatiable craving for the absent thing), death is the essence of the stage of symbol. Reigning at the center of the world of symbols is the phallus; phallocentrism, that is, the phallus as the most stable and permanent of all signs. As noted, the Freudian concept of castration is the theoretical cornerstone of Lacan's perception of the phallic psychic structure: the male's dread of the future loss of his penis; woman's affliction over the loss of penis. Woman's lack of phallus (compensated by the insertion of the male penis or the birth of a baby as phallus substitute emerging from the vaginal canal) and the male's dread of losing the penis—that is the basic structure from which the other psychic structures emerge, the various other signing procedures, according to Lacan. That which is absent from the body exists in the imagination: the female craving for a phallus, the male craving for a monumental erection. The phallus is the ideal sign, combining presence (physical protuberance) and absence (as contraction or hole). As supersign, the phallus is the great promise of significance. The phallus, absent and present, unites thought and body.[1]

I believe that the foregoing can elucidate why Derrida invests the phallus with supreme epistemological status (combining Platonic logo-centrality with phallo-centrality); why the experience of castration underlies his Oedipal quest for the truth, and his incisive stance vis-à-vis his absent father; and why the experience of the absent in the present—the diminution of the sex organ in the act of circumcision—functions as virtual Cartesian axis in uniting body and soul. Thus are death and circumcision mutually interwoven, Derrida comparing the rabbi's ritual ripping of the mourner's apparel with "the ripping of the skin" by the *mohel's* knife (*Circonfession*, 157). The existential situation thus becomes one of permanent victim "as though I were someOne whom the One God incessantly circumcises" (208). Knowing yourself entails knowing the secret of your circumcision. Learning to love entails reopening the circumcision wound and analyzing the secret (212).

We revert to Derrida and his *Circonfession* (and the "Book of Élie" included therein): the book of the secret, the secret that hinges upon the absent foreskin. In this book-within-a-book, Derrida identifies, in the sacrifice of his member, the banquet of wine and blood intermingled and mixed with semen and saliva. "Describing my member over thousands of years of Judaism, describing it . . . until the paper is ripped . . . if possible leaving nothing in the shade of what it is that connects me to Judaism" wrote Derrida (145). It was a cannibal repast that also underlies the seminar "Eating the Other" that he taught in the late 1980s.

Circumcision is the experience of the eternal scar that will never heal; eternal eschatology, eternal injury (91) a never-ending crucifixion (222), an ocean of blood and a mighty sponge, as in St. Augustine's *Confessions* (*Circonfession*, 101–2). *Yom Kippur* and *Yom Coupure* [Day of Atonement and day of incision. Trans.] mutually intermingled (188) to become an eternal *Yom Kippur* in Derrida's life. Indeed, the philosopher rampages madly around the ring of his foreskin. He, baby Derrida, is in the arms of his uncle (similarly named "Elijah," like Jacques's own middle name), who is seated in "Elijah's chair": the seventh day in Algeria, 1930 (seventh? Has Derrida mistakenly omitted the additional eighth day?),[2] the blood soaked up in a scrap of cottonwool, the bandage around the mutilated penis, the orange petal ointment sprinkled to assuage the pain; that relentless pain, the burning, the terrible inflammation of the flesh, the torment forever arising vis à vis the pain of the Other (his mother in particular). Like now, when the son offers his dying mother the bandage soaked in orange water to assuage her pains.

The mother is guilty. She is to blame for her son's circumcision (*Circonfession*, 73), for the act of violent cannibalism that the father perpetrated upon his son (and which, it will be recalled, Derrida would refuse to inflict upon his own sons). "[T]he role of the mother in the circumcision . . . her fawning pose as the desire to carry out the circumcision blends with the suppressed desire to murder the child . . ." (176). The mother, in a typically Lacanian act, seeks to make up for the lack of phallus by the act of its insertion, albeit in a substitute hole, the mouth: here she, the mother, carries out the circumcision, as in the biblical tale ("Then Zipporah took a sharp stone, and cut off the foreskin of her son, and cast it at his feet, and said, 'Surely a bloody husband art thou to me'" [Exod. 4:25]). Georgette Esther is in the role of Zipporah, Jacques in that of Moses' son, and the covenant between mother and son is as an awesome bloody wedding: "slowly provoking the ejaculation in her mouth at the moment that she swallows the bloody circle of skin with the sperm as mark of an exultant alliance, her arms open, hers enclosed in mine, laughing, both laughing, passing the skins from mouth to mouth, like a ring (203).

The "parchment" on which Derrida wrote the confessions of his *Circonfession* is the foreskin, the writing carried out in a posture of oral copulation with the mother in the course of the circumcision (213). But pointing an accusing finger at the mother is merely a substitute for the true culprit, the great absentee (who is replaced by the son, taking over the sexual role), Derrida's giant Other, the father (who passed away in 1970). After all, the accused is the beloved mother, whereas the vanished father represents the painful emotional account (which all of Derrida's books are an attempt to resolve). Is it a reckoning with God?

It is only a reading of *Glas* (1974) that makes plain the true allocation of blame between mother, father, and son. *Glas* relates Hegel's version of the mythical event that inaugurated human society: prior to the Flood, man lived in harmony with nature, his mother. This idyll was disrupted by the Flood. Henceforth, Mother Nature would turn against mankind. The sole way of overcoming the fury of the rising waters was by taming nature through the power of thought. For the concept of reason (the dialectical "spirit" at its raw level) will reunite that which is divided. In fact, that is Noah's accomplishment. He builds his ark as realization of a concept and as unification of opposites (opposite sexes, warring animal species, etc.). Nimrod, king of Shenar, went further in the same direction, but he applied force to found a uniform society. The Tower of Babel that he constructed (see below the chapter "Tower of Babel") is a forceful-uniform response to an enraged Mother Nature. This marks the onset of the conflict between Jewish and Greek cultures, for this stance is entirely unlike the gentle affection displayed by Deucalion and Pyrrha, who, on the morrow of the Flood, summoned mankind to renew its friendship with Nature.

The Jew's attitude toward nature (the Hegelian assumption is that Noah and Nimrod were Jews) is harsh and unfriendly. The absence of harmony with nature is the absence of a sense of beauty. The Jew remains divided and torn, that being the source of his ugliness. And indeed, as illustrated likewise by the annals of the patriarch Abraham, his departure from Ur of the Chaldees in effect cut him off from family, from natural love. The act of separation is thus the very essence of the birth of the Jewish people. Abraham's story is a tale of divorce from nature, of eternal alienness: desert, wilderness, wandering, war with the peoples whose domains he invaded, even the search for a bride for his son among the alien people of Canaan.[3] Thus, against this Hegelian setting to circumcision, the latter act should be seen as mark of isolation, mark of an identity of separation and excision characterizing Abraham and his people (*Glas*, 50). Circumcision facilitates the act of excision, but simultaneously condemns you to remain bound to the incision. The circumcision covenant is a covenant of excision. Abraham remained bound to the "cutting" of one of his bodily members, as were his descendants who underwent the *milah*.

Abraham capitulated to the infinite divine power, becoming its slave. Incapable of loving his God, he could only fear Him. Neither was he capable of loving his own son. For according to the Hegelian interpretation, having circumcised his son Isaac, he cut himself off from him. The sacrificial offering up of Isaac is thus merely the other side of the coin to the circumcision: castration of the son, the absence of love for him, the slave's subservience to the cruel God (*Glas*, 51). In this incarnation, nonpaternal, ugly, and detached, the Jew is death. His heart is a heart of stone (and he petrifies into stone all who come into contact with him). He was chosen to be God's favorite (in time, the "Chosen People") solely because the Jewish God is an equally cruel and detached (concealed) father (54). Being imprinted with the simulacrum of castration (circumcision), the Jew exists for the purpose of enduring emasculation. "He exhibits his castration as though it were an erection as challenge to another" (56). Derrida ostensibly adopts Hegel's interpretation, which renders philosophical support to Lacan's aforementioned view. The combination leaves Derrida no way out at the level of the autobiographical narrative. Elisabeth Weber reminded him of his comments on circumcision as a consistent thread in his writings, and of his statement that "Every man is 'circumcised by language . . . and so is every woman'" (*Circonfession*, 188), asking him to explain this ideological persistence. Derrida responded by pointing to the paradox in the expression "turning about"—which is the unity of contradictions between the obsession (arising from the adherence to the thing about which one revolves endlessly) and desisting (arising from the movement around the thing, without touching it). A dual relationship of attachment and remoteness. Particularly when one is revolving around something that remains an injury" (Weber, *Questions au judaïsme* [Paris: Desclée de Brouwer 1996], 74). The injury does not enable you to withdraw from your body, but simultaneously, there is enormous difficulty in describing the experience of your attachment to the injury ("my experience, or the experience of my connection with—I dare not say 'to Judaism'—let's say, to the circumcision" [75]).

The level of detachment from the injury is also the level of Derrida's impersonal, general, and universal understanding. For to him (as he explains in reply to Weber) circumcision is more than a mere mark of the Covenant between God and the people of Israel. It is a universal mark applying to any person insofar as he is a person (man or woman), and indeed, a mark applying to every people (ibid.)—Judaism as universality, as supra-Judaism. Thus, if circumcision is the root of the lingual rupture, we face a Jewish ritual phenomenon representing a supra-Jewish truth.

Elucidation and expansion of the dimension of universality of the circumcision found expression in Derrida's book on Nietzsche, *Éperons* (Spurs) [1978a]. After presenting and interpreting Nietzsche's perception (in *The Gay Science*) of woman as "style"—as manifestation, superficial, vision, appearance, remoteness, beauty—that is, as something beyond truth, Derrida linked Nietzsche with Lacan to associate truth with phallocentrality, and thus accepted woman as aphallic and removed from the domain of actual castration, which is a masculine domain (unless we are dealing with feminists . . . *Éperons*, 50). The feminine is the domain of the virtual, exhibition and beauty, not the domain of penetration to the profundities of permanent and absolute truth, the domain of the true erection or its emasculation (corroboration or refutation of the truth). The feminine is the domain of an imagined castration. This explains the significance of the imagined castration arising from the mother's touch in *Circonfession*. At this point, Derrida is able to set Nietzsche in the Lacanian formula vis-à-vis the phenomenon of Judaism. Here we find Nietzsche categorizing Jews and women in the camp of nontruth, along with actors and other "pretend" persons ("Is there today a good actor who is not Jewish?" Nietzsche, *The Gay Science*, sect. 361).

Women and Jews represent the simulacrum of emasculation, and what is emasculation if not circumcision? (*Éperons*, 54) Is woman the fulfillment of Judaism? As antiphallus, she is the foundation of Derrida's analogy between Jew and woman: "The Jew is merely a woman, the Jew is feminization or femininity of society, a threat to all the virile values reigning in a community, an army, a nation, etc." (Weber, *Questions au judaïsme* [Paris: Desclée Brouwer, 1996], 89). Derrida sets this unity (woman = Judaism) and this contradiction (Judaism as against army, state, etc.) as challenge to all the nations of the world, Israel included (ibid.) In this context, he calls for a reassessment of woman's role and the role of the army in Israel:

> What does a woman become there? What becomes of the value of femininity? I don't pretend to claim that there is unanimity on the subject, for example in the state of Israel. But there are various movements of which some can be analyzed or suspected of sharing in these schemes. There are numerous ways of thinking about the Israeli nation or state, numerous ways of thinking about the army, the purpose of the Israeli army, numerous ways of thinking about the attitude to woman in that society, in that religion, but also in its army. I don't have any cut-and-dried conclusion, but I would like to pose the issue. (ibid.)

How is one to reconcile Hegel's Jew with Nietzsche's? If woman has been appropriated to the camp of beauty, while the Jew is expelled, how is one to reunite Jew and woman after all the claims put forward hitherto? Nietzsche regarded Jews as "actors," whereas Hegel set an abyss between Jews and beauty or art. Derrida does not attempt to reconcile the two interpretations, even if he is inclined to identify the Jew with the feminine. Furthermore, Lévinas (in his *Totality and Infinity*) identified the feminine with the principle of domesticity, inclusiveness, hospitality. How does Derrida reconcile this "femininity" with Jewish "femininity," that is, with the Jewish people's status as refugee, stranger, and guest? Is the Jewish people in essence a hospitable people?

6

Countenance Averted

Here and there, we have observed an asymmetrical division in the writing:
. . . on the one hand, the theological encyclopedia . . . the book of man; on
the other, a tissue of traces marking the disappearance of God exceeded, or
man effaced. . . .

Original writing, writing tracing the original tracking the signs of its
disappearance, the lost writing of the original.

"Writing is having the passion for the original." [Edmond Jabès, *Return of the Book* (1965). Au.]

But what affects writing, we now know, is not the original but that
which replaces it. This is not absence in place of presence, rather, a trace
that replaces a presence that was never present . . .

Something invisible is lacking in the grammar of repetition. This repetition is writing, for what disappears in it is the original's own identity, the
independent presence of what is known as living speech. That is the center.
The lure upon which the first book, the mythical book preceding any repetition, became lifelike, was that the center is protected from any game:
irreplaceable . . . the invariable first name to be invoked but not repeated. . . . The moment . . . it is written . . . it becomes an abyss, a
bottomless pit of infinite duplication. The other is in the similar . . .

The moment a sign appears, it begins by repeating itself. Otherwise, it
would not be a sign . . . that nonidentity with self forever reverting to the
same. That is to say, denoting another sign itself born of self-division. The
graphic sign, in repeating itself thus, has neither natural place nor center. . . . Is not this center, this absence of game and difference, another
name for death? . . .

An absent presence, a black sun . . . (From the chapter titled "Ellipsis," *L'écriture et la différence*, 429–32)

Otherness is nothingness, absence, death. Any Other is "alive" and
"dead" (even when I say "we," it is one who is saying the word
while the others are absent (*Résistances de la psychanalyse* [1996e], 61). Ever

present is the lingual tension between the presence and absence of the Other, between the sign and the signified.

As far back as 1968, "Plato's Pharmacy" (*La dissémination* [1972a]) presented the connection between "writing" and *logos* as the unbalanced relationship between son and father. Derrida's interpretation of several of Plato's texts depict "writing" as the craving for orphanhood, for liberation from the *logos* (which features in Plato's writings as organic truth and virtue). Goodness (the father, the primary sun) is the concealed and ambivalent source, shining or dazzling (burning the eyes). "The *logos*," concludes Derrida, "is thus the resource, one should turn toward it, not merely when the solar source is present and threatens to scorch our eyes if we fix them on it . . . but also when the sun appears to be absent during an eclipse. Dead, extinguished, or concealed, that star is more dangerous than ever" (95).

The relationship between "writing" and *logos* is equally the connection between "writing" and "speech." Speech is the original divine voice, whereas writing is a secondary product, a substitute, like the moon vis-à-vis the sun. We can easily match such relationships with the affinity between Tuth, the Egyptian god of writing, and his father Amon-Ra. Tuth is simultaneously the god of death, and, as the Egyptian *Book of the Dead* relates, death is the path to the sun, to taking up position face-to-face with it. But Tuth, god of writing and death, is also a healing deity, "*pharmakon.*" It should be recalled that in Plato's writings (as Derrida construed them, of course) the man preoccupied with intoxicating drugs and poisons is the trickster, the swindler. Indeed, writing, the expanse of signs, is an act of deceit. It repeats, in artificial imitation, something genuine that preceded it. However, it is a dead repetition, for it cannot stand the test of living speech, the *logos*. In Derrida's interpretation, Plato's texts project writing as magic simulacrum, as mask or grease paint, or, to be precise, the makeup smeared on the faces of the dead to endow them with a semblance of life. To revert to the model of the father-son relationship, writing is an illegitimate son, a bastard not acknowledged by his father. Writing is thus a son abandoned by his father, but also the son's violence toward his father. The remoteness between father and son is mutual. Concomitantly, father and son are condemned to one another. The primary truth (as presence of the idea) is contingent upon the connection with the nonpresence, with nontruth (which is language, writing):

> If truth is the presence of the *eidos*, it must always connect, other than the mortal blindness brought on by the fire of the sun, with the . . . nonpresence, and thus, with the non-truth . . .

> The absolute invisibility of the origin of the visible, of the good-sun-father . . . all the presences will be mere substitutes for the absent origin. . . . the forbidden intuition of the visage of the father . . . The disappearance of the visage is the movement from the *différance* which violently launches writing. (*La dissémination,* 192–93)

At the same time, Derrida writes there: "The disappearance of the truth as presence, the concealment of the present origin of presence, is the condition for any (revelation) of the truth. Untruth is truth. Non-presence is presence" (194).

Revelation of these relationships in Plato's writings merely marked the launch of an *exposé* of relationships of father-and-son, original-and-copy, sign-and-signified, in Western culture and its philosophical and religious traditions. In between Derrida's hermeneutics and his theology runs this line of the concealment of the primary truth. Indeed, in many of his works, where he refers to the remoteness of these relationships, one can detect residues of Jewish mystical philosophy hinging upon the "the Divine countenance averted." Thus, for example, Derrida's discussion of Hegel's doctrine illuminates the disparate father-son relationships in Christianity and Judaism: according to Hegel (who regarded the revelation of truth as the revelation of light) the Christian revelation of light is the revelation of the Son of God and his return to his Father in heaven—a kind of family reunion. Such unity is not to be found in Judaism, argues Hegel (as interpreted by Derrida); Judaism condemns father and son to eternal conflict. The Christian is required to believe in the light as condition for his being transformed into light. The disciples of Jesus (who is the light) were united in his flame, as twigs are united in the central trunk of the vine. But Jesus' death (his crucifixion) is precondition for their achievement of light. In other words: only when the vine branch is sheared off will the barrier separating father (God) from his sons be removed. Jesus is the barrier blocking the way to the divine light, hence the inevitability of his death (*Glas* [1974], 95). By contrast, Judaism leaves the father (God) inaccessible, without any mediation. The hidden light (*or ganuz*), the primeval infinite light, is reserved for the righteous alone. God's concealment of His countenance is eternal. God's inner withdrawal "from Himself to Himself" in an act of "contraction" was not a temporary act.

God is source of all significance and law; it was He who granted the text, the laws, the Torah. The question is whether Derrida's possibly most renowned sentence, "*Il n'y a pas dehors text*" (Nothing exists beyond the text) (*De la grammatologie* [1967a], 227), signifies (inter alia) that there is no God outside the text. But how are we to reconcile the concept of God with the aforementioned condemnation of the term "writing" as nontruth? Clearly, this was not what he meant. Derrida appears to have intended to say: God is not revealed in "writing" and we are condemned to be blind, deaf, and dumb. It is this setting that explains the Cohen's [priest's] Blessing (uttered while concealing his face beneath the *talith*, i.e., his "blindness"): "May God illuminate His countenance toward you and grant you grace" as a benediction associated with the notion of revelation of the divine light, which illuminates the righteous ("light strewn for the righteous") and that is the meaning of the prayer (uttered as the Torah scroll is removed from the ark, i.e., revealed): "And let us see Him eye to eye when He returns to his oasis, as it is written: for they shall see eye to eye, when the Lord shall bring again Zion. And we shall utter and reveal the honor of the Lord and all flesh shall see together that the mouth of the Lord has spoken" (from the prayers for *Rosh Hashana,* Jewish New Year)—the revelation of the Torah as verbal preparation for the visual revelation of the Blessed Lord.

But at the same time, the Jewish point of departure is the self-concealment of God, or, in Kabbalah terms, the contraction and the secret. Not even Moses saw God face-to-face, only from behind (like Plato seeing Socrates from the rear in the primary postcard of *La carte postale* [1980]: "No connection . . . S. does not see P., who sees S., but (here's the truth of philosophy) solely *from the rear.* There exists nothing but the *rear,* the view from the rear in what is written, that's the final word" (55). Derrida also recalls (*L'écriture et la différence* [1967b]) the words of Emanuel Lévinas, that the countenance of God is the total presence of "the eternal speech to Moses face-to-face" but also that the countenance tells Moses: "Thou canst not see my face: for there shall no man see me, and live. And the Lord said, Behold, there is a place by me, and thou shalt stand upon a rock: And it shall come to pass, while my glory passeth by, that I will put thee in a clift of the rock, and will cover thee with my hand while I pass by: And I will take away mine hand, and they shalt see my back parts: but my face shall not be seen" (Exod. 33:20–23). That should be borne in mind in reading this chapter and its claim that underlying Derrida's writings is the assumption, simultaneously monotheistic and radical, that the source is unattainable. Accordingly, Derrida's reiterated resort to negative theology is a resort to the sphere of vacuity, the realm of the infinite Other, God.

But we must not forget that the sphere of discourse with God as possible impossibility is the cornerstone of deconstruction (*Sauf le nom* [1993c], 31). For since deconstruction is the experience of the impossible, that means venturing into the world of "death" and "absence," with the object of proving the absence, and the infinite self-concealment of the source, of the Other, as finite and infinite. The absence of the primary voice, the voice of God, is behind the signs, the "writing." Thus does negative theology become the domain of conversation with the dead, or of evocation of spirits. In these contexts, Derrida again recalls that Heidegger defines death as the possibility of the impossibility of *Dasein,* adding: "This whole mysterious silence can also be understood as potent discourse about death, as discourse about the (impossible) possibility of the own death of the being who speaks" (34).

Deconstruction and negative theology are thus allied. Indeed, Derrida identifies in deconstruction "the last witness," a kind of late-twentieth-century *martyre de foi* (martyr of faith). We should thus not experience surprise if "the last Jew" (the last witness—see chapter 1) is Derrida the Deconstructivist, for whom the paths of negativism and paradox rest upon the rationale of theology (see the chapter titled "How Not to speak?" *Psyché* [1987c], 539).

Notwithstanding its character—analytical (in the dismantling of the argument, the institution, etc.) and "archeological" (in the quest for the ancient origin), deconstruction rejects the possibility of reverting to the source, or the feasibility of a unifying synthesis. In his *Résistances de la psychanalyse* [1997e] Derrida deals with these traits of deconstruction, pointing to the inevitable conflict between deconstruction and analysis (41–42). The latter, Derrida stresses, seeks some kind of synthesis at the end of the analysis, whereas the process of disassembling in deconstruction is eternal. Separation, or *divisibilité,* is thus a fundamental principle of deconstruction. Accordingly, it will acknowledge no element of simple origin (no *logos,* no *Geist,* no substance) that is indivisible, that is, that completes the process of disassembling (48). In other words, bottomless chasms separate the seeker-after-truth from the primary truth. Any additional abyss leaves the seeker-after-truth with an additional ruin of truth. This approach entails a theological position, no less than a hermeneutic one, as it condemns the concept of God (as source, *logos*) to everlasting division, everlasting separation, or—to resort to the concepts of Jewish mysticism—to the eternal averting of divine countenance; or, as the Kabbala puts it: *Reisha delo yada* (the unattainable head).

Derrida homes in on the very essence of the negative theology paradox, which sets silence and absence at the heart of the dialogue with God, and is condemned, at best, to negative reference (negativism of subtraction and evacuation) in relation to the divine traits.[1] It is the paradox of knowledge of the unknown, and blind testimony (prayer as testimony). Thus, in his *Sauf le nom* (1993c) the title already suggests the riddle of that which cannot be named (*l'innomable*). Derrida does not overlook Heidegger's statement that the *logos* is "the *logos* of no one" and that "if man must one day arrive in the neighborhood of Being, he must first learn to exist in that which has no name." In regard to which Derrida comments: "Did not the Kabbala also speak of the unnamable possibility of the Name?" (*Writing and difference* [Chicago: Univ. of Chicago Press, 1978], 137).[2]

With that, Derrida does not link negative theology specifically with Judaism—not directly, at least. On the contrary, the center of gravity of his discussion in these contexts rests upon ancient Christian-mystic sources, including the writings of Angelus Silesius (*The Cherubial Wanderer*); St. Augustine (*Confessions*); the Revelation of St. John (Apocalypse); Pseudo-Dionysius (*The Divine Names*); Meister Eckhart (*Sermons*); and so on. These mystical texts, Derrida stresses, do not prove "knowledge of God," for He is beyond knowing. The confession genre, for example, supplants the knowledge of God with the awakening of love (*Sauf le nom*, 23) in addressing a friend (28). But that love confirms separation from the beloved.

Derrida's reiterated question relating to the crossing of borders (a question simultaneously geographical, existential and cognitive)—the question of the refugee, the homeless (*Schibboleth* [1986c]; *De l'hospitalité* [1997b])—now impinges upon the border zone between the being and the beyond being (*Sauf le nom*, 18). The formula ("slogan") of the transition or border-crossing is now perceived as an archival series of mechanistic or canonical utterances of empty speech (46–47), for the devotional text is evidently incapable of representing the existence of the self-concealed divinity. The negative theological expanse remains a desert (see the chapter "The Other *Kippa*"); that is, an expanse of utter silence, where God is dumb, and His Name alone is known.

During his sojourn in Jerusalem in June 1986 as guest of the Hebrew University, Derrida delivered a lecture entitled "How Not to Speak?" His discussion revolved around the negative theology of neo-Platonic Christian mysticism, focusing upon the "divine names" of Pseudo-Dionysius (attributed to Dionysus the Areopagite). With these perceptions, Derrida again pinpointed the paradox of the nonentity Divinity, or the negative affirmation (*Psyché* [1987c], 540).[3] As he put it, negative theology enables intuition, or the eye, to unveil the concealed divine essence; mysticism guarantees presence and unity with the essence, through silence and deafness. Recalling Ludwig Wittgenstein's conclusion in *Tractatus* that one should keep silent about whatsoever cannot be talked about, Derrida affirms that, like any negative theology, the negative theological mysticism of Pseudo-Dionysius considers this silence in relation to the secret that must be preserved. Whosoever preserves the secret condemns himself to silence. As there is a secret, it must have a location: the place of God; A location that is nonlocation; a location beyond vision and appearance (see the chapter titled "The Place of *Makom*"); a location that cannot be reached, whose border cannot be crossed, and which is protected by the lingual barricade of "Shibboleth" (i.e., an expression whose test is withstood by a mere few: a sanctified few, the mystics). We are therefore dealing with opposites: location and nonlocation, total unity and infinite remoteness, silence and speech, becoming in the course of deletion.

Speech about, or to, God, that is, prayer to the Deity, presumes God as entity antedating language or preceded, by language, as something that was or something that will be, as promise. That coincides with the assumption that the true meaning of a text precedes the text and/or is revealed after its termination. At all events, the negative-theological movement of the psyche is the movement where the eye crosses the threshold of being to nonbeing so as to see that which does not presence itself. But this is merely the ego addressing the Other, the impossible, incapable of crossing the threshold, but concomitantly, of loving the unattainable Other, albeit merely at a lingual level; the name (*nom*) of God as name that represents nothing ("*qui ne nomme rien*"), "boundless desertification of language" (*Sauf le nom,* 56). Prayer maintains God as Platonic "*khôra*", a bodiless body, as absent body, and simultaneously, as body (place) of all. In this context, even if Derrida prefers to limit the expression "negative theology" exclusively to the Greek and Christian traditions (60), he refers to Judaism as a religion that combines the concept of "God" with the concepts of "location" and "the desert" (58). However, we should not forget that this is not a geographical location; rather, it is a place existing within ourselves, principally within our speech. "The here of eternity is located there" (60). It is language that bids us go to the concealed place, to the "there" (*là*), the inaccessible place, to the there (*là*) that is the name (*nom*) that is beyond the name (*nom*), to that which is within the name (*nom*) to that which preceded name and language (60). Beyond any doubt, the ambiguities of the two-letter Hebrew root shin mem (which combine into both *sham* (there) and *shem* (name). Trans.) enrich Derrida's interpretation, even if he is unfamiliar therewith. But in relation to the imperative of theological language, Derrida reminds us that the French *il faut* means both "it is necessary" and "he is absent."

The principle of negation is the principle of self-destruction at work at the heart of faith. It is the double bind of affirmation of God (communication with Him) and His denial as secret (*saufle nom,* 77). For an address to the name (*nom*) is, as already noted, simultaneously an address to that which is beyond the name. Thus is negative theology constructed on a discourse of abysses: the abyss of the ego calling the abyss of God (97); calling from abyss to abyss without crossing the threshold border between the two;

the call of the soul to the infinite Other, while leaving the Other in his Otherness; love as abandoning the Other (101). Simultaneously, negative theology is love and abandonment; the paradox of faith and atheism. Thus, the Name of God remains inaccessible secret. According to Derrida, names belong neither to those who endow them, nor to those who receive them. And as Derrida has already taught us, every signifier entails the death of the signified, giving a name is giving absence, giving lack of the essence of giving (112). An abyss yawns beyond the name of God.

Revelation of the divine secret is the ambition of the mystics. From his earlier works onwards, Derrida is forever ambiguous in relation to mystics, or magicians or *pharmakons* (*La dissémination* [1972a]). Thus, for example, his 1984 booklet *D'un ton apocalyptique adopté naguere en philosophie* recalls that Kant accused Plato of killing philosophy by introducing the mystical dimension into it. The mystics, argued Kant (as interpreted by Derrida) draw attention to the apparent mystery, the apparent (theatrical) sun, by keeping the secret of revelation as their private secret, as knowledge confined to a noble few. What need have they of philosophical thought if they are capable of bridging the gap between the listener's ear, the oracle, and the secret? They have no cause to analyze a concept, they can make do with a "leap" (to use Kierkegaard's term) into the heart of the vision. Thus, in Kant's view, Plato connived with these swindlers who shelter in the dark shadow of Isis's veil, diverting the masses away from the voice of reason. Indeed, in contrast with this Platonic tradition, which evolved into the various hues of neoPlatonism (Plotinus and his successors), Kant set about divesting metaphysics of the mystic envelope as the challenge of reason and enlightenment.

Derrida expands the domain of mysticism to embrace the concept of apocalypse, in mutual dependency. As he puts it, Christian and Jewish apocalypses rest upon mystical doctrines of numbers, revelation, and so forth (see *D'un ton apocalyptique*, 41). He claims that both, in their false claims, emasculate philosophy. In their visions, we shall forever encounter merely "the emissaries" of light, we are forever left with the promise of the advent of the Redeemer. Nevertheless, apocalypse infiltrated post-Kantian thought, as can be deduced from the philosophy of personages like Hegel, Nietzsche, Marx and so on, and postmodernists' apocalyptic talk of "the end of history," "the end of mankind," and so forth. In this context, Derrida refers to Nietzsche's oration about "the last man," and we recall Derrida's declaration that he is "the last Jew." However, his deconstructionist critique, partially directed at mystical-apocalyptic thought and the false promise of presencing divine light (the Revelation of St. John is an obvious example of such a promise) seems to backfire on Derrida himself: how can he define himself with so apocalyptic a sentence as "I am the last Jew" while simultaneously denying the concept of apocalypse? However, contradiction is not necessarily a fatal factor in Derridean thought. After all, he is in the habit of withdrawing out of himself so as to know himself; furthermore, from his point of view, his statement about "the last Jew" is largely ironical. Here, too, we must seek the solution of the contradiction between Derrida's critique of mysticism and his theologized resort to Christian mystics: he crosses borders, quitting the domain of philosophy for its mystical Other, just as he leaves it for literature, for example. Without countering the arguments against the pairing of mysticism and philosophy, Derrida delves into mystical literature—not as mystic, heaven forbid, nor to bring redemption and light; but rather, as essay, critical and interpretative, as paradoxical elucidation of preservation of the secret and its revelation, silence and speech, and so on. In other words, he adopts a paradoxical strategy (as antimystical philosopher preoccupying himself with mystical literature) with the aim of illuminating paradoxes—Derrida pure and unadulterated (with just a smattering of the later Heidegger).

In his *Résistances* (1996e) Derrida wrote (after Freud) that, in spite of any possible analysis, every dream bears within it an impenetrable place, the place of the unknown and the irresolvable (24).[4] Similarly, he also writes there that an additional principal force defying analysis is to be found in the subconscious urge to repetition: the craving for patterns, the unchangeable, and death (37). Patterns denote an absence of progress, or elevation (*Aufhebung*) or dialectics. By analogy, certainly upon the basis of the link between religion and dream that Freud pointed out, certain conclusions are called for in relation to the impossibility of knowing the impenetrable place of faith, the place of God. In a further parallel, there is room for the concept that the patternlike nature of all writing (the devotional genre in particular) merely guarantees remoteness, and death, between the believer and the self-concealed object of his faith. It should be added within this Freudian context that the connection between faith and repression signifies that the repressed is that which is concealed. Furthermore, the Freudian theological notion of parricide (*Totem and Taboo*) condemns God to death, preserved as living by the disciple-son.

Derrida does not turn away from the abyss, the ruins, the graves, the ashes (see the chapter "Fire"). His interpretation (1982) of Kafka's story "Before the Gate of the Law" likewise focuses upon the eternal absence of the source of authority, of the sovereign, of the father of the law. Directly influenced by Freud's perception of moral law as repression (concealment), Kafka already expressed the notion in the title of his story: "Before" the gate of the law, at a distance from it. The authoritative nature of the law requires that it be removed from any "history," or any context of motive (see Kant's "purging" of moral law of any motives or purpose; Derrida points to this parallel, whereas we, his readers, recall the Kantian connection between goodness and God, between morals and religion). The villager who comes to meet the law will never achieve his purpose. The law will remain mysterious, invisible, concealed, dumb. The guard at the gate is there to block the way before the man who comes to meet the law. The gate is indeed open (the law is open to all), but the way is blocked. The distinction between man (the villager, the guard, and all the rest) and the source of the law is eternal. The place (*topos*) of the source of the law will never be known. The source is here as *différance*— delaying the significance beyond, after. Every additional guard is a further distancing, till death, of the encounter with the father of the law.

It is the double bind: the gate simultaneously open and closed. Within the law and outside it (after all, Derrida has taught us that truth is forever between the within and the without, somewhere in the *passe-partout* [matting] surrounding the painting beneath its frame [*La verité en peinture*, 1978b]). "[T]he law . . . has no essence . . . truth without truth . . . guarded by a guardian who guards nothing, the gate remaining open and it opens on nothing" ("Préjugés" [1985b], 123). We thus know nothing of the substance of the law. Like the villager, we are left without an iota of acquaintance with the identity of the law.

Derrida is interested primarily in the hermeneutic object of his parable: the text as guard and the open-closed gate that interdicts entry to the substance of the meaning behind the text ("Préjugés" [1985b], 128). Equally, however, he invites theological connections. In his view, the story ends "at the most religious moment," that is, when the villager, reduced to childhood (on all fours) and almost blind, nevertheless finds light in the darkness enveloping him (126). We recall the link that Derrida found between blindness and religious revelation (sight) (*Mémoires d'aveugle* [1990e]). He also reminds us that the text of the story is repeated in full in Kafka's *The Trial*, related by a priest, and he adds a comment about the talmudic nature of the scene between the priest and Josef K. (135, 137). The priest now strikes Derrida as resembling one of the rabbis of the Talmud.

Not fortuitously, Derrida concludes his interpretation on a Jewish theological note (his quotes from *The Trial* remind him of laying stones on the Maharal's tomb at the Jewish cemetery in Prague), for throughout his discussion, he has referred to the Jewish context of the "the divine countenance averted." He commences the connection by mentioning the remarks of Jean-Francois Lyotard (in *The Righteous*) on the Jew's obligation to obey God's law without knowing Him. The Jewish God commands obedience, but he who obeys knows nothing of Him who commands, nor the significance of His commands ("Préjugés" [1985b] 107). Later, he continues the connection, in reference to the Jewish "Holy of Holies," as illuminated in Hegel's doctrine: the emptiness at the heart of the Temple, the absence of essence, the absence of the meaning of the secret (126).

Derrida, who dwelled at length (in his *Glas* [1974]) on Hegel's attitude to Judaism, focuses his study on the Tent of Congregation, wherein Hegel perceived the major "aesthetic omission" of ancient Israel. According to Hegel, the people of Israel, naturally deficient in its ability to synthesize finite with infinite, or unite the abstract and the sensual, exhibited its infirmity in its main aesthetic architectural creation, the Tent of Congregation, which is nothing but an envelope surrounding emptiness and death. According to Derrida's reading of Hegel, the Tent of Congregation is a signifier without signified, an empty house, that is, the absence of a sensual form. The Jewish attempt to construct a home for the infinite terminated in the envelopment of emptiness, enclosing an inner "desert." The Tent of Congregation reveals nothing. It houses emptiness, a black hole, death—to employ Derrida's terms. Beyond the curtain (the *parochet* of the Holy of Holies) lies no center, no heart, empty space, nothing (*Glas,* 58). This emptiness expresses the Jew's total alienation, his estrangement from any tangibility or sensuality. The house that was to have guaranteed a cosy *Heimlischkeit* [warm homeliness], turned out to be *unheimlich* (uncanny), which is the anxiety of the "menaced."

Ostensibly, Derrida adopts no normative position in relation to Hegel's *critique.* But we have already observed how difficult it is to draw a distinction between Derrida and the text on which his interpretative discussion turns (unless his reservation is outspoken). In view of the manifest connection between Derrida's philosophy and Hegel's concept of the castrating father-God (see the chapter titled "Derrida's Yom Coupure" in this volume) the distinction is particularly difficult when the topic is a Hegelian text. The various texts of Derrida mentioned in this chapter seem to confirm the Hegelian observation regarding the envelope of emptiness, though without the normative residue denouncing Judaism (as "nation of slaves," etc.). Here we have Derrida's triple thread: deconstruction, negative theology, and Kabbalistic "divine countenance averted."

But as we have discovered, we cannot attribute mysticism, Jewish or otherwise, to a Derrida forever divided from his God by the principle of remoteness and abyss (in contrast with mystic unity). In a radio interview (in Germany in 1986, with Florian Ritzer) Derrida had the following to say in this context:

Anyway, fortunately or unfortunately for me, whichever you prefer, I am no mystic and there is no mystical element whatsoever in my work. In fact, my work is the deconstruction of values established by mystics . . . of the unspeakable. When I say I am no mystic, especially not a Jewish mystic, as Habermas claims, I do not say that in order to defend myself, just simply establish a fact. It's not just that personally I'm not a mystic; I also doubt whether anything written by me is touched with mysticism. As things stand, there have been numerous misunderstandings, not just between Habermas and me, but also with many German readers, as far as I can see. The reason is that the German philosophers don't read my texts directly, they resort to second-hand interpretations, American as a rule. For example: if Habermas speaks of my Jewish mysticism, he uses a book by Susan Handelman, which in my opinion is certainly interesting, but highly problematical in its claim that I am a stray scion of Judaism. . . . I am well aware that there is forever an attribution to the text of internal schemes and interventions, accordingly I don't demand to be read in such a way that my texts bring you to a kind of intuitive ecstasy; however, I do demand greater caution and criticality in relation to translations and contextual bypasses which are frequently remote from me. (translated from a Hebrew version of the text as quoted on the Internet)

7

The Place of Makom

Where does meaning lurk? That original truth, which is deferred and guaranteed in language, which is buried and/or messianic—where is it to be found? Where is its hiding-place? Unlike the energetic detective in Poe's "The Purloined Letter," who discovers the letter in a tiny cubbyhole in the kitchen (Poe's story, which featured in Jacque Lacan's study, also served Derrida in his essay "The Postman of Truth"), Derrida fails to find it. But, like that detective, it is evident to him that the location he seeks has to be a space of absence, empty, a kind of vagina constituting a negative phallus and castration:[1]

> The letter has a place of origin and a destination. It is not a subject, rather, a hole; an absence in relation to which the subject is constituted. The contour of that hole can be determined, and it magnetizes the entire trajectory of the bypass leading from hole to hole, from hole back to itself, and which thus has a *circular* form. It is thus clearly a matter of regulated *circulation* that organizes the return of the detour toward the hole. (*La carte postale* [1980], 465)

Is the hole the location of the *logos*? But we have learned that logocentric centers are empty. That argument was the foundation for Derrida's critique of structuralism (the latter assumed a center of structure).[2] All the same, whither has speech been banished? The vaginal space of absence suggests the place sought is feminine. We should stress again: we are considering a metaphysical place, the place of "sun," "light," "substance," "essence," and other concepts of absolute truth (represented in Western culture by masculine images!) of the annals of metaphysics. Derrida seemed to be seeking the place of the Almighty.

The place of God? But *makom* (Hebrew: place) is also a euphemism for God. In the first century, Philo of Alexandria interpreted the Biblical phrase "And he [Jacob] lighted upon a certain place" (Gen. 28:11) at three levels: (*a*) a place as a space filled in material form; (*b*) a place as divine word filling the being with potential (So far, the interpretations are entirely Aristotlean); and (c) place is God containing things, without Himself being contained (Philo, "On Dreams", in *The Concept of Place in Neoplatonism,* ed. and trans. S. Sambursky (Jerusalem: Israel Academy of Sciences and Humanities, 1982), 35.

The Jewish sages of antiquity supported the third of those interpretations, though it is highly doubtful whether they attributed them to Philo.[3] In "B'reshit Raba," (chap. 68, 28, 11) we read: "And he lighted upon a certain place. Rabbi Hona in the name of Rabbi Ami: Why is the Almighty given the appellation place? For He is the place of His world. Rabbi Yossi son of Rabbi Halafta said: We know not if the Almighty is the place of His world, if His world is His place. From the text: 'the place by me' (Exod. 33:21) the Almighty is the place of His world and His world is not His place." This was written after the destruction of the Second Temple, God's place-and-home. Now that Hadrian had constructed Iliya Capitolina on the ruins of the Temple, and God no longer dwelled at the "place of the Temple," the question of His location became more acute. The sages answered: "The place of His world and His world is not His place." God dwells above and beyond any geographical location. This is God as the principle of inclusion, enfolding the entire world (but never identified with the world).

Jewish traditions (and their non-Jewish counterparts, if we take, for example, Plotinus and his *Ennead* 6; or John Scotus Erigena and his *De divisione naturae*; or Meister Eckhart and his *Commentary on the Book of Genesis*),[4] all neo-Platonist, primarily Maimonedes' *Guide for the Perplexed* written in the late twelfth century, propagated the notion of the intangible place of God as a place of the intellect: "Place as level of study and intellectual outlook" (*Guide for the Perplexed,* trans. David Kapach [Jerusalem: Mosad Harav Kook, 1977], chap. 1, 8) and proximity of the place as scientific reservation/query. The nonphysicality of God does not allow Him to be defined or understood in terms of time and space, accordingly "there is no relation between Him and a place" (1:12).

Thus, God is a placeless place; place as inclusive principle and pure spirituality; the Aristotelian principle of the soul as bodily form (and accordingly, inclusive of the body). In his *Commentary on the Book of Genesis* (49.LW 1: 220, ll. 2–7) Meister Eckhart argues that place has a sense of purpose, but the nature of purpose is such that all things for which it was purpose are included therein.

However, identification of the Divinity with place should be attributed to a pre-Aristotelian source, namely, Plato's concept of *khôra*. In his *Timaeus* we read: "For that which includes all other intelligible creatures cannot have a second or a companion; in that case there would be need of another living being which would include both, and of which they would be parts; and the likeness would be more truly said to resemble not them but that *other* which included them" (31, by the Stephanus categories; *Plato: The Collected Dialogues*, eds. Edith Hamilton and Huntingdon Cairns [Princeton: Princeton Univ. Press, 1961], 1163).

Derrida identified this "other living being," known as *khôra*, as the place of concealment of the *logos*. In 1993 he published his *Khôra*, devoted entirely to illumination of this elusive concept, even Plato being too perplexed to discuss it, writing: "at the commencement of my discourse, I call upon God and beg him to be our savior out of a strange and unwonted inquiry, and bring us to the haven of probability. . . . But now the argument seems to require that we should set forth in words of another kind, which is difficult of explanation and dimly seen" (*Timaeus*, 48–49; *Plato: The Collected Dialogues*, 1175–76). This "difficult" kind is the *khôra*. It is a third species transcending the great Platonic categorical dualities of essence and appearance, idea and matter, spirit and body, and so on—the third metaphysical element. Derrida scrutinizes *Timaeus*, confirming the total elusiveness of the concept of *khôra*, and its principled resistance to any definition, interpretation, or translation. There are as many definitions of the term as there are interpretations. All the same, the Platonic concept is plainly connected to the metaphor of mother, or nanny, or vessel, or—place; the feminine place.

Following in Plato's footsteps, Derrida is able to discuss *khôra* exclusively in negative terms, in keeping with the tradition of negative theology: *khôra* is neither idea, nor tangible, nor rational: it possesses no entity, it is neither *logos* nor myth. What is it then? *Khôra* is that which facilitates a concept of place, without itself occupying any place. A placeless place, or, in the terms of the Jewish sages of antiquity, "the place of His world and His world is not His place." Pepita Haezrachi has written:

> The *khôra* is thus the empty place, where things come into being, it is amorphous matter where forms appear and vanish, it is the vessel and sustainer of design, being without design or definition, and infinite. . . . Just as the idea of good, like the sun, sends out rays of light, and is the supreme purpose to which the entire Universe yearns and aspires, so does the idea of *khôra* send out rays of darkness, and it is the lower under-casing from which everything defined and designed takes flight. It is the source of the rejection. The light-beams of the good show up things as familiar, known. In the *khôra*'s beams of darkness, forms are muddied, forfeiting their clarity and distinction. (*On the Perfect Being* [in Hebrew] Jerusalem: Academon, 1964], 260, 262)

The place of the *logos* must perforce reject any characterization employing the binaries grown customary in post-Platonic Western thought. We will never comprehend this place so long as we think in terms of being and nonbeing, body and soul, matter and spirit, and so forth. As already noted, *khôra* is a third term, transcending all binaries, and "daughter of a sly consciousness" (Haezrachi, *On the Perfect Being*, 260); it is an interim domain, place, and vessel between the tangible and intangible, between world and supraworld. Furthermore, as metaphysical maternal womb rejecting any conceptualization or concretization, *khôra* is the yawning chasm opening up between *logos* and myth.

Indeed, *khôra* works as abyss. The place of the *logos* is an abyss. Derrida illustrates the darkness of that chasm with an ancient tale related by Solon (*Timaeus*, 23–24) about the aging Egyptian priest who teased the Greeks over the infantile mythology of their culture, which lacked any written tradition (the absence of a signifying tradition of memory). It is a story that has been told and retold in various versions: Cryton related a tale from his childhood, concerning his conversation with Solon, who told of his conversation with an Egyptian priest, who narrated his memories of Greece . . . Any narrative substance is a vessel incorporating a different story, from a different place, a *khôra* (but *khôra* itself never becomes a story; it is a principle of inclusion, the principle of enfolding the story). According to Derrida, the *Timaeus* experience is one of infinite regression to the nonoriginal origin.

> Audacity here consists of again evoking the origin, or the birth-place, of the necessity that neither generated nor engendered and which bears philosophy that "pre-dates" (ahead of past time, or eternal time prior to history) and "accepts" the effect, here the images of the opposites (intelligible and tangible): philosophy. . . . This necessity (surnamed *khôra*) seems so virginal it does not even have a virgin's form. (*Khôra* [1993a], 95)

Khôra is a hole. Is this the *Nukba*, the *Shekhina* (Holy Spirit), the feminine aspect of the Divinity, the aspect of the void, the Divinity's feminine absence? Gershom Scholem wrote: "Appearance of the *Shekhina* as female . . . the final sphere is regarded . . . as a vessel enfolding all the other spheres, and anyway was accepted from the outset by the Kabbalah scholars as a feminine element. . . . In an interesting passage of *Sefer Ha-Bahir* (the Book of the Clear) the bride in the Song of Solomon is interpreted as 'she-devil' (*sheda*) and 'closet' (*shida*), that is, the vessel into which the higher spheres flow" (*Elements of the Kabbalah and Its Symbolism* [Jerusalem: 1977], 176–78; translated from the Hebrew). In identifying the *Nukba* (Aramaic for both "female" and "hole") as a version of *Khôra*, as *Shekhina*

(Holy Spirit), are we saying that *Shekhina*—derived from the Hebrew root "to dwell"—denotes "occupying a place"? Of course, Kabbalah devotees reply, identifying the *Shekhina* with the immanent, "occupying" aspect of the Divinity. But we would rather associate *Shekhina* with *hashkana*—that is, giving the place to the world.

Shekhina. Derrida's book *Demeure* (Dwelling) [1988a] does indeed discuss Maurice Blanchot's work, but it is indebted to the concepts of dwelling, house, and home of Heidegger and Lévinas. The principle of dread, homelessness, the *Unheimlich* (uncanny) that enfolds the concept of home (*Heimlisch*) is specified by Heidegger in *Being and Time* (trans. John Macquarrie and Eduard Robinson [San Francisco: HarperCollins, 1962], 233–34), while Lévinas's *Totality and Infinity* identifies the dwelling principle with feminine Otherness. The *khôra* concept thus matches both these interpretations. Derrida goes further, adding the lingual connection between the words *demeure* and *meurt* (dead). Death resides within the home (*Demeure* [1998a], 101–3). We have learned from Freud's 1919 essay "Das Unheimliche" that the terror of *Unheimlichkeit* (uncanniness) is the dread of ghosts (which haunt the familiar, customary location: the home).[5]

Be all that as it may, *khôra* is metaphysical place as eternal secret, as total spiritual condition of all matter, as "place" unknown and intangible that proceeds any place. Derrida wrote:

> We witness a secret without substance, without substance that can be distinguished from its performed experience. . . . There is a secret. . . . It remains inviolable even when one thinks to have revealed it. Not that it lies forever in an untraceable tomb, or behind an absolute curtain. . . . One can speak of it endlessly, tell stories about it . . . for the secret often makes one think of secret stories. . . . And the secret will remain secret, mute, impassive as the *khôra*, like the *khôra* a stranger to any story . . . "the secret is that which, within speech, is estranged from speech." . . . And whether or not one respects it, the impassive secret remains there, far beyond reach . . . there, is neither time, nor place . . . if . . . I like anything in literature . . . it is the place of the secret. The place of an absolute secret. There dwells passion. . . . [The secret] is that which does not respond. It has no *responsiveness*. Should one call it death? (*Passions* [1993b], 56–70)

The place is the place of the *logos*, the Jewish principle of inclusion, the Platonic *khôra*, death. It is the original vessel for creation of all things, but equally, it is the dark "place" to which all things arrive: the Promised Land, the place where the messiahs reiterate their promises; desert-within-desert, Derrida would say. Death, he would add again.

8

Tower of Babel

"—One always speaks but one single language . . . (yes but)—One never speaks one single language that isn't just the selfsame law of what is called translation . . . I've always suspected that law, like language, of being crazy . . . (*Le monolinguisme de l'autre* [1996c], 25)

In one sense, nothing is untranslatable; in another sense, everything is untranslatable, translation is another name for the impossible. (ibid., 103)

When we refer to the Tower of Babel, Derrida reminds us ("Des Tours de Babel," in *Psyché* 1987c) we refer to numerous languages mutually distinguishable, and therefore requiring translation. The Tower of Babel, he adds, also denotes the inability to complete a multiple assignment on a large architectural scale. Accordingly, the inevitable collapse of the Tower of Babel seems to foreshadow the launching of deconstructivist architecture. But the Tower of Babel interests Derrida largely in the context of language and translation.[1] "Babel" denotes babble (a confused mixture) but "Babel" also serves as a proper noun, the name of God: (*ba—av*—father; *bel*—God). Consequently, "Babel" denotes "divine father," but also "confusion." We thus come across another paradoxical coupling in the series of "double binds" (Derrida forever insists on using the English term) that the philosopher cherishes: the Heavenly Father grants His Name (it's always fathers who grant names, Derrida adds) and thus constitutes the source of language. But in His anger at the builders of the Tower, He also withdraws the gift of language and imposes the multiplicity and diversity of languages.

Prior to God's demolition of the Tower, the family of Shem (Hebrew: "name" = word,) sought to found a lingual empire, uniform and universal. Shem aspired to grant the name to the world, Derrida explains, but God did not forgive a presumption that the Almighty reserves unto Himself. The tale of the Tower of Babel is thus the story of His jealousy.[2] God demolished (French: *détruire, destruction,* hence *deconstruction*) the Tower, thereby de-

68

molishing human aspirations to a single language and imposing lingual diversity and, consequently, the need for translation (which comprises lingering remnants of the avidity to unify languages) as well as the inability to fully translate from one language to another. In Derrida's creed, the concept of the Tower of Babel represents the problem of translation. In fact, his previous work, *Dissémination* (1972a) sketched out and delineated this key concept in a similar tone: "The Tower of Babel where multiple languages and writings clash with one another or blend with one another, changing and being generated from their most irreconcilable otherness . . . for multiplicity . . . is not experienced as negative, in the nostalgia for a lost unity. . . . The Tower of Babel, that vertebral column of text, is also a phallic column woven in the thread of creativity" (379).

The text remains in the middle, halfway between total translation which is impossible, and utter confusion (Babel), equally impossible.[3] Translation is out of the question when the text comprises several languages (as in the works of James Joyce; this may explain Derrida's fascination with them, notably *Finnegans Wake,* to which we shall refer below) or when the identical word has different meanings in different languages (e.g., "war"— English: *armed conflict*; German: *was*). Equally untranslatable are proper nouns ("Londres" is not a translation of "London," affirms Derrida [*Dissémination,* 209]). Some would therefore say they are better excluded from the domain of language; but what is the value of language if it does not permit application of proper nouns? We thus find ourselves (by divine decree) in a paradoxical quandary between the obligation to translate, and the impossibility of perfect translation.

In casting the "Tower of Babel" image, Derrida falls back on "The Task of the Translator" (introduction to the translation of Baudelaire's *Tableaux Parisiens*) that Walter Benjamin wrote in 1923. In fact, he could equally have found that image in an earlier essay of Benjamin's, "On Language as Such and the Language of Man," written in 1916. As Benjamin put it in 1916, man's lingual essence is expressed in his ability to call things by name. Of all the world's creatures, man alone gives names to members of his own species and objects in his environment. By this act, man's spiritual essence supposedly proclaims its divine nature. God's act of creation achieves completion only when objects receive their name from man. Man thus completes the divine language. Accordingly, perfect language is the exclusive province of man. God's lingual essence is speech as creation. Human language is ostensibly a mere reflection of divine speech in the name. Indeed, language is limited in its power of creation and its infinity. Concomitantly, translation of the language of things (things as they exist in the world) into human language is translation of lifeless matter into the audible, and translation of the nameless into a name, an act whereby cognition is introduced. God created Man from dust, but endowed him with the gift of language. The presence of Adam and Eve in the Garden of Eden dictated resort to a single language. Man's Garden of Eden language, stated Benjamin, was a language of perfect recognition. It was only with Original Sin that the human word was born. It was thus Original Sin that laid the foundation for the multiplicity of language, by making it a means. Henceforth, Benjamin elaborates:

> it could be only a step to linguistic confusion. Since men had injured the purity of name, the turning away from the contemplation of things in which their language passes into man, needed only to be completed in order to deprive men of the common foundation of an already shaken language-mind. Signs must become confused where things are entangled. The enslavement of language in prattle is joined by the enslavement of things in folly almost as its inevitable consequence. In this turning away from things which was enslavement, the plan for the Tower of Babel came into being and linguistic confusion with it. (W. Benjamin, "On Language as Such and on the Language of Man," in *Reflections,* ed. P. Demetz [New York: Harcourt Brace Jovanovich, 1978], 328–29)

In applying his lingual (translation-linked) concept to Benjamin's subsequent "The Task of the Translator," Derrida clung to the Tower of Babel image. According to Benjamin's essay, the translator is duty-bound to restore something he has received; he has to restore the meaning of the original. But in his view, this is an impossible task. After all, translation is not reproduction of an original. The relationship between the translation and the original is essential, but the translation is not a representation re-creating ("resembling") the original. Translation is a form whose guiding rule (the translation's duty) dwells within the original version (as translated) like a kind of genetic code, whereas the translation is merely a phase in the development of the original.

This accordingly brings out the theological aspect within translation— the primary origin as regulation and demand for translation (which, we recall, is impossible).[4] God, who grants His Name ("Babel" as "Father-God"), simultaneously demands its translation into "babble," the multiplicity of tongues that do not permit of translation of the One Name. According to Derrida—and with a close affinity to Maimonides' ideas in *Guide to the Perplexed* concerning the Names of God—the holiest text of all, the Name of God, "Babel," is untranslatable ("Des Tours de Babel," in *Psyché* [1987c], 219). Benjamin resorts to the metaphor of the dividing wall between the original language and the language of translation (although he does open up a passageway—"*arcade*"—through the wall).[5] "From the origin of the original to be translated, there is a fall and exile" (222). Thus does Derrida point up the definition of the translator's task as set by Benjamin: "Redeeming in its own language this pure language held captive in the work, that is the translator's task" (222 [Translated from the French quotation in the Hebrew text. Trans.].

Liberation of the pure language is also the liberation and vocation of the translator, whose contact with the meaning of the original is minuscule and short-lived, like a light caress. The relationship between the translated text and the original is that of collating fragments and gluing them together to match the concept of the perfect jar (which does not exist). The fragments of various languages come together in translation to create a broader language (simultaneously, in the course of the translation—a mere "gluing together"—the fragments change, the translator's language changes). According to Benjamin, translation calls for adapting the fruit to the peel, but at the same time, precludes recognition of the kernel. The core of the fruit (the original meaning) is therefore untouchable, invisible, unattainable. According to Benjamin, translation resembles the sewing of a regal garment, without the presence of the monarch: the emperor's new clothes.

A kingdom without monarchy, translation holds out promise of a "Babelian" kingdom unifying all languages. But the promise is not fulfilled. "[T]he pure language remains concealed, hidden (*verborgen*), walled up in the nocturnal intimacy of the 'core'" (*Psyché* [1987c], 233)

Translation promises redemption of the pure language. It contains something of the divine, messianic, religious promise. Any translation is a paraphrase of sacred text, demanding its pure and perfect translation, but it is also a paraphrase of its infinite remoteness (233). The original text declares itself translatable and calls for its translation, as though it were a sacred text demanding translation, but any such text is also a Tower of Babel condemned to demolition, to pulverization (to "Ruins": see the chapter of that name), to deconstruction.

An illustration of the dual lingual *démarche* of Tower of Babel is to be found in Derrida's *Ulysse gramophone* (1987d), whose first chapter ("Two Words for Joyce") hinges upon a pair of words Derrida fished out of *Finnegans Wake:* HE WAR. "An especially Babelian scene" is how Derrida defines the lines from which he extracted the two words. How are they to be translated? Is WAR to be understood as the English "armed conflict" (whereupon HE WAR denotes "he war") or as the German "was" (which makes HE WAR "he was")? Derrida continues to seek God behind human language: "I AM THAT I AM," is the Almighty's definition of Himself; and now "he was" is merely one of the dual aspects of God as "he is war" and "he was." For the true essence of God, says Derrida, is the declaration of war, we recall, against language and by means thereof. (Need we recall here that one of God's Hebrew names is *elohey tzevaot*—"God of Hosts"?) "Here is the truth of Babel," Derrida concludes (*Ulysse gramophone* 17).

The attention required by language, by "HE WAR," like any other attention, is a matter of obedience; obedience to a father who raises his voice: "The audio-phonic dimension of divine law and its sublime height" (35–36). Derrida also notes the parodying of the biblical style in Joyce's work, where the reversal of the word "Babel" ("And shall not Babel be with Lebab") demonstrates the divinely imposed lingual confusion prevailing throughout Joyce's book (books?). The following extracts from *Finnegans Wake* are provided by Derrida to illustrate Joyce's "Babelism," or at least, the Babelism surrounding the riddle of "HE WAR": "The babbelers with their thangas vain have been (confusion hold them!) they were and went; thigging thugs were and houhnhymn songtoms were and comely norgels were and pollyfool fiansees. . . . And they feel upong one another, and themselves they have Fallen." Or "Alist, as she bibs us, by the waters of babalong" (*Olysse gramophone* [1987d], 38).

"HE WAR" is an elucidation of the demand to translate the untranslatable. The divine ban on fulfillment—at the human plane—of the single language, is an echo of God who—alone—is One with no other. The ban is a taking back, but the demand for translation—is a giving.[6] Derrida concludes with the sentence "*Alliance et* double bind" (40), which, containing two languages, is in any case untranslatable. Joyce's ghost, and consequently, the ghost of Babel, too, constantly haunts the pages of Derrida's books. We are therefore not surprised to discover Joyce and the Tower of Babel again in *La carte postale* (1980); this time, the philosopher is fascinated by the pair of brothers in *Finnegans Wake:* Shem and Shaun, the writer and the postman, one preoccupied with names, words, language; the other with the dissemination of texts (letters). They represent the double bind—the single language and the multiplicity of languages, the translation and the impossibility of total translation. Here, too, (*Ulysse gramophone* [1987d], 32–36) there is mention of the conflict between the two brothers, immediately followed by "HE WAR," and closely thereafter (still within the same section) the story of the Tower of Babel, God's anger, and His punishment of those who aspire to a single language: "I call myself, and impose my name as father . . . try, I beg you, to translate it, but I really hope you won't be able to" (33). Is the Tower of Babel metaphor restricted exclusively to the domain of translation? The negative reply is in fact suggested by Derrida when he drags Babel into the postman's domain of the transfer of texts from one place to another, that is, the Babelian expanse with its "double bind" is the expanse of all textual migrations. Geoffrey Ben-nington's book on Derrida expands Derrida's view of translation to an over-all perception of reading and interpretation. In relating to Benjamin's notion of the translator's debt to the original, Bennington wrote: "The same could be said of reading in general. . . . Any text is indebted to its future readers, while remaining . . . indifferent to the death of any empirical addressee."[7] Furthermore, "It could also be said, somewhat generalizing on the sense of the word 'translation', that all of Derrida's own texts are (merely) readings or translations of "originals"; but one would say of the originality of these readings that they in turn demand to be translated—and that is the case notably of the term 'deconstruction' proposed as translation of the Heideggerian *Destruktion* . . . which also requires a certain measure of translation."[8]

Now we have a clarification of Derrida's reply to Benjamin and "On Language as Such and the Language of Man." He does not accept the superiority with which Benjamin endowed man over God in the act of nam-ing. Human language is not superior to divine language. According to Der-rida, attributing such superiority is hubris, which incurs the heavy price of the demolition of the Tower, the "confusion," the dissemination and mul-tiplicity of languages. Human language does not reflect the divine pro-nouncement of name, it is a poor and fragmentary shadow of the supreme nominal pronouncement. Human language, in its full extent (in the expanse of writing, reading, interpretation, and translation) is longing for the divine language (for "speech") but also acknowledgment of the impossibility of reverting to the divine language.

We are still close to Babel. We are in Persia, and still preoccupied with the Bible and its interpretation. But now we turn—with Derrida's help of course—to the Book of Esther, to encounter given names: "Esther"—Persian; "Hadassah"—Jewish. Two different names for the same woman: Is this not another instance of the problem of meaning and origin, the prob-lem of dispatch and transfer that so engaged Derrida in *La carte postale* (1980)? Indeed, we read: "the posts . . . went out, being hastened and pressed on . . ." from city to city, from country to country, from governor to governor, bearing the royal command, the decree against the Jews, the ho-locaust ("holocaust without fire or flame" [*La carte postale* (1980), 79]). Derrida stresses the written correspondence, quoting André Chouraqui who translated the Book of Esther: "The Book of Esther should be read in the synagogues as one reads a letter." Is not every translation a form of letter? They are texts ("letters") conveyed from here to there.

Admittedly, God's name does not appear in the Book of Esther, but the letters are signed with the royal seal (Ahasuerus, Xerxes) and their origin lies in the royal decree, as supreme authority. As ever, God is in hiding. The substance of the letters is condemned to chance, to "a lot." For, as Derrida stresses, falling back on historical and interpretative sources, the fate of Persia's Jews (which was the subject of the king's letters) was decided less by their devout faith than by political machination. Within this expanse of fortuity, the Book of Esther is not unequivocal: "Everything in this book is 'difficult to tell'," Derrida cites the *Interpreter's Dictionary of the Bible* (could not the same be said of any one of Derrida's own works?). As though that were not sufficient, he quotes further: "It seems probable that the book of Esther is primarily romance, not history" (*La carte postale* [1980], 83). (In fact, Ahasuerus's "historical" wife was named neither Vashti nor Esther; her name was Amestris). Romance rather than history. We remind the reader that a similar dilemma confronted Derrida in *Mal d'archive* (was Freud's book on Moses history or a novel?). The movement from historical fidelity to the "origin," to the freedom of the "novel" or "romance," is the liberation of the interpreter (or translator). The debt to the historical "source" is thus eroded, as is the commitment to the father, to the royal command. The message of the original letter has been changed. Total translation is out of the question. Total interpretation is equally impossible. In spite of all that, there is the great commitment to Esther, Esther Safar, (Jacques Derrida's mother), the fidelity to his beloved mother and to Purim as a further resurrection of the mother (see *Circonfession* [1991a], 211).

9

Scroll of Eros and Death

Although the biblical Book of Esther (in Hebrew "the Scroll of Esther") does not once mention God's name, the term *dath* (religion) appears there eighteen times. Contrary to the conventional view that the Scroll has no religious content, we will argue that its theme is divine authority and the question of its representation therein. Although this reconsideration of the scroll was prompted by Derrida's *La carte postale* (1980), it should be stated in fairness that the following interpretation is an attempt to extend his reading, his works, his authority (his religion? see below)—the reading of a reading, on the subject of writing and books.

As already noted, Derrida displayed a particular interest in the Book of Esther, "Esther" being his mother's name. Furthermore, the biblical Esther saved her people from "a holocaust without fire or flame." But, as evidenced by four pages of *La carte postale,* the prime motive for his interest should be sought in motifs such as promulgation of the royal decree through dispatch by messengers of the royal books and letters, embossed with the royal seal. As already noted, he considered that writing is also to be found in the "dispatch" that is, conveyance of an overt message, recalling the open format of the postcard. From his point of view, the plot's center of gravity is the replacement of one letter by another (the letter relating to the annihilation of the Jews is superseded by the missive concerning the massacre of their enemies). Moreover, says Derrida, quoting André Chouraqui, the translator of the scroll, it should be read in the synagogues as one reads a letter. It is thus not fortuitous that the Book of Esther reminds Derrida of Edgar Allan Poe's "The Purloined Letter," whose theme is "the return of the letter"—a theme to which we will revert in the course of our discussion.

The multiple meanings of the term *dath* (rendered into English in the King James Version as "law." Trans.) already become apparent in the first chapter of the scroll. *Dath* is "command" (Esther 1:8: "And the drinking was according to the law; none did compel . . ."; that is, on the order of the king, all restrictions on drinking were removed); *dath* is also "law," the royal law (Esther 1:13: "the king's manner toward all that knew law and judgment"); *dath* is judgment, the law of the land (Esther 1:15: "What shall we do unto the queen Vashti according to law"); *dath* is the code of laws (Esther 1:19: "and let it be written among the laws of the Persians and the Medes"). By contrast, the more prevalent meaning of the word *dath* appears solely in Esther 3:8: "There is a certain people scattered abroad and dispersed among the people in all the provinces of thy kingdom; and their laws are diverse from all people, neither keep they the king's laws." Granted, here, too, the term "the king's laws" denotes the royal decrees; but now there is a possible—if not to say necessary—analogy between *dath* as book of laws (*patsheguen*: letter; legal code) and as belief system committed to a set of laws, whether positive commands or interdictions.

The books are written by scribes, at the behest of the king or ruler, the holder of the seal of office. The authoritative seal of office is the primary mold that dictates all other writings. In Esther 8:8 we read: "Write ye also for the Jews, as it liketh you, in the king's name, and seal it with the king's ring; for the writing which is written in the king's name, and sealed with the king's ring, may no man reverse." But the sole source, primary and holding supreme authority, is condemned to division into numerous books, in the process of translating speech into writing that is, in fact, the process of fragmentation, differentiation, and shattering (the shattering of the Tablets of the Law): "For he sent letters into all the king's provinces, into every province according to the writing thereof, and to every people after their language, that every man should bear rule in his own house, and that it should be published according to the language of every people" (Esther 1:21). Once again we encounter the penalty of lingual multiplicity and division, incurred by the tragedy of the Tower of Babel (Derrida, "Des Tours de Babel" in *Psyché* [1987c]): the tension between the divine father (Ba-bel; Abba-Bel; Abba-father-El-God), the sole and unique granter-of-names, and the members of the Shem family aspiring to a single language, that is, to granting names in their own right. Writing is, accordingly, an outcome of this lingual multiplicity, and of the requirement of translation that will never be fulfilled in full. Lingual multiplicity and division are an internal and essential lingual fracture.

This lingual expanse between the One (the pronouncement of the Father—God, king) and the multitude (writing, books, languages) pervades the Book of Esther as subversive lingual force, resting upon the combination of dissident authority and book. Compare that last verse of the first chapter of the Book of Esther with the following passage near the end of the book: "and it was written according to all that Mordecai commanded unto the Jews and to the lieutenants, and the deputies and rulers of the provinces which are from India unto Ethiopia, an hundred twenty and seven provinces, unto every province according to the writing thereof, and unto every people after their language, and to the Jews according to their writing, and according to their language" (Esther 8:9). In other words: the archival command concluding the book is now a Jewish command, and the multiplicity of books and languages now refers to the individual Otherness of the Jewish tongue, a fact that was not mentioned in the parallel verse of the first chapter.

What happened between the first and the eighth chapter, what is the significance of this Jewish Otherness of authority (book, religion)? Let us revert to the fundamental lingual formula of the Book of Esther: (*a*) writing is legislation and letter: "The copy of the writing for a commandment to be given in every province . . ." (Esther 8:13 or 9:26). In other words: writing is fate dispatched, signed by the signs of writing; (*b*) writing and religion are united in the *patsheguen,* the royal letter: "the copy of the writing of the decree that was given at Shushan to destroy them . . ." (Esther 4:8); (*c*) writing is united with religion, that is, the religion of the king, the sovereign, in his name or on his behalf (by the royal viceroy equipped with the royal seal-ring): "Then were the king's scribes called . . . and there was written according to all that Haman had commanded . . . in the name of the king Ahasuerus was it written, and sealed with the king's ring. And the letters were sent by posts" (Esther 3:12–13); (*d*) every archive signifies the *arche* (the past) that created it. The Book of Esther reverts to the theme of the Book of Chronicles at the inspiration of the king and/or Mordecai: "and he commanded to bring the book of records of the chronicles; and they were read before the king" (Esther 6:1); (*e*) however, every archive signifies future, no less than past (Derrida, *Mal d'archive* [1995a]). Here, the Book of Esther stresses the connection between the writing of books and destiny: writing books, writing religion/royal decree, implies a verdict of perdition, in general—of death. The book spreads death: "And in every province, whithersoever the king's commandments and his decree came, there was great mourning among the Jews" (Esther 4:3).

The king is sovereign by divine right; furthermore, the supreme authority of primary speech and seal is divine authority. Consequently, the royal command (*dath*: religion) immediately becomes the divine command/religion. The seal ring is thus the ring of the covenant between man and God (in *Mal d'archive*, it will be recalled, this ring is reincarnated in the "seal" of the circumcision that inscribes Jewishness with the ring of the foreskin). Delegating the ring of covenant is the right of the father—the heavenly father, or the king, or the paterfamilias. In the Book of Esther, the seal ring is delegated initially to Haman, and ultimately to Mordecai ("And the king took off his ring, which he had taken from Haman, and gave it unto Mordecai" [8:2, and previously 3:10]).

The progression from Haman's ring to Mordecai's ring is thus progression between two "religions," two books of law: the "Agagite" book of law as against the Jewish law, the Torah. Each bears death to the unbelievers, that is, the Others. The triumph of one "religion" over another is conditional upon penetration and inner alliance with the source of power, the authority, the king; alliance with the phallus. Indeed, the "religious" turnabout in the Book of Esther rests upon Esther's introduction into the royal court, and the king's penetration of Esther ("In the evening she went, and on the morrow she returned into the second house of the women" [2:14]). Haman knew the secret of authority, hence his attempt to rape Esther ("and Haman was fallen upon the bed whereon Esther was" [7:8]). At this point, we should recall that in *La carte postale,* Derrida compares Esther to the queen in Poe's "The Purloined Letter," which also engaged the attention of the psychoanalyst Jacques Lacan. Indeed, the post-Freudian interpretation of the story stresses the role of the royal phallus, including the queen's betrayal of the king, and concealment of the letter of betrayal in a vagina-like hiding place. Derrida found it necessary to stress the role of the letter as phallus (as suprasignifier). However, any erotic alliance with authority, alliance with erection and penetration, begins with sex and ends in death. After all, the phallus is both being and nothingness, erection and contraction (absence), monumentality and circumcision (cutting, removal, excision). The phallus is thus the supreme signifier, but also the signifier of absence. Any writing is a hope of phallic significance, bearing with it the sign of nothingness and mutilation.

The origin of writing is refusal—denial, Otherness. Law and authority demand and expect the similar, the same. Concretizing the law (in the original speech) in writing is condemned to Otherness. This is the dual tension between writing the truth, and the truth. The Book of Esther represents Otherness with expressions of refusal by those subject to the law. Thus, for example, Vashti refuses to attend the royal banquet (1:12). Later, Mordecai refuses to bow to the royal viceroy (3:2). Without the recalcitrant Otherness of the signifiers (the subjects) toward the signified (the king)—there is no writing (of books of law, commandments, jurisprudence "religion"). The book, religion, jurisprudence, bear the verdict of total dismissal of the signers from the signed (Vashti's dethronement), the death sentence signed with every sign (the sign being a memorial to the absence—the death—of the signed): "let it be written to reverse the letters devised by Haman the son of Hammedatha the Agagite which he wrote to destroy the Jews" (8:5). The writing of the new books (letters) that supplant Haman's books (letters) entails the massacre of the Others: the slaughter of the non-Jews. Seventy-five thousand subjects of the Medes and Persians were massacred by the vengeful Jews (9:16), on top of the hanging of Haman's ten sons and the murder of eight hundred persons in Shushan (8:6, 15). It was genocide. A holocaust.

In the book, in writing, in the law—dwells violence, death. This theme can be found at greater length in Derrida's *Force de loi* (1994), dealing with the issue of human rights and the Holocaust. The book, whose subject is legal philosophy no less than theology, considers human law, divine law, and human authority as reflections of divine authority. The crux of the book is Derrida's commentary on Walter Benjamin's essay "On the Critique of Violence" and the desire to identify the violence residing within any law (indeed, in any definition of right), whether human or divine. Benjamin's essay concludes: "Divine violence, which is the sign and seal but never the means of sacred execution, may be called sovereign violence" (*Reflections,* ed. Peter Demetz [New York: Harcourt Brace Jovanovich, 1989], 300), whereas Derrida writes of the destruction brought about in all writing and in any legal "structure." With that, he follows Benjamin in drawing a distinction between the violence of Greek mythology, which gave rise to laws and human rights, and divine Jewish violence, whose nonrecognition of separate human law demolishes law and human rights. Jewish divine violence is interpreted as annihilation for the sake of life, as coming to terms with the sacrifice in order to save life. Judaism consecrates life and justice, whereas Greek violence sacrifices life for the satisfaction of violence. Accordingly, as he puts it, Greek violence did constitute human rights, but simultaneously perpetuated violence; whereas Jewish divine violence ravaged human rights, but affirmed life in the name of divine justice.

Is this, then, the message of the Book of Esther? Is Agagian religion (books of law) distinguishable, as violence for its own sake, from the "religion" of Mordecai the Jew, the affirmation of human sacrifice for the purpose of affirming and sanctifying life? Haman's violence stems from his anger over the flouting of the law, and furthermore, from the blow to his personal dignity: "And when Haman saw that Mordecai bowed not, nor did him reverence, then was Haman full of wrath" (Esther 3:5). The transition from the disobedience of the individual, Mordecai, to punishment of the multitude, the entire Jewish people, seems capricious, seizing upon the temptation of plundering the victims ("and I will pay ten thousand talents of silver to the hands of those that have the charge of the business, to bring it into the king's treasuries" [Esther 3:9]. Commentators note the enormity of the sum: three million ancient shekels). By contrast, the text stresses that the Jews massacred their "enemies" (Esther 9:2, 5 and elsewhere), while being particular not to engage in plunder (Esther 9:10, 15, 16) despite the royal sanction to pillage their victims (Esther 8:11). Moreover, the Purim festival would henceforth be marked by the dispatch of "gifts to the poor" (Esther 9:22).

Here we have the difference: Agagian law rests upon "the Pur," casting lots on days, weeks, and months: "the Agagite, the enemy of all the Jews, had devised against the Jews to destroy them, and had cast the Pur, that is, the lot, to consume them, and to destroy them;" (Esther 9:24; see also 3:7) whereas the Jewish religion is based upon fasting and crying (Esther 9:31); the crying of Mordecai, clad in sackcloth and ashes, and concomitantly, the mourning and weeping of the entire Jewish community (Esther 4:1–3) and a great fast (Esther 4:16). The arbitrary nature of the Pur is contrasted with ritual resting upon sacrifice, diminution, and absence. Without mentioning the Lord's name, such ritual must presume a transcendental sovereignty. We therefore disagree with André Chouraqui, who discerns in the Book of Esther political machination against a setting of an absent religious content (Chouraqui stresses that the Jews' fasting mentioned in the narrative involves no prayer). The salvation of the Jews of Persia and Media is divine salvation, whose terrible cruelty—we used the term "holocaust"—affirms life, as against those who sought to end life and bring about a holocaust by the arbitrary means of casting lots, that is, holocaust as end to itself. The calamity of the Jewish massacre of non-Jews is horrifying to any person of sensibility, but it is not wanting in a moral and "religious" lesson. For our reading of the Book of Esther has discovered the triumph of the Other religion, the Other authority, the Other law, the Other book.

And what of the absence of God's Name from the book? Faithful to the Derridean context, we would reply: the absence of God is like the self-concealment of the *logos,* the source, the onto-theological "divine countenance averted" that condemns us to the "footprints" of God in the signs of language, in books. In other words, God's "self-concealment" in the Book of Esther is a substantial aspect of a Derridean reading thereof. Possibly also, it is this aspect that spans the traditional interpretation of the Book of Esther, which dwells on concealment of Esther's Jewish origins, and the philosophical interpretation marked by self-concealment of the truth. In this context, we should quote the Jerusalem Talmud: "and why was her name called Esther, because she 'concealed' ["Esther" and "concealed" comprise the identical root in Hebrew. Trans.] her words, as it is written 'Esther had not shewed her people, etc.'" (Masechet "Megillah," 13, 1). Derrida would have also referred to the manner of the scroll's reading: its closing is also its opening (it is rolled open and rolled closed) as a metaphorical action representing the simultaneous presence and absence of the truth.

10

Ruins

"Writing is itself written, but also ruined, made into an abyss, in its own representation" (*Writing and Difference* [*L'écriture et la différence*] [Chicago: Univ. of Chicago Press, 1978], 65). Derrida's writings associate the image of the ruin—piles of stones, rubble, remnants of a collapsed house—with the concept of abyss, but equally, as early as 1967, with the metaphor of the shattered Tablets of the Covenant, as image of poetry. From the very outset of his hermeneutic endeavor, the poet's autonomy was interpreted in terms of the shattered tablets of divine law: "Between the fragments of the broken Tables, the poem grows and the right to speech takes root" (67). This autonomy is not merely a matter of aesthetic distance, of the kind to be found in Kantian artistic autonomy; it is rather a rupture of principle between divinity and "writing," which is an internal fissure within the divinity:

> The breaking of the Tables articulates, first of all, a rupture within God as the origin of history. . . . God separated himself from himself in order to let us speak, in order to astonish and to interrogate us. He did so not by speaking but by keeping still, by letting silence interrupt his voice and his signs, by letting the Tables be broken. . . . Writing is, thus, originally hermetic and secondary. (ibid.)

Man is thus divided from God, "writing" from "speech," by rupture, destruction, ruins. Man's path to God must accordingly run through the ruins (*La religion* [1996b]).[1]

Derrida identifies the ruin—as image of destruction applied to the principle of representation—in every cultural system whose purpose is representation of the world. Thus, for example, he discerns in the artist's act of drawing (*Mémoires d'aveugle* [1990e]) the inability to see that which is in concealment, declining to be seen or be present. This holds true whether it is a flesh-and-blood person or some transcendental Other. Indeed, the artist's "blindness" is identified with the "blindness" of the visionary who witnesses a revelation of divinity (frequently, as in the case of Saul of Tarsus, his blindness is real). Derrida connected the darkness of this blindness (as the true content of the creative work) with the image of ruin: "It is like a ruin that does not come *after* the work, rather, it remains . . . *at its source*. . . . In the beginning there was the ruin . . . with no promise of restoration" (68–69).

Elsewhere, in an interview with Elisabeth Weber (*Questions au judaïsme* [Paris: Desclée de Brouwer, 1996]) Derrida took this position to an extreme, linking together creativity, memory, and deconstruction: "The disruptive force of deconstruction will always find itself already within the work's architecture . . . a work of memory to know deconstruction, a work of memory to recall the tombs" (90).

No wonder he draws such a radical conclusion: "Memory without the risk of forgetting is not memory" (*Questions au judaïsme*, 93). The ruin at the foundation of any artistic work thus symbolizes the failure to recognize that which is represented, the Otherness beyond the "writing" (whether drawing, painting, etc.). Derrida writes: "There are only ghosts . . . the ghost of the invisible that the work lets us see without ever presenting it" (*Mémoires d'aveugle*, [1990e], 69). Any representation of the human face (whether as portrait of the Other or as self-portrait) is a face in ruin to an extent more profound than any marks of aging and bodily deterioration: "Ruin is that which overtakes the image from the very first glance. Ruin is the self-portrait, this defaced face like a memory of itself, that which remains, or returns like a ghost from the first glance at self, representation of an eclipse" (72). Derrida also suggests that paintings of ruins be regarded as portrait images, or even self-portraits (ibid.). Accordingly, he asks: "How can one love anything but the possibility of ruin? But the impossible totality?"(ibid.) This "masochistic" declaration of love, to be repeated in *Force de loi* (1994a), applies to a totally beloved object, and the infinite secret separating it from the lover. The ruin is more than mere image, more than something revealed to the eye. The ruin is the experience itself and the self-concealed totality in person. Love is love of God, and accordingly, the ruin is the ruin of the Temple, mark of the divine absence.

In *Lignées* (1996d) Derrida's brief philosophical and poetic remarks on two hundred sketches by Micaëla Henich, he translates vistas of devastation into vistas of text. He contemplates the miniatures, with their abundance of short, dense lines, representing ruined houses huddled on a cliff, but discovers a large envelope tumbling from heaven (No. 801) to be transformed into one of the village ruins which, amazingly, is nothing but letters and books in the form of houses. The vista of devastation is therefore a lingual landscape, a stone archive (No. 872), a silent library (No. 838). And the entire cliff rises up like a prayer from the books to the book (No. 803), from ruins to a (Kafka-like?) castle and to a supreme Father who does not reveal His Name. In reverse too, the vistas of devastation reveal the heavenly fury, the anger of the supreme Father who has pulled down the houses and the castle, the lingual claim to familiarity with the original, leaving only the distress of homelessness—*Unheimlichkeit*. Again we thus confront what could be termed the syndrome of the collapsing Tower of Babel (Nos. 832 and 959. See the discussion above in the chapter titled "Tower of Babel"). The piled-up books frequently recall graves, the village as a whole conjures up a cemetery, reminding Derrida of the Jewish cemetery in Prague (Nos. 809, 836, 900). Thus, the hill of the ruins is also a downward slope, and the lines likewise sign derailment and philosophical plunge into the abyss (No. 851).

The solid house has collapsed. The surviving hope is to build the lines of boards into shelter to host ancestors of antiquity (*ushpizin* [strangers made welcome]. Trans.). Derrida relates to the festival of *Succot* (No. 818) (when the family in the tabernacle awaits *ushpizin*) but stresses the nothingness present within the *succa* (tabernacle). The architecture of the ruins contains no center (No. 820) and the blockades of rubble close in on the secret. The visit to the village of ruins—of stone and of language—is the visit of the universal worshipper. The stones of the ruins are the stones of prayer (of synagogue, cathedral, mosque—No. 834) enfolding memories of destruction, such as concentration camps (No. 834). The architecture is that of memory. The stones of the ruins, like the headstones in the Jewish cemetery in Prague, are frozen, silent shrieks, souls cast in stone, clinging together in desperation vis-à-vis the dark skies. The worshipper visiting the "village of ruins" (yet another Derridean "place" that is "not-a-geographical-place"; instead, it is a nonplace denoting a divine promise) momentarily imagines that he sees the Tablets of the Covenant, signs of the divine law, appearing from the heavens (No. 850), but the end result is ever more ruins: a pile of tiles of a collapsed roof, shattered like the fragments of the Tablets of the Covenant (No. 868). Thus, there is no hope of tidings enclosed in a heavenly envelope; nothing but an aerial cemetery of dead letters (of the alphabet, but equally, missives) (No. 887). The envelope's contents are unknown; they remain a secret buried between the ruins (No. 954), a fatal secret encompassed by death. The promise will not be fulfilled: Moses will not come to the Promised Land, the Tables of the Covenant will be shattered, the *talith* (prayer shawl) is a veil concealing the worshipper from the object of his prayers—God (No. 939). The worshipper knows and sees nothing but the ruins.

The structure demolishes (deconstructs) itself even as it is being built. Construction as deconstruction (the text "*se ruine*" to become a mere specter of itself [*Force de loi* (1994), 104]). Here we hold the key to some of Derrida's writings, a bridge joining romanticism, (negative) theology, and deconstructivist architecture. Is the structure of a work like *Moscou aller-retour* (1995b) anything more than the ground-plan of a "cathedral"?—but we are left with ruins! The text, composed as a lecture (in California) following a ten-day trip to Moscow (as guest of the Soviet Institute of Philosophy), can be characterized as a description of the impossibility of describing the trip to Moscow. Referring to three journals on the theme of "return from the Soviet Union" (by, respectively, Etiemble [1934 and 1958]; A. Gide [1936]; and W. Benjamin [1926]) and uncovering the three myths that constitute their underlying structure (Oedipus, Demeter, and Tiresias)—myths of promises broken—Derrida condemns himself likewise to reneging on a promise (the promise to describe the trip to Moscow). Accordingly, as the book progresses and the words pile up ("writing") the nothingness (of the *logos,* the *eidos*) becomes increasingly plain. We are left with "ruins."

Nevertheless, the "ruin" is of course not restricted to Moscow. The model of the trip to the utopian city parallels the model of the "pilgrimage" to "Paradise Lost," to the "Promised Land," and of course, "to all the utopias, to the ancient or new Jerusalem, Athens, Rome" *(Moscou aller-retour* [1995b], 19). Derrida mentions W. Benjamin's *Moscow Diary,* which also holds (in the preface by Gershom Scholem) an account of his letters from Moscow to Jerusalem. Derrida uncovers the elliptic connection between Oedipal Greek mythology (the secret behind Benjamin's journey to Moscow) and messianic (or "Mosaic" [21]) revelation, writing: "In 1926–1927, Benjamin found himself between Moscow and Jerusalem, between the German Communist Party that he hesitated to join, and the Zionism to which he would never adhere" (ibid.). The empty space between these promises likewise is the expanse of ruins.

Moscow, Jerusalem, and so on—these are promises enfolding the principle of their nonfulfillment. "Next year in rebuilt Jerusalem!" even as one walks the streets of a rebuilt Jerusalem. "What are the conditions for one's presence in Jerusalem?" Derrida demanded of his audience at his 1986 Jerusalem lecture ("How Not to Speak?" *Psyché,* [1987c]), adding:

and where is the place so named? How to measure the distance that separates us, or brings us together? Here is the reply of Dionysius [Christian mystic of Roman times, the first bishop of Paris. Au.] who quotes Scripture in his *Ecclesiastic Hierarchy:* "Do not draw away from Jerusalem, rather await the promise of the Father that you have heard from my mouth, and

by which you shall be baptized by the Holy Spirit' (512c, 303). . . . [Jesus]
spoke of Jerusalem as a place that has remained a place of expectation of
fulfillment of the promise. (581)

From all these angles, Jerusalem, Moscow (and other "pilgrimage" sites
in East or West) remain a vista of ruins, a demolished Temple encased in
hopes of redemption, in promise. Derrida's Jerusalem thus remains true to
the city's romantic image and its representation in etchings, paintings, photographs, and so forth, executed by pilgrims over the centuries. Although he
has visited Jerusalem four times, Derrida has left the city—in philosophical
terms—"in ruins." It was as though he reduced Jerusalem to the Western
Wall—a relic of the Temple and the departed Divinity (see below in the
chapter "Jerusalem").

Modern study of the ruins metaphor rests upon the writings of Walter
Benjamin; to be precise, on his "Origin of German Tragic Drama" (1925).
Here, Derrida could (and most certainly did) read the following lines:

[T]he allegory exposes to the observer's eyes the *Facies Hippocratica* [face
of the dying] of history as a kind of frozen primordial landscape . . . that is
the kernel of the allegorical regard, the Baroque, secular performance of
history, as the world's *via dolorosa:* only at its stations of destruction does it
possess meaning, such great meaning, such a great addiction to death, for
death etches the deepest border-line between *physis* and meaning . . . the
false glamour of totality is brought to an end. For the *eidos* has been extinguished, the parable wilts, the internal universe dries up. In the riddles of
the remaining arid pictures, lies insight . . . [t]he observation of the absence
of freedom, of the incompleteness and fragility of the physical and the sensual. . . . The allegorical visage of nature history, exhibited on the stage by a
melancholy pageant, is indeed present there in the form of ruins. . . . Indeed, history finds expression, in this form, not as a process in eternity, but
rather as a process of constant destruction that cannot be arrested. . . .
Hence the Baroque cult of ruins . . . The perfect vision of this novelty was:
the ruin. . . . The incarnation of things going to their ruin is the most
extreme opposite to the concept of sublime nature, as held by the early
Renaissance.[2]

Benjamin regarded the departure from classical beauty as taking leave of
the infinite glory of the *physis,* Nature, and its replacement by the fracture
and fragments of the ruins. Derrida adopted the image, connecting it with
postmodernism, whose links with the Baroque were frequently noted in discourse of the 1980s. Thus, in his reading of an earlier Walter Benjamin essay
("On the Critique of Violence," [1921]) Derrida wrote:

> One could write, perhaps with, or according to, Benjamin, perhaps against him, a short treatise on the love of ruins. Anyway, what else can one love? One can love a monument, architecture, an institution as it is, but within its own precarious experience of its fragility: it has not always been there, it will not always be there, it is finite. Precisely for that reason one loves its mortality, across its birth and its death, across the phantom or the silhouette of its ruin, of mine. (*Force de loi* [1994a], 105)

Indeed, Derrida dredged the ruins from the depths of Benjamin's soul. Thus, in a lecture during a 1990 symposium on "Nazism and the 'Final Solution': The Limits of Representation," held at the University of California, he referred to one of Benjamin's earlier essays (see the chapter titled "Benjamin's Given Name," in *Force du loi* [1994a]). As Derrida puts it, this essay is "haunted by the theme of radical destruction, extermination, total annihilation; and above all, the annihilation of rights, if not to say justice; and among those rights, the rights of man" (67). Derrida refers to a "haunted" text, having identified a specter connected to Benjamin's Jewish origins, or in Derrida's terms: "a Jewish perspective that sets just, divine (Jewish) violence, which destroys the law, against the mythical violence (of Greek tradition) which underpins and preserve the law" (68). In other words, Derrida detects within the foundations of Judaism a certain power of destruction and havoc. Not for the first time, it should be recalled.

Derrida commences with the final words of the Benjamin essay: "Divine violence (*die göttliche Gewalt*) which is the insignia and seal (*Insignium und Siegel*) but never a means of sacred execution, could be called sovereign (*mag die Waltende heissen*)." For these words, Derrida explains "ring in the ears like the blasts of the *shofar* on the termination or eve of worship" (75).

The signature "Walter" appended to the essay reminds Derrida of the German *Waltend* (sovereignty). Political sovereignty? Walter (Benjamin) as sovereignty? Which of the two? According to Derrida's creed, Benjamin's essay can be construed as a grafting of neo-messianic mysticism onto neo-Marxism, but also vice versa. Either way, the duality is of historical forces whose message is ruin.

Derrida, with his peculiar predilection for "double binds," for contrasting paired concepts, does not omit to list the two types of historical violence set out in Benjamin's essay: that is, the violence that elevates social law (revolution, strikes, war, etc.) and protects it (by the violent sanctions of the regime); and the divine violence whose effect is the destruction of social law. The first type rests upon Greek myth, the second, on its Jewish counterpart. Both types work their effect upon human history, guaranteeing a bizarre interdependence between law and violence, that is, violence as expression of the law, and law as expression of violence.

In Derrida's view, this pairing of violence and law thus guarantees deconstruction, the law's self-destruction (*Force de loi* [1994a], 93). At the very heart of every law, says Benjamin, the rot is at work, adding that this rot condemns the law from the very outset to ruin; for the law, by virtue of being the law, defends itself by means of violence that demolishes the law from within (police, military conscription, the death penalty, etc.). "Every judicial contract (*Rechtsvertrag*) rests upon violence" (112). In similar vein, Derrida writes elsewhere: "[I]n origin as in conclusion, in introduction as in preservation, the law is inseparable from violence, immediate or deferred, present or represented" (115). Thus, in relation to the future universal justice that Benjamin identified with God and His wrath, Derrida claims that this is the Jewish God whose violence, by its very essence, destroys laws (in contrast with the gods of Greek mythology—Prometheus, Apollo, Artemis, et al.—who laid foundations for social law [122]). But as already noted, there is a fundamental distinction between the two forms of violence. Benjamin shows no hesitation in taking the side of one against the other: the violence of Greek myth causes bloodshed for its own sake and against life; by contrast, the violence of the Jewish divinity offers up life in order to save life and for the sake of life. The victims notwithstanding, "Thou shalt not kill" remains the foundation and cornerstone of Judaism, whose essence is consecration of life, and whose hallmark is justice. The essence of the Jew's existence is fulfillment of the potential for justice; the sanctity in his life is not in life: rather, it is in the justice of life (126).

In the philosophy of the early Benjamin, messianic utopianism overcame Marxist historicism: the optimism overshadowing Benjamin's dualistic pessimism required that history ultimately side with the justice of divine violence. History shall contrive the victory of divine violence (which demolishes laws, but simultaneously affirms life) over mythological violence (which elevates the laws of states and societies, but perpetuates violence). Political authority and its violence will crumble before heavenly sovereignty, which enfolds the incarnation of historical justice (even if it is beyond man's powers to understand heavenly justice, and he can merely witness its outcome). Having concluded on that ringing note, Benjamin denounces the violence of social law, his words, as Derrida puts it, resounding like the *shofar* (ram's horn) call at the termination of worship (153); now comes the wordplay on Walter-*Waltend* to ensure that God, sovereignty in its full incarnation, is the signatory to the essay of W. (Benjamin), not Walter. "Authority, justice, power and violence are among those [names]" (134).[3] It is common knowledge that the *shofar* concludes worship at the termination of the services for *Yom Kippur* and the Jewish New Year. It is therefore very probable that Derrida's *shofar* association (twice!) occurred on *Yom Kippur,* to be extended to Judgment Day and history overall. The human sin of resort to violence for the purpose of enforcing human law will be punished by the violence of the heavenly sovereign. Thus, whereas the Jewish *shofar* is sounded to open the gates of Heaven to forgiveness and *Kippur* (inscription in the Book of Life), the *shofar* that Derrida hears is the trumpet call of Judgment Day from the Revelation of St. John (the "Apocalypse").

Walter Benjamin committed suicide on the Spanish border, two years before the Wansee conference formulated the Nazi "Final Solution." How can the appalling Nazi violence be reconciled with these observations of Benjamin? Derrida regards the Nazis as employing one type of violence against the other. As incarnation of mythological violence, social and political, Nazism arose to annihilate the witnesses of the other logic, that is, the Jews (141). But conversely, one cannot shake off the temptation to regard the Holocaust as expression of divine violence, unintelligible and demanding sacrifice of atonement; annihilating but ostensibly without bloodshed, merely with lethal gas. The power of this temptation is easy to detect if we recall that Benjamin associated divine violence with bloodless annihilation, as in the instance of the biblical Korah and his company. But Derrida hastens to reject such a shocking interpretation, as he writes: "When one thinks of the gas chambers and crematoria, how can one hear without horror this allusion to an extermination of an expiatory nature because it was bloodless? One is terrified at the notion of an interpretation which renders the Holocaust an expiation and an indecipherable signature of God's just and violent wrath" (145).

Be that as it may, even if Benjamin's essay evoked Derrida's reservations (which he expressed at least three times in the course of this chapter), there can be no doubt that, deep inside, he did imbibe this principle of Jewish divine destruction as a deconstructivist principle. In this context, it should be noted further that a certain equation between holocaust and God does nevertheless stand out in Derrida's writings, notably in *Glas* (1974). Here, in his interpretative study of the Hegelian concept of God, Derrida defines the spirit of "natural religion" in terms of a holocaust:

> At the first moment of the natural religion, that of the luminous essence (*Lichtwesen*) the spirit is nothing more than its own concept . . . dwelling within undefined abstraction, it has yet to be deployed, manifested, produced. It is preserved within "the night of its essence" (*die Nacht seines Wesens*). In the first sundering that reveals its secret (*Geheim-*

nis) of the spirit . . . it appears . . . pure sunlight . . . a sun purely visible, therefore invisible, which allows of vision without showing itself . . . consuming all with its appearance. . . . Pure and without form, this light burns all (*brûle-tout*). It burns in the all-burning that it is, leaving of itself nothing, nothing at all, no trace, no mark, no sign of its passing. Pure and all-consuming . . . (*Glas* [1974], 265)

"A burning of everything" (*brûle-tout*) is the term Derrida coined to denote the onto-theological concept of holocaust (*holos caustos* [burnt whole]). There is thus some equation between God and holocaust. The two constitute an example-without-example,[4] that is, they are without essence, signifiers that cannot be attached to the signified; on the one hand, the absence of any figurative vestige of God; and on the other, the uniqueness of the Holocaust, transcending any imaginable historical concept (other than the principle of Otherness): "The all-burning is 'an essenceless by-play, pure accessory of the substance rises without ever setting' . . . pure example, without essence, without law. Therefore without example, like God about which Hegel says that an example cannot be made, but because he, God, merges with the pure essence, pure essence is also without example."[5]

The essenceless absence, leaving us with the ruins, could serve as model for an architectural approach. For the absent-presence in deconstructivist architecture has theological significance, if only in its full compliance with the Jewish perception of God. Derrida stresses this connection, as he linked Peter Eisenman's architecture with the Temple or synagogue: "[W]hat distinguishes your architectural space from that of the temple, indeed of the synagogue (by this word I mean a Greek word used for a Jewish concept)?" (Letter to Peter Eisenman in *Art and Its Significance*, ed. Stephen David Ross [Albany: State Univ. of New York Press, 1994], 430).

Derrida drew a line from Benjamin's concept of "ruins" (in this instance, relating to his 1924 study of the allegory of the baroque tragic play) to the Platonic concept of *khôra* (which, elsewhere—in "How Not to Speak?" [*Psyché* (1987d)—he compared with God's absence in negative theology). As metaphysical, nonentity principle of containment, *khôra* took on a metaphorically apocalyptic hue, both *Khôra* and "ruins" being called upon in contemporary architecture, as construction bearing within it the seeds of its own destruction (whether future or past destruction). Any memory is a kind of ruin, writes Derrida, as it constitutes something that was and is no longer. Contemporary architecture is an architecture of memory bearing within it destruction:

[W]hat would again bring the architecture of "the period" . . . back to the ruin, to the experience of "its own" ruin? In the past, great architec-

tural inventions constituted their essential destructability, even their fragility, as a resistance to destruction or as a monumentalization of the ruin
itself (the baroque according to Benjamin, right?) Is a new image of the
ruin to come already sketching itself in the design of the architecture that
we would like to recognize as the architecture of our present, of our future.
(*Art and Its Significance*, 435)

Derrida continues to underpin the concept of ruin with Judaism. The
ruin image turns into the image of ashes, and it is but a short path to
memories of the Holocaust and references to the "Jewish Museum" in Berlin (Daniel Libeskind, architect). Indeed, Derrida goes so far as to quote the
Israeli architect: "And in turn the void materializes itself in the space outside
as something that has been ruined, or rather as the solid remainder of an
independent structure, which is a voided void. . . . The past fatality of the
German Jewish cultural relation to Berlin is enacted now in the realm of the
invisible. It is this invisibility which I have tried to bring to visibility" (*Art
and Its Significance*, 36).

The foregoing lines were written in Jerusalem, a city whose Jewish spiritual center is the "ruin" of the Temple, the surviving wall of the Temple of
antiquity. Ever since the destruction of the Second Temple, Jewish culture
has constantly hinged upon the memory of that ruin. The Talmud composed in Babylon and completed in the fifth century tirelessly wove a match
to that ruin, concomitantly relating to the concept of ruin overall. Thus, for
example, the Talmud relates: "There are three watches in the night, and at
each watch the Almighty sits and roars like a lion, saying: Woe upon those
sons for whose sins I destroyed my house and burned my temple and banished them among the nations of the world" (*Masechet "Brachot,"* 3, 71).
Shortly thereafter, the story of the Jerusalem ruin appears: Rabbi Yosi the
Babylonian entered the Jerusalem ruin and prayed there, whereupon the
prophet Elijah was revealed unto him, teaching him, inter alia that one
should not enter a ruin. The ban on entering a ruin ("because of suspicion,
because of [the danger of] collapse, because of evil spirits" [*Masechet "Brachot,"* 3, 71]) leaves little ontological chance of a *locus* in the Land of Israel,
condemned simultaneously to nothingness and to transcendence (prayer
rules drawn up in Babylon conformed with memories of the regulations in
force at the Temple, just as hopes of redemption were all directed to reconstruction of the Temple. But in between mythical past and mythical future,
stretches history, as reflection of myth in time, at the level of ruin). Henceforth, the Babylonian Talmud was entirely dedicated to injecting the replica
of the Babylonian "here" into the suspended, devastated original of the
Jerusalem "there."

The here-there relationship between Babylon and Jerusalem is, in effect, the relationship between replica and the absent, resting upon the expectation of fulfillment of the messianic promise (reconstruction of the Temple, the Return to Zion, etc.). This was the model the Jewish people bore for two thousand years, injecting its consciousness of the destruction into prayers, days of fasting and commemoration, bans on various types of celebration, breaking a glass at weddings, avoiding completion of plastering and painting the home, and so forth. In all these aspects, Derrida's concept of destruction could reflect a further Jewish aspect in the submerged countenance lurking behind the armor of the French philosopher. But principally, this countenance, emerging perforce in his philosophical work, is camouflaged as "writing."

11

The Fire

Discussing Edmond Jabès's *Return of the Book* in the chapter "Ellipse" (*L'écriture et la différence* [1967b]), Derrida referred to the theme of the absent center (in the original topical sense) citing Jabès:

> Reb Naman said: "God is the center . . . ."
> And Yukel said: The center is failure."
> "Where is the center?"
> "Under ashes."
> Reb Selah: "The center is mourning." (*Writing and difference* [*L'écriture et la différence*] [Chicago: Univ. of Chicago Press, 1978], 297)

Fire is the absent center, the original meaning, divine speech; whereas the ashes, identified as written signifiers, are the dead "traces" of that meaning. Writing is therefore akin to ashes, to mourning. In effect, we have here Derrida's first reference to the fire theme, which would continue to grow and expand, permeating all his writings, with connections to the sun (rising and setting), holocaust, the Holocaust, memory, and so on

Derrida's concept of "trace" (originally, one of E. Lévinas's basic concepts) emerged as part of his critique of Platonic metaphysics and its offshoots in Western thought, as a philosophy that promises revelation of the truth as presence (present). Thus, the chapter in *Margins of philosophy* [*Marges de la philosophie*] [Chicago: Univ. of Chicago Press, 1982], 31–67) dealing with the relationship between the concept of time and the concept of being in Heidegger, Hegel, and Aristotle concludes by injecting the concept of "trace" into the very heart (text) of metaphysics: "In order to exceed metaphysics, it is necessary that a trace be inscribed within the text of metaphysics, a trace that continues to signal not in the direction of another presence, or another form of presence. . . . The trace is produced as its own erasure. And it belongs to the trace to erase itself, to elude that which might maintain it in presence" (ibid. p. 65).

In fact, without resorting to the terms "fire" and "ashes," these affirmations already contain identification of the sun as revelatory fire that uncovers the truth (the truth itself is like the sun, like fire. The truth is as the movement of self-revelation, exposure.) and simultaneously, identification of the ashes as trace, as erasure of the revelation, that is, extinguishing the fire to leave it as memory of truth that was and is no longer. Indeed, in 1980, Derrida conceded: "I would like to write to you so simply . . . effacing all the traits . . . so that the language above all remains secret in relation to the evident . . . as though it caught fire the moment a third person set eyes upon it" (*La carte postale*, 15).

Language and fire. Fire burns all matter, erasing all characteristics, whereas language, vis à vis the fire, being a "burning" conflagration, is banished from the world of certainty, truth, source. Derrida's world seems to be going up in smoke. The crematoria of language burn incessantly in this great holocaust where he pinpoints truth (which hides itself as it is consumed by the fire) of language and consciousness, until he steps forward to do everything in his power to safeguard the fire. What we have here is the conscious act of free will of the pyromaniac: "The sole 'decision' possible to me—which I obey at any moment . . . : burn everything, forget everything, to examine the force of departure without trace. . . . The symbol? a great holocaust-like conflagration, finally burning all, into which we would fling, with all our memory, our names, letters, photos, the little articles, the keys, the fetishes (*La carte postale* [1980], 46).

This is burning so as to guarantee the disappearance of being, as realization of its broadest significance (which is the absence of being the significance); burning so as to guarantee the ash which is the memory of fire; burning so as to experience the dual aspect, and the great inner contradiction, of the fire: revelation of being (through its illumination) and annihilation of being (through its burning). This is Derrida's paradoxical response to the Platonic ladder of cognition, at whose pinnacle the sun shines: destruction of metaphysics (of the sun) by burning it in its own fire.

In 1987, when Derrida decided to publish *Feu, la cendre* (Fire, the ashes)[1] as text and recording, he chose, in effect, the dualism of writing and voice, or the tension between eye and ear. Indeed, this dualism also permeated the text with two parallel pages: to the right, a duet, or douale of male and female (that is to say, a further duality); to the left, passages from Derrida's earlier works—*Glas, La dissémination,* and *La carte postale*—on the theme of fire, burning, and ashes. Collated, the quotations constitute a kind of archive, or the powdered ashes of the fire that burned, went out, and left ashes of memory. Alongside all this is the recording—the voices of Derrida and Carole Bouquet, of the writer and the reader. One voice evoking the other, one voice reaching out to the other, "almost a prayer" notes Derrida in his introduction to what strikes our ear as hermeneutic-existential-theological elegy.

Over fifteen years after completing *La dissémination* (1972a), Derrida was taken with a sentence he wrote at the end of the chapter on "Plato's Pharmacy," a sentence that haunted him, so he claims, seeming to have been dictated to him by some superior authority: "There are ashes there." Ghostlike, that sentence reverberates in his mind, concluding the book like a "signature" where he wrote of the total collapse of his signature (which marks his personal presence). "Far from the center, when the secrets were scattered and turning to ash," he wrote, naming the four thinkers to whom he was indebted, and thereafter—that sentence. It seems open to the following interpretation: the disintegrated text is ash, which is indebted to a previous fire. Prior to this dedication dating from December 1971, he concluded the chapter with a fictitious letter, written moments before a holocaust, before the arrival of the executioners:

> The greatest safeguard of all will be not to write, but rather, to learn by heart . . . because it is impossible that the writings will not end up falling into the public domain. . . . Goodbye and obey me. As soon as you have read and re-read this letter—burn it . . .

> I hope this doesn't get lost. Quick, a copy . . . lead . . . charcoal . . . re-read this letter . . . burn it . . . There are ashes there. . . .

> Night passes. In the morning, knocks are heard at the door. They seem to come from the outside this time, the knocks . . .

> Two knocks . . . four . . . (197).

The text stands therefore as intermediary entity, between the fire that was and the fire that will be, between two holocausts—the ash between two holocausts, before and after. "*Il y a la cendre*": the "there" (*là*) seems to erase itself in speech in French, *la* sounding like *là*. The place—*là* (there)—has erased itself in speech—the duality of revelation and erasure. The ash is there, in the place that erases itself. The ash image itself crumbles like ashes. It is distinct from what was. It has been consumed. The ash is that which no longer exists, that has vanished like smoke, leaving behind nothing. The ash is "there," it has been shunted into the past, the ash as memory of the fire; as memory. But—what has burned? Who? The ash does not reveal the answer. The ash is a closed secret, "being without presence," in Derrida's term. The veil of the ash will not be removed. Ash, being erasure, is the place of the nothing and the *es gibt* (German, "there is," but literally "it gives." Trans.) that gives nothing. Ash is destruction without possibility of restoration or re-turn; ashes as sign of the past to which no return is ever possible.

Ashes as text, text as ashes—both contain within themselves their remoteness from their origins. Ashes and text are residual traces of the "all-burning" that has annihilated all, leaving no hope of renewal. Ashes are thus the negation of the phoenix arising from its ashes. The fire concealed behind the ashes is disguised in a "*pharmakon*" mask of ash, which is, as we have noted, language. Sentences and words are ash, even the word "ash" is the ash of the actual ash. The language's sentences scatter the ash, while simultaneously preserving its existence "there." Every sentence separates the "dead" (victims of the fire) from the reader. Thus does language become a kind of mourning work; the language as grave of grave (for the fire's burning annihilates); language as traces of dead being (every sign is a trace of a dead signified) and false hope of the return of the fire of being; memory enfolding forgetting.

Is this memory of holocaust? Expectation of holocaust? Of which holocaust, which fire, which ashes—does Derrida speak? "Holocaust, crematoria—in German and in all existing Jewish languages," as though Derrida refers to a known historical Holocaust. But at the same time, Derrida dissociates the holocaust from its historical context, expanding it, as holocaust with a small *h*, into the universal, metaphorical level of the meaning of language, cognition, and religion. Thus does the philosopher become pyromaniac, obsessive arsonist. "Playing with words as one plays with fire," or, as he repeatedly urges his secret love in *La carte postale:* "Burn everything!" But in truth, Derrida is condemned to ashes, rather than to fire. He is condemned to language and its memories (despite the paradox of ashes as memoryless memory: for ashes lack any figuration of fire and/or of the object consumed by the fire), condemned to writing: for writing is the language of "traces," traces of death. More writing means more holocaust.

In *Ulysse gramophon* (1987d), Derrida wrote one of those sentences that defy translation: "*Avant d'être, c'est-a-dire un présent, cela fut, fut Il, fuit, feu le Dieu de feu le dieu jaloux*" (40). The origin of being is the divine fire that eludes (*fuit*) its essence. That being so, it leaves ashes: as memory, as trace of something that was and has been erased. Should we say: divine ash? In his 1986 lecture in Jerusalem on negative theology, Derrida spoke of ashes as lingual trace of the language of prayer, prayer as sign of the divine absence (*Psyché* [1987c], 561). "There are ashes there." Not here, "there." Is this a reference to "there" as in the text of *Sauf le nom* (see above, the chapter titled "Countenance Averted")? The divine "there"? Again, we recall the Hebrew ambiguity of *sham* and *shem*. And what if "there" nothing remains but ashes, without fire?

As is his wont, Derrida answers these questions in his interpretation of another philosopher, in this instance: Hegel. According to Hegel (as interpreted in *Glas* [1974]) "natural religion" developed as various stages of cognition. The earliest is the stage of the abstract, undefined concept, of the nonemergence of light from "the night of its essence." The emergence of the religious spirit from the darkness of the unconscious commences with the eruption of fire as pure light, sunlight, the visual sun (which is also unobservable, i.e., unrevealed, and burns all [265]).[2] This is the sun rising in the east, all-inclusive and all-exhaustive (ibid.). At this early phase of the religious spirit, light is pure, shadow-less, without any resistance or antithesis: bodiless light, total burning (*brûle-tout*, holocaust) burning up and burned up. It is a pure, essence-less burning: "*brûle-tout* is 'a game without essence'" (266). A game? Indeed it is, but only in the sense of the free, aimless play of division and destruction (*dissémination*) that the fire bears in its flames—a "game"—exclusively in the sense of the free expanse of the elimination of any representation (entailed in burning of matter, or the world) and crushing any unification or generalization:

> The burn-all (*brûle-tout*)—which only occurred once, and which meanwhile is repeated *ad infinitum*—so excels in drawing away from any essential generalization that it resembles the pure separation of a complete accident. Play and pure separation, here we have the secret of an imperceptible burn-all, the torrent of fire igniting itself . . . a sort of sign without signed, an ornament wasted without a proper body, the total absence of propriety, of truth, of meaning, of a deployment of forms that are promptly destroyed. This is One simultaneously infinitely multiplied and absolutely different, different from itself. (266)

How is the fire to be doused? How is the destructive fire of holocaust to be contained? How is the sun of *brûle-tout* to realize its decline and fall? How is it to bring forth from within itself the fire, the dynamics of the worst of all, any stable body, a monument to preserve the traces of death? Casting around after the body to preserve both living and extinguished fire for a monument born thereof and preserving its traces, Derrida found it in the pyramid: the tomb whose hallmark is the sun and whose form perpetuates the point of the flame. The pyramid completes the duality of the fire's contradictions. In order to be what it is—a fire that consumes, disintegrates, and ensures "differences"—the *brûle-tout* is required to fulfill its contradictions: to be preserved in the movement of its self-destruction, to appear in its disappearance. For that is the secret of fire: survival within its own perdition. This internal contradiction is the source of the movement of time—from sunrise to sunset. Sunrise enfolds sunset, east enfolds west—the movement of history. In his article "The Pit and the Pyramid" (*Marges de la philosophie* [1972b]) the pyramid represents the sign (see below, the appendix, "The Black Academy").

Construction of the pyramid as temple-of-solar-cycle signs the victim preserving the *brûle-tout* while simultaneously annulling it. The victim does not destroy the *brûle-tout*; rather, he permits it—by virtue of its transformation into monument—to become *pour soi*, "for itself" and self-knowing. The *brûle-tout* is sacrificed in a holocaust "for itself." It is offered up to ensure its preservation. The fire flickers and goes out, the fire burns down, the sun begins to decline, moving in an orbit of increasing internalization to the west (the West internalizes the sun into its consciousness). This sacrificial offering belongs, like its negation, to the logic of *brûle-tout*; in other words: if you wish to burn everything, you must burn the conflagration, to prevent its continued existence as presence. It is vital to extinguish the fire, to preserve it for the sake of its annulment, or its annulment for the sake of its preservation. They are mutually dependent. The movement of history, the sun's progress from east to west, the dialectic—all bear the hallmark of holocaust, *brûle-tout*, cycles of self-fulfillment and self-effacement. Therefore, "The dialectic of religion, history and philosophy (etc.) is created as effect and reflection of a victim of the Holocaust" (*Glas*, 270).

If this is the movement of the spirit, and the truth, the task of the intellectual is clear: to ensure the duality of the fire and its extinguishing (ashes). And wherever there is no fire, it is his duty to set a blaze, to annihilate, to offer up sacrifice, to burn—to exercise a holocaust. Otherwise, without fire and its victim (including its self-sacrifice, i.e., the burning of the fire) there is no truth. Hence the obsession surrounding the burning of letters in *La carte postale* comes. From first to last, "it should have all been burned, everything, right up to the ashes of unconsciousness—and 'they' would never know anything" (*La carte postale* [1980], 11). Burning letters, burning photographs, burning any representation (any "dispatch")—even if it is the writer himself—must occur: "Before my death I will give instructions. If you aren't there, they'll retrieve my corpse from the lake, burn it, and send you my ashes, a well-protected urn ('fragile'). . . . It will be a shipment from me that will no longer come from me . . . Well, you'll like mixing my ashes in with your food" (211).

Burning completes the act of writing. Writing, sending the message, is done overtly; it is exposed, like the postcard, an open letter, a text revealing itself. But the truth of writing (a postcard) is not in the ash (for the text, we recall, is ash); rather, it is in the fire. "If I write on the card . . . that will be to destroy, so that nothing shall be kept but an illegible support. . . . And if we don't destroy all the traces, we are saved, that is to say, lost" (*La carte postale*, 38). "Saved, that is to say, lost"—the dual aspect of the truth of fire. "Keep what you burn, I beg you. Mourn that which I send you" (67)—language as mourning, as the rite of tombs. Mourning? Furthermore, language as fan for the flames of holocaust, the fatal fire. To kill and mourn. Preserving the vitality of truth is thus setting it on fire, safeguarding it in the dual condition of revelation and perdition.

> If you'd listen to me, you'd burn it all and nothing would have arrived. I would like to say the opposite, that something ineffaceable would have arrived, in place of that endless misery in which we are dying. . . . [Y]ou did clearly hear the other voice . . . that urged you not to burn, to burn so as to save. Nothing arrived because you wanted to keep (and thus lose) . . . I recall the ashes. What luck, burning, yes, yes. (28)

Truth is condemned to the contradiction of fanning the flames and dousing them—the duality of truth to God and man: "God himself only had the choice of two crematoria: where to start? When? Catastrophe is always imminent . . . I write bent in two with a double instrument, fickle, perfidious, perjured. I scratch and erase everything with the other hand" (156). Therefore, knowledge of the truth arises from its denial, memory from forgetfulness. "Amnesia, what strength. One should forget, know how to forget, to know how to forget without knowing. To forget, d'you hear, not to confuse" (85). Concomitantly, the experience of ashes resembles the experience of memory. What is the meaning of recalling out of forgetfulness? To forget so as to start over: "Our only chance of survival . . . is in burning everything, so as to return to our first desires . . . oblivion, our only chance isn't it . . . it will allow us to start over" (185), or:

> I would like to be sure that you, and only you and nobody else, who has accepted (without a moment's thought) the idea of this final great fire, call it "the burning"; that up to the letter nothing remains of everything we have sent, all this eternity, that some day or other we shall again become younger than ever, and that after the burning of the letters I should run into you . . . I forget everything so as to love, I forget you, you, up to the moment when I will fling myself at you. (187)

The fire metaphor is thus one of Derrida's basic images (along with ruins, abyss, wound, etc.). It is startling to discover that, in a departure from his familiar resort to historical and philosophical discussion of matters close to his philosophical domains, Derrida refrained on this occasion from the rather self-evident mention of the pre-Socratic "fire philosopher" Heraclitus, particularly as the latter frequently engaged the attention of a man to whose writings Derrida incessantly reverts: Martin Heidegger.[3] At Freiburg between 1966 and 1967, Heidegger held a "Heraclitus seminar" that highlighted, inter alia, the fire theme. As one of the four elements, fire was connected in his discussion with the dialectics of life and death, resting upon fragment 76 by Heraclitus: "Fire resurrects the death of the earth, and the air resurrects the death of fire; water resurrects the death of air, and the earth resurrects the death of water" (Martin Heidegger and Eugen Fink, *Heraclitus Seminar 1966–67* [University: Univ. of Alabama Press, 1979], 89; translated from Hebrew). Eugen Fink, who shared with Heidegger in moderating the seminar, offered his own interpretation: "Can we imagine life and death interwoven, not in the sense of life becoming death, but in the sense of seeing the change as 'living the death of another'? It doesn't mean: coming from death to life."

Quite central to the seminar was the concept of lightning—the fire the flashes out of the night sky, divine fire lighting up the world. Lightning is the light of Zeus, dynamic fire-and-light that imposes unity upon the multiplicity of things and reveals the totality of the world. Heidegger interpreted the heavenly-and-nocturnal light in terms of the relationship between language and the world: Zeus's lighting illuminating the world is calling things by their names. Endowing names illuminates things and presents them to consciousness.[4] The nocturnal lightning striking things causes them to appear, and to become visible under Zeus's name—so did Heidegger interpret it (ibid.). In his opinion, in the modern era, we are inclined to avoid lightning, to lull our anxiety, to do everything to make the storm subside. The German philosopher, finding it difficult to accept this inclination, yearns for lightning and fire: "We shall see this lightning only if we place ourselves at the heart of the tempest of existence" (78, translated from Hebrew). However, the fire of revelation is merely one aspect of being. Heidegger dwells at length on a line from Homer's *Odyssey* which relates how, on hearing a poem, Odysseus hid his tears before those in attendance at the palace. In Heidegger's view, this scene, with Odysseus hiding his face in his robe, represented the pre-Platonic Greek notion of presencing as self-concealment: "Presencing is a glowing self-concealment . . . remaining concealed before the enclosedness of the present" (108, translated from Hebrew). We would add: note the *talith* as approximating concealment (see below, the chapter titled "Father's *Talith*").

Heidegger thus links the principle of the self-concealment of being with the concept of oblivion. Oblivion as self-concealment. Not merely does modern man often forget: he has even forgotten the essence of "oblivion";

oblivion, says Heidegger, rests upon its own essence, that is, the present sinks into hiding, the essence of this hideaway being that it hides from me. In other words: oblivion itself sinks into concealment. According to Heidegger's interpretation, Heraclitus in his fragments relates to this principle of oblivion in terms of the sun setting at eventide: the great ball of fire conceals itself within the clouds of night.

This fire concept, as seen by Heraclitus and Heidegger, bears close parallels to Derrida's ideas. The fire of self-revelation, which is the divine fire endowing things with their names, bears the dimension of self-concealment: "Presencing is a glowing self-concealment." And concealment is as oblivion, knowledge is as its erasure, sunrise is as sunset. Beyond being an "existentialist" call, is Heidegger's appeal to man to stand at the storm center, in danger of the lightning—an affirmation of "holocaust"? Is he who is struck by lightning (turning him charcoal-black) the one who was illuminated by the divine light?

Derrida is sparing in endowing his fire notions with Jewish associations. Unlike his other catastrophe images, to which he grants a Jewish hue, however slight, his discussion of fire is rarely lit up by a glimmer of Judaism (equally, it bears no associations from Christianity or Greek mythology, etc.). This is surprising in view of the centrality of the fire concept in Judaism, and the powerful links between God and fire. For God is revealed in fire: speaking to Moses from the fiery bush; as "burning lamp that passed between those pieces" in preparation of the Lord's Covenant with Abraham; in the pillar of fire that went ahead of the Children of Israel in the wilderness; in the vision of the fire resting upon the Temple at eventide; in the prophet Ezekiel's testimony concerning the divine appearance ("I saw as it were the appearance of fire" [Eziek. 1:27]); and so on. The "eternal flame" burning at the Temple altar is the constant divine presence. But it is not just visual presence. Divine fire is revelation that speaks: "the voice of God speaking out of the midst of the fire" (Deut. 4:33); "the word of the living God speaking out of the midst of the fire" (Deut. 5:23/26); "The voice of the Lord divideth the flames of fire" (Ps. 29:7); and so on. With that, God is neither fire nor voice, as He proves in His revelation to the prophet Elijah: "[T]he Lord was not in the fire. And after the fire a still small voice" (1 Kings 19:12). Furthermore, the Bible twice repeats the same words in characterizing fire as nothingness and vacuum: "the people shall labor in the very fire, and the people shall weary themselves for very vanity" (Jer. 51:58 and Hab. 2:13).

God's revelation in fire is therefore His externalization, His mode of communication with His people. In fire is He revealed, in fire does He speak, by fire does He punish. This is the divine fire, fire that consumes.

"For the Lord thy God is a consuming fire" (Deut. 4:24); or "And the fire of God came down from heaven, and consumed" (1 Kings 1:12, 14); and so on. The consuming divine fire is also the fire of the altar and the sacrifices. It is also the fire that changes, from merciful light and knowledge ("light is sown for the righteous," the hidden light of the Act of Creation, the fire that purges impurity, etc.) into punitive fire: "And the light of Israel shall be for a fire, and his Holy One for a flame: and it shall burn and devour his thorns and his briers in one day" (Isa. 10:17).

In other words, God is fire as nothingness; fire revealed to eye and ear; fire as harbinger of annihilation. Are we to deduce that, deep within the divine fire that consumes itself as it burns, there is no dialectic? Not if we are to believe the Book of Zohar, which employs self-devouring terms to interpret "For the Lord thy God is a consuming fire" as:

> For there is fire that consumes fire, consumes fire and destroys it, for there is fire stronger than fire. That is the fire of the sphere of majesty, which is justice, sustained by the fire of the angels and destroying the fire of the force of evil. The Zohar draws a distinction between two lights shining from the flames: one white, that illuminates, the other tinged with black or pale blue. The white light is the superior, while the black or blue is inferior. The inferior light (which is a "chair" for the other) forever consumes and destroys whatever is beneath it (in generating the blue-black light) whereas the white light shining above does not consume and is never destroyed, its light never changing. "That is the secret of the sacrifice, the rising smoke arouses the blue light to be ignited, and when it is ignited, it is joined to the white light." (Y. Tishbi, *Chapters of Zohar* [Jerusalem; Mosad Bialik, 1972], 1:160)

All this is a far cry from the "concealed light" (*or ganuz*), the light of Creation, the original, pure light, the light that rose from one end of the world to the other, and was concealed for the sole use of the righteous.

Derrida cannot accept the concept of "concealed light," countering it with the primal, pure light of the fire that burns all. At the same time, there are parallels between his fire concept and the Jewish notion of fire, which construes heaven as a fusion of fire and water (see "*Midrash Raba*," Rashi, "Likutey Moharan" et al.) and refers to the Torah as *esh dath* ("fiery law" [Deut. 33:2]); sundry commentaries of rabbinical Midrash literature, and the literature of Jewish mysticism, speak of the Torah being written in white fire and black fire.[5] In other words, writing is a fire of dual aspect: white and black, illuminating and consuming (corresponding to the duality of the flame's light). Probably, Derrida would have gladly accepted such a distinction at the level of hermeneutic allegory. In fact, this aspect of white and black fire features in his writings, being the sole Jewish association he injects into his fire concept. He would probably sign on to the triple Jewish link between fiery light, the skin, and the foreskin of circumcision, as set out by Rabbi Nachman of Breslau: "For there are three evil spirits, the wind of tempest, a great cloud, and fire flaring up. . . . And a thin fourth skin as brightness . . . and that is the secret of circumcision."[6] His words permit us to connect the Heraclitean-Heideggerian concept of lightning (tempest, cloud, and fire flaring) with the Derridean concept of circumcision: inscription of the wound into the body as divine fire, simultaneously consuming and writing; circumcision as the brightness of the fire of contradiction between revelation and concealment, giving and taking. Should we then say that the craving for burning (including, we should recall, self-immolation) is in fact the Derridean craving for "martyrdom"? As for the divine fire, which gives things their names, concomitantly the fire that burns things, submission to the fire guarantees the augmentation of the greatest divine flame, the light and the meaning (name-giving).[7]

12

Derrida's Sacrificial Offering

Arguably the most profound and pivotal motif in the creed of Jacques Derrida is the troubled relationship between father and son: Jackie (as the young Jacques was nicknamed) in relation to (the patriarch) Jacob. Derrida's father, Aimé, who died in 1970, aged seventy-four, is virtually nonexistent in most of his writings. And if his father is present, he represents absence, death (See a few mentions of the father in *La carte postale* [1980]: "Why is it that I think now of the *eau de cologne* that we pour by the liter over the deceased before he is placed in the coffin? About my father, to be precise?" [86] Similarly, there is mention of the father in a dream about someone terminally ill [231–32.) The father's absence contrasts with the looming image of the mother, Georgette-Esther. A familiar Freudian interpretation, of decisive importance in Derrida's philosophy, would explain all this away in patricidal terms.

The patricide theme never relinquishes its grip on Derrida's writing. Assuredly, there is his reiterated preoccupation with Freud's *Totem and Taboo* (see Jacques Derrida and Gianni Vattimo, *La religion* [1996b]) and *Moses and Monotheism* (see *Mal d'archive* [1995a]), not to mention his constant preoccupation with deicide, and of course, his reiterated studies of the theory of the psychoanalyst Jacques Lacan. In his lecture on Lacan ("Lacan and the Philosophers" [1992], published in his *Résistances de la psychanalyse* [1996e]) Derrida cites a remark made about him by the renowned French psychoanalyst: "The sentence where Lacan speaks of a 'father' and that is I, of a father who did not recognize . . . the blind alley into which he himself coaxed the Other, while playing dead" (69), and Derrida adds that Lacan regarded him as the father, but was blind to the perspective of the son: Derrida as son, or Lacan as son. Another decisive line: "Between me and Lacan lay death" (70), as if to say: between father and son lies death.

Lacan was right: Derrida frequently "played" dead; certainly he often "played" with death. We should recall that Derrida defined both "death" and "deconstruction"—a key term in his early interpretative theory—in the identical words, as "the experience of the impossible" (see, for instance, *Résistances de la psychanalyse*, 73). Death is always the death of the father (murdered by his son) or of the son (sacrificial offering rendered by his father).

Father and son: Derrida would identify that bilateral relationship wherever he looked: Socrates and Plato as father and son (*La carte postale* [1980]); the relation between idea (*logos*) and representation as a father-son relationship ("Plato's Pharmacy," in *La dissémination* [1972a]); even the theatrical relations between words (playwright) and body (actors) recall the father-son relationship (thus, in analyzing the writings of A. Artaud, Derrida points to the patricidal dimension in the theater rebelling against the playwright's primal and definitive speech. See the chapter titled "The Theater of Cruelty and the Closure of Representation," in *L'écriture et la différence* [1967b]). The metaphor is a representation of the vanished father (*Margins of Philosophy* [Chicago: Univ. of Chicago Press, 1982, 244); Stalin is the father of the socialists (*Moscou tour-retour* [1995b], 50); Greek philosophy of antiquity is a great father that Lévinas wishes to kill (*Writing and Difference* [Chicago: Univ. of Chicago Press, 1978], 89); "Babel" is the name of the divine father (*Tower of Babel* [Paris: 1985]); artwork is the offspring of its creator (Derrida following Lévinas in *Psyché* [1987c]); and so foth

Who is mistreating whom? Is it father tormenting son, or vice versa? Did Plato sentence Socrates to death? Did Y. H. Yerushalmi perform a circumcision upon Freud (see the chapter titled "Shibboleth of Evil")? Does writing "sentence to death" the original speech? Or did the God of the Jews, the Father, mistreat his offspring, the Jewish people (as Hegel claimed; see Derrida's study in *Glas* [1974])? Does the Platonic sun (father) enslave all the shadows (sons)? The key issue reiterated in virtually all of Derrida's writings is: the impossible route from father to son, from son to father. Certainly, the overriding motif of circumcision in Derrida's writings sets the father-son relationship in its utter starkness: the father's castration urge (*Glas*) and, by contrast, the son's fury at his mangled foreskin (*Circonfession* [1991a]). Derrida's overall philosophy thus emerges as an impossible encounter with the absence, or murder, of the father. The divine countenance concealed, the impossibility of penetrating "the gates of the Law" (as claimed in Derrida's interpretation of the Kafka story) in showing "writing" as a veil that precludes the transition from signs to the *logos*, leave an enormous void of nothingness, above or beneath which (or behind whose back) the writing is devised. The father is unknown, mysterious, cryptic (father, even if his gender is unknown to us, as set out in his interpretation of the identity of the "Law" in the aforementioned Kafka story).

Here is Derrida's great secret, a "secret" underlying an interpretative venture. In some instances, Derrida refers to it by the name "secret" (*Pas-*

sions [1993b]); in others, he tags it with the Greek name *khôra* (*Khôra* [1993a]). The former, we would suggest, is the abstraction of the vanished father. The latter, in Derrida's own words, is the "mother": a mother in quotes. We should stress again that Plato's *Timaeus* identifies *khôra* as the location of the initial fount of forms, a concept even predating Plato's fundamental distinction between idea (truth) and world (phenomenon). Plato understood this *khôra* exclusively in the metaphysical terms of "nursing," "containing," "motherhood." However,

> the thought of writing did not aim to rehabilitate writing . . . rather to regard writing as something already created by the voice: it is therefore not a matter of setting a maternal force against a paternal force, rather, to demonstrate that that which was always understood as "father" . . . exists only beyond that previous thing that may be termed "mother," just as long as it is not confused with the conventional sense of "mother." . . . Thus, there is something of the mother in the father." (J.Bennington, *Derrida* [Paris: Les contemporains seuil, 1991], 196–97)

Be that as it may, the mysterious mother is the space of the primordial fount, infinite voluminity rejecting any attribute of its own—a place that is antiplace: *khôra* leaves room for everything, but itself is without place—an anonymous and unlimited womb, this total maternity (to be identified also with the God of "negative theology"; see "How Not to Speak?" in *Psyché* [1987c]) of memory flowing out of memory ad infinitum, without commencement or beginning.

In his *Otobiographies* (1984b), Derrida traces the autobiographical route of Friedrich Nietzsche, who returns to father and mother as principles of death and life. Derrida writes (of Nietzsche? of himself?):

> in a word, my dead father, my living mother, my dead father or death, my living mother or life. As for me, I'm between the two of them. . . . and in that place, my truth, my double truth, is attached to them both . . . "in me my father is dead, but my mother is alive and aging." Insofar as *I am* my father, I am dead, I am the dead and I am death. Insofar as *I am* my mother, I am life that goes on, the living, the living woman. I am my father, my mother and I . . . death and life, the dead and the living and so on. (61–62)

Thus, setting out to pursue the secretiveness of the vanished father, we have discovered—death. In Derrida's teachings, paternity is coupled with its loss, with the loss of the father's primordial voice, with his "death":

> To write is not just to know that the Book does not exist and that forever there are books, against which the meaning of a world not con-

ceived by an absolute subject is shattered . . . it is not just to have lost the
theological certainty of seeing every page bind itself into the unique text of
the truth. . . . This lost certainty, this absence of divine writing, that is to
say, first of all, the absence of the Jewish God (who himself writes when
necessary). (*Writing and Difference* [Chicago: Univ. of Chicago Press,
1978], 10)

There we have him, Derrida's father: simultaneously lurking and castrating. Although Derrida should not be saddled with Hegel's notions about the
Jewish God (cruel, demanding obedience, punitive, loveless), we should bear
in mind that Derrida could have borrowed the concept of the castrating God
from Hegel. According to Derrida, the religious experience is dual: simultaneously phallic and castrating. On the one hand, the holy and the sanctified imply potency, creative power, fertility, might, erection (*La religion*
[1996b], 64); on the other, all three great monotheistic religions are embossed with the seal of the Covenant, invariably the Covenant of circumcision, external or internal, explicit or implicit (65). Here we find the duality, if
not the "double bind," of religion: affirmation of life ("Thou shall not kill")
and the command to sacrifice (67). It is the alliance of religion and death;
death that lies at the root of everything transcendent, all Otherness, fetishism
and messianic *spectralité* [ghostliness], the infrastructure of religion; the substantive link between religion and sacrifice (69). Even the vogue of "return
to religion" is interpreted by Derrida in terms of subconscious "death impulse": the typical urge to return, the impulse of the pattern.

Our theme is the "double bind," the mutual interdependence of contradictions that Derrida pinpoints in various discourses, among them Freudian psychoanalysis. His *Résistances de la psychanalyse* (1996e) diagnoses the
psychoanalytical method of disclosing a duality of two knots entangled with
one another: on the one hand, the principle of analysis and division; on the
other, reverting to the primal, indivisible source. Derrida identifies this
"double bind" with deconstruction (50). Even more intriguing to our subject is the footnote (51) where Derrida draws a parallel between the "double bind" and the sacrifice of Isaac; or, to be precise, the relationship
between Abraham and Isaac in the course of the sacrifice. In his words, a
"double bind" cannot be unraveled entirely. It is impossible to untie one of
the knots without tightening the other. These are the complex relationship
between sacrificer and sacrificed: the duality of the sacrificer binding, and
the sacrificer cutting and unbinding. Abraham binding his son, and Abraham cutting (quartering) with the knife he holds—is a set of paradoxes (see
below) to blame for a "snarl" ("double bind") of growing complexity. We
should stress that Derrida refers to the sacrifice of Isaac at the very conclu-

sion of his discussion of psychoanalysis in *Résistances*. If you wish, that is a kind of Jewish *Aufhebung* (levitation) of the discussion (even if the "ascent" was a descent to a mere footnote). Jacques Derrida and his Jewish "double bind" . . . (see the chapter titled "The Other *Kippa*").

Religion and sacrifice: Derrida's study of the philosophy of the Czech theologian Patocka ("Donner la mort" [1992]) hinges upon the moment of the revival of the spirit and its willingness to accept death (in French *donner la mort* means "giving death"—a man surrendering his life and opting for death). It is a moment of taking responsibility ("[G]iving death is the alliance between responsibility and faith." See "Donner la mort," in *L'éthique du don,* an anthology of essays on Jacques Derrida's philosophy of giving, eds. J. M. Rabaté and M. Wetzel [1992], 15). We can locate the roots of this mood as far back as Socrates, who surrendered his life on the altar of the Other and responsibility (19). From that viewpoint, the Platonic tradition resembles the attainment of eternal life by looking death straight in the eye (23). However, Derrida is more closely linked to a different Patockian religious dialogue concerning death: "Another way of giving, or yielding to, death, this time, the word 'giving' is stressed. This different manner of comprehending death . . . relates to a gift received from the Other, from him who, within his absolute transcendence, sees me without me seeing him, grasps me with his hand while remaining inaccessible to me" ("Donner la mort," 44). Giving death is Lévinas's double adieu: the leavetaking from God and giving oneself up to Him (*à Dieu*) (51). That is a definition of a man's acceptance of maximum responsibility by surrendering himself to death, surrendering his life.

Responsibility rests upon goodness no longer being objective transcendentalism, like the relationship between objective things; rather, it is the attitude to the Other, the answer to the Other. Moreover, the goodness of supreme responsibility is the goodness of self-oblivion above and beyond any calculation, a goodness founded upon infinite love for the Other. This responsibility demands an irreplaceable singularity. Nothing but death, nothing but one's death, can guarantee such singularity. Only offering up one's life is the complete giving of infinite love to the Other; the transcendental Other, unattainable, silent: the father.

Here, Derrida evolves his discourse about Kierkegaard and the sacrifice of Isaac (in Kierkegaard's renowned *Fear and Trembling,* which he published under the pseudonym of Johannes de Silentio—John the Silent!). Kierkegaard relates, albeit obliquely, to St. Paul's leavetaking of his disciples, when he demands their obedience in his absence. This is Paul-Saul, the converted Jew, saying "adieu" and rendering the demand of the absent, concealed, taciturn, secret God. Paul represents the Jewish perception of divinity, the Father-God in hiding, the God dictating to Abraham the impossible, unexplained imperative to sacrifice his son.

Derrida addresses the experience of the sacrificial offering; the sacrifice in the Hebrew lingual sense (Derrida specifically resorts to the Hebrew term *korban,* with its affinity to "closeness" ["Donner la mort," 60) but principally in the sense of surrendering the unique, the most precious, the most irreplaceable. The duality of sacrifice and secret: Abraham guards his secret. He tells no one of the command he has received. Taking responsibility is a singularly personal act. Talk would strip the act of its singularity. Talk would strip the ego of its exclusive egoness, to the general. Just as no one can die in my place, so can no one take a fateful decision in my place. It is incumbent upon me to be alone with my responsibility, my secret. A relationship of faith between man and God, between son and father, is a relationship dictating sacrifice and secrecy equally.

The Other, as total Other, God, is committed to His transcendentalism, remaining concealed, secretive and jealous of His love (by setting Abraham's love of Isaac in opposition to Abraham's love of God). The secret is essential to the acceptance of absolute responsibility, a sacrificial responsibility that is a consummation of love.

Contradictions are essential to the "double bind" between the son (Abraham) and his father (God), and/or between Abraham and his son Isaac. Responsibility is a manner of response, response to a call (*responsabilité*—response is a duality equally present in French; in Hebrew, there is a startling presence of "the Other"—*aher*—within "responsibility"—*ahrayut*). Responsibility is therefore a manner of speaking, language. At the same time, as noted, taking responsibility denies language, for language removes the speaker from the domain of the private ego. That is the clash between the duty of silence (Abraham's duty toward a concealed divine totality) and the duty of speech (Abraham's duty toward Isaac and toward his own family). Furthermore, Abraham's total duty toward God cannot be discharged within the framework of what is termed in a social context "duty." For faith is not discharge of a duty in the conventional social sense. Total duty demands giving or self-sacrifice, which is an act of faith beyond social duty. The kind of sacrifice demanded of Abraham was that he was required to "hate" his beloved son, to sacrifice him. Of course, Abraham was far from hating Isaac. On the contrary: it is his enormous love for his son that alone illuminates the horror of his sacrifice. And here we have a further contradiction: Abraham operates outside of any social morality (he sacrifices morality, says Derrida). However, for the act of sacrifice to have meaning, morality has to be integrated into the event. The horror of the act will be understood exclusively in a moral context. "The moment I am in a relationship with the Other, with the regard, the demand, the love, the order, the appeal of the Other, I know that I can respond only by sacrificing morality. . . . Day and night, at every moment, upon all of the world's Mount Moriahs, I am in the course of doing this: hoisting the knife over him whom I love and am bound to love, over the Other" ("Donner la mort," 68).

Here, Derrida drew his conclusions in relation to morality. Abraham's relationship with God is a model of accepting moral responsibility. That is the required relationship between any man and any other person (a total Other) and the relationship with those close to me, who are remote and "secret," "*tout autre*." A key sentence in Derrida's morality is thus: "*tout autre est tout autre*" (each Other is utterly different). But equally, each Other is a total Other (the absolute Other, God). The influence of Lévinas is evident, and Derrida makes no effort to conceal it. He mentions the Lévinasian term "visage" (80–81): the parallel between the countenance of God and the face of the one near you, between God's infinite Otherness and the infinite Otherness of the Other (see the chapter titled "Facing Lévinas").

Derrida is aware of what everyone knows: no father nowadays would sacrifice his son on the Montmartre mount (82). With that, he knows well that Isaac's sacrifice remains pending. He recalls that the sacrifice site, Mount Moriah in Jerusalem, is the site of the Temple, just as it is the location of the Omar Mosque, and very close to Christ's Via Dolorosa. The al-Aksa mosque, the Western Wall, the Church of the Holy Sepulcher—the three Abrahamite monotheistic creeds lay claim to the location, having fought and continuing to fight for it with fire and blood. Each religion has its historical-political interpretation of messianity and the sacrifice of Isaac. "Isaac's sacrifice continues every day," says Derrida (70). The following lines were written against the setting of the Gulf War:

> We do not even speak of wars, more or less recent, when one could wait eternally for morality or international justice . . . to determine responsibility or culpability for the hundreds of thousands of victims sacrificed, one doesn't even know to what end, innumerable victims, of whom each individual is infinitely singular, each one being entirely different, whether it is the victims of the Iraqi state or the victims of the worldwide coalition that accused Iraq of failure to respect legal right. In the discourse dominating these wars . . . it was strictly impossible to distinguish the religious from the moral, the juridical, and the political. The belligerents were all irreconcilable coreligionists within religion supposedly [derived] from the Holy Book. Does this not converge into what we term the fight to the death still raging on Mount Moriah for the purpose of appropriating the secret of the sacrifice of an Abraham who never uttered a word? (*L'éthique du don* [1992], 83)

Three years on, in 1994, on the isle of Capri for a French-German-Italian-Spanish symposium on the essence of religion, Derrida referred to the Baruch Goldstein massacre in Hebron as a further example of a relentless sacrificial offering: "It is difficult to say 'Europe' without the connotation of Athens-Jerusalem-Rome-Byzantium, wars of religion, unresolved war on the issue of the appropriation of Jerusalem and Mount Moriah, the "Here I am" of Abraham or Ibrahim before the extreme "sacrifice" demanded, the absolute sacrifice of the beloved son. . . . Yesterday (yes, last night, truly, it's scarcely a few hours) there was the massacre in Hebron, in the Tomb of the Patriarchs, a site jointly sanctified by the religions termed Abrahamic" (*La religion* [1996b], 13).

The sacrifice of Isaac has not ended, even if Derrida does not extend the fate of that sacrifice to the pogroms and the Holocaust, as is customary in Israeli literature, poetry, and art.[1] From his viewpoint, the fate of that sacrifice is linked to a religious commitment and an affinity to Mount Moriah and the heroes of that episode (who are buried in Hebron). In other words, the fate of the present-day sacrifice is mainly the fate of Jews and Moslems, waging their political-religious conflict in the Middle East. He would probably have expanded the discussion to include Moslem Shi'ite parents proudly sending their booby-trapped offspring to mount an Israeli bus.

If Derrida had a "solution" to the archetypal problem under discussion, it appears utopian-moral, clinging to the horns of the ram from the sacrifice of Isaac. For, when faced with infinite hatred, what can Derrida do other than confront it with infinite love towards the son and the Other, toward God and man. Accordingly, *tout autre est tout autre;* in other words, each encounter with the Other must pick out its "Mount Moriah," the responsibility toward the Other as absolute Other demanding of me that I sacrifice all for Him. The reader knows: right up to now, the sacrifice of Isaac goes on, the Isaacs, Jewish and Moslem, are offered up without a redemptive ram.

The onto-theological secret that is hidden at the bottom of literature was linked by Derrida to the secret covenant of God and Abraham at the time of the Binding of Isaac. In his 1999 version of *Donner la mort* (formerly titled *The Ethics of Giving*), Derrida added a large new chapter, "Literature as a Secret," in which he describes Abraham's religious experience of sacrificing his son as being located at the very root of the literary experience. Derrida, who proposed that experience as an alternative to Western literature's affinity with the Greek seed, extended the religious secret of the *mys-*

terium tremendum (of the three Abrahamic religions) to the sphere of reading: between the reader and the literary work there lies a secret of significance, the secret of the literary truth. Like Abraham's betrayal of God (his paradoxical betrayal of Godly ethics by his willingness to obey God and kill his son), the reader asks for a certain forgiveness for his own betrayal of literature, "As if the source of literature, in the Western sense of the word, is not Greek at root. As if literature lives on the memory of that impossible forgiveness" (*Donner la mort*, [Paris: Galilée, 1999], 117). The reader's betrayal is his daring attempt to reveal the literary secret. The secret's abyss is the place of the unreachable signified, which is literature's supreme messianic promise. At the same time, this abyss is literature's tomb, as the literary experience is based on the absence of an answer (although there is the expectation for the answer). Did not Lévinas define death as "that which does not answer"?

Trying to answer the question "What is poetry?" ("Che cosé la poesia," [Berlin: Brinkmann und Bosa, 1990]), Derrida interpreted the poetic experience in the image of a hedgehog's night-accident, the moment it is hit by a car's lights. The spiny hedgehog is the poem. According to Derrida, there is no poem without an accident, no poem without an open wound, as there is no poem that does not wound. The encounter between the reader and the poem is a fatal one: it "kills" the "speech"; it puts to death the original authenticity that is concealed under the spines (the poem's letters).

Literature, Derrida claims, constitutes special relationships between a son (the reader) and a spectral father (the author): "Literature begins when we can no more tell who the writer is and who is signed on the text, on the 'I am!' that occurs between absolute father and son" (*Donner la mort*, 179). The literary relationships between the two resemble those of Franz Kafka and his father, who would not answer his son's letter to him. Derrida, who elaborated on this letter, focused on Kafka's asking forgiveness from his absent father, while identifying with this unseen father. Such is the secret of the author: a concealed source whose presence in the work is but an assumption. Therefore, the reader makes a covenant with the vanished author, but simultaneously betrays him by interpreting the work and trying to reveal its utmost secret. Indeed, the reader is a sinner, betraying his father the same way that Ham betrayed Noah when casting an eye on his nakedness: "No doubt, literature is the heir of a holy story, in which the Abrahamic moment was left as an essential secret . . . but literature also denies this story, this belonging, this heritage. . . . It betrays it . . . it is not loyal to it, turning its back the moment it discloses the 'truth,' the secret. . . . For such a double betrayal literature cannot but ask forgiveness. At the beginning there was forgiveness" (208–9).

13

Derrida's Ruah

*R*uah is the Hebrew word for "wind," "spirit," "ghost," "phantom," "specter"; the Humanities are called "Sciences of the *Ruah*"; an intellectual is called a "man of *ruah.*" Solomon Mandelkern's *Concordance to the Tanakh* (the Hebrew Bible), which prints Latin (and occasionally Greek) meanings of the various appearances of each word it indexes, lists the following under ruah: spiritus narium, anhelitus; ira, superbia; spiritus oris; s. vitalis, halitus, s. aeris, aura, aer; ventus, procella; coeli plagi; res inanis; anima, vita; animus, sedes sensum, affectum; sentiendiagendique ratio; voluntas et consilium; intellectus; animus fortis; ingenium; spiritus sanctus, vis divina. It also seems relevant to the *ruah* of the present essay to note that *ruah* is in most cases a feminine noun (in Hebrew almost all nouns are either masculine or feminine, while a few nouns, *ruah* among them are both. In the *Tanakh,* in those cases where the gender of the noun can be read from the gender of the allied verb or adjective, *ruah* is most often feminine, beginning from its first appearance in "veruah elohim merahefet al pnei hamayim," generally translated "And the Spirit of God moved upon [or hovered over] the face of the waters" (Gen. 1:2). Trans.]

Ruhot [the plural of *ruah*] wander about abundantly in the books and lectures of Jacques Derrida. He, who told us about how Kant blames Plato for introducing mysticism into philosophy, that is, for putting philosophy to death (*D'un ton apocalyptic adopté naguère en philosophie* [1984a]), is he whose pages are illumined with a cautious and radiant understanding by the light of the Enlightenment no less than by the heavy shadow of a great secret. About the centrality of the "secret" in interpretation he has written an entire book: *Passions* [1993b]. Indeed, this is the great magic of Derrida's writings: the blend that they create between the rational and the metaphors of the invisible, the abyss, the ruin, the secret, and their congeners. It is an undeniable fact that his recurring concepts—*spectre* and *fantomes*—

Translated by Richard Flantz.

are frequently invoked, and represent his hermeneutic soul's desire since 1967: "the essential shadow of the unsaid" (*L'écriture et la différence* [1967b])—the *ruah* [ghost] of Hamlet's father, the *ruah* [ghost] of the dead Commander in *Don Juan*—the name of his book from 1993—*Spectres de Marx* (1993d), and many more. And of course, deconstruction itself is an act of "turning the text into a phantom of itself" [in Hebrew: into a *ruah* of itself] (*Force de loi* [1994a], 104). Not infrequently the feeling arises (as from a spell?) that the *ruah* that haunts Derrida most is a particular *ruah* of Judaism that he tasted as a child in El-Biar, Algeria, and which demands reparation from him for offenses it has suffered. In any case, the champion of languages does not speak Hebrew, and only rarely will we find in his writings Hebrew words such as *hazon* [vision], *milah* [word, circumcision], *shem* [name, God] or *ruah*. Excellent French, much mixed with Heideggerian German, here and there translations into English, frequent etymological forays into Greek and Latin—yes, the Derridean experience is also a "Berlitzian" experience. And there appears only a tiny fraction of Hebrew. Even though he learned Hebrew when a boy, as mentioned in *Circonfession*, Hebrew is Chinese to him, as he admits in his book *Donner la mort* (Paris: Metailie-Transition, 1992, 85). He has never mentioned the Hebrew word *ruah* in reference to his specters and phantoms. Nonetheless, as far as I know, in his books Derrida has used the Hebrew term *ruah*—*ruah* as *esprit*—twice only, and it is about these two times that I wish to write.

His philosophical revolution, which attained the popular name of "deconstruction," and which was philosophically deformed beyond recognition, to the philosopher's chagrin—this revolution was formulated by Derrida between the years 1967 and 1971 in books like *De la grammatologie* (1967a), *L'écriture et la différence* (1967b), *Marges de la philosophie* (1972b), *La dissémination* (1972a), and others. Already in the first pages of *L'écriture et la différence*, the attack on structuralism is declared, in the words: "Structure then can be *methodically* threatened in order to be comprehended more clearly and to reveal not only its supports but also that secret place in which it is neither construction nor ruin but liability" (13). If so, then every structure has a secret place, through which the interpreter will filter the text. At this stage, in which imagination conducts us to dark tunnels, into closets and beyond the mirror, it is quite surprising to discover Kant as inspiration for this "secret place" of art. Derrida refers to Kant's conception of art as a cognitive autonomy, as a retreat from the everyday actuality (of purposiveness, interestedness, and conceptual knowledge). It is an indisputable fact that the prince of the *Aufklärung* from Koenigsberg, who in the future would yet be represented by Derrida as a "Jewish philosopher" (Derrida knows full well how much Kant is a total and utter gentile, but his studies of Hermann Cohen's essay "Germanism and Judaism," or of Hegel's attitude to Judaism, reveal philosophical exercises in the "Judaizing" of Kant. To explain: in Derrida's study, *Kant, le juif, l'allemand* (1990d), Cohen, the ultra-Kantian Jewish philosopher, "Judaizes" Kant when he unifies the spirit of the Enlightenment and Judaism. In his book *Glas* (1974), Derrida shows how Hegel smeared Kant with the same blame with which he smeared Judaism: slavish, blind obedience to an evil and demanding God, without any real sensitivity to infinity and love. The Kantian link between religious faith and the moral imperative suffices Hegel to ostracize Kant as a "Jew.") This "Enlightenment" Kant, then, is a point from which Derrida sets out on a journey that ends in a mystery: "We must therefore turn to the invisible which is at the core of poetic freedom. We must separate, in order to reunite in the work's blind night of origin" (17). And, later, on the same page: "only pure absence—not the absence of one thing or another—but the absence of anything that heralds presence—has the power to be inspiration. . . . The pure book turns naturally toward this absence . . . which is its real and primary content."

Which is to say: no meaning is prior to the act of writing. No voice dictates the written meaning; rather, the writing itself is the act of creation of the meaning, before which there is nothing, only nothing, absence. Speech, as a kind of "primal voice," has therefore turned into a Kantian "thing in itself" (18), something which is unattainable in writing:

> Writing stifles and rapes speech in advance. Writing is the oppression of the Hebrew *ruah* (Derrida italicizes this word, which is printed in Latin characters)—*ruah* in the test of human responsibility and solitude; in the test of Jeremiah who surrendered to the divine dictate ("Take a scroll of a book and write upon it all the words that I have spoken to you") or of Baruch, who copies down what was dictated to Jeremiah, etc. (Jer. 36:2, 4) [. . .] This is the moment when we must *decide* whether to engrave what we have heard—and whether engraving it rescues or loses what was spoken. (19)

This, then, is Derrida's first Hebrew *ruah*. Let it be clear: by "Hebrew *ruah*" Derrida means "the concept which in the Hebrew language is called '*ruah*,'" not by any means some Hegelian *Volkgeist*. Nonetheless, it is not by chance that Derrida made use of the Hebrew term. For the theological conclusions that stem from the thesis of "absence" strike directly at the Jewish *ruah*, as Derrida himself was to write: "This absence of the divine writing, that is, of the Jewish God, who himself sometimes writes" (21). In his book from 1967, *De la grammatologie* (27–28), Dérrida quoted Lévinas, who quotes the talmudic *midrash* by Rabbi Eliezer that says that if all the seas and lakes were of ink, and the sky and the earth were all sheets of parchment, and all human beings excelled in writing, they still would never attain to more than a tiny drop (like a paintbrush dipped in the sea) of the *Torah*—the *Torah* as the primal and total truth. Yes, the absence of the primal voice from the text signifies a challenge to the divine dictation, to the celestial book (in the Christian sense as well, of course, such as that of the Revelation of St. John the Divine, St. Augustine, St. Thomas Aquinas, etc.), and, if we like, a challenge to the metaphysical status of the Book of Books as a primal source of meaning.

Here, a long-standing and respected Platonic and Neoplatonic tradition (Hellenistic, Jewish, Christian, Muslim) receives a "root-canal treatment," if not an extraction of the tooth: no longer the book as an expression of the totality of the universe (as in Leibniz's *Discourse on Metaphysics*); no longer "In the beginning was the Word"; no longer the Kabbalistic *Sefer Yeetzirah* [Book of Creation]; no longer the world and man as a secret texture of combinations of divine letters and words, a challenge to decipher the sainted "Ari" [Rabbi Isaac Luria, the systemizer of the Zohar], Rabbi Abraham Abulafia, and all the rest. Derrida wrote, "We have to know that the Book [*Le Livre,* the transcendental Book. Au.] does not exist" (20), and if for a moment we thought that the thesis applies to "all of modernist aesthetics and criticism" (21), we soon read the resolute words, which state as follows: "to write—means to know that all that has not yet been created in the letter has no other place to reside in, and does not await us as a prescription in some supernal place or in a divine understanding of any kind. Meaning is obliged to wait to be spoken or written, so it may become that which it itself is in its differentiation from itself: meaning" (22).

Let us hasten to clarify: Jacques Derrida may be considered one of the most theological philosophers in contemporary philosophy, despite his utter secularity. A dualism of this kind is not unknown in modern philosophy. Derrida himself deals with this issue in reference to Heidegger, who distinguishes philosophy and theology, yet is at the same time a theological philosopher (*La Religion* [1996b], 78–81. See elaboration in the chapter titled "The Other *Kippa*"). Only someone who has read his *Circonfession* (1991a), his autobiographical confession in the manner of St. Augustine, will understand the depth of the religious-secular dualism Derrida lives in. In *De la grammatologie* he expatiates on the theological meaning of the subordination of the signified to a transcendental *logos,* and it is thus evident that he is walking upon paths that have been covered with many layers of theology. The voiding of the "origin"—a thesis that will haunt the philosopher in most of his books—does not mean the murder (once more, after who knows how many times?) of God. For between belief and this hermeneutic voiding, which we will call, simply, "the absent," there passes the bridge of negative theology, which occupies Derrida a great deal, especially in his book *Sauf le nom* (1993c). Referring to Augustine's *Confessions* (his discussion of the negative theology concentrates on Angelus Silesius and Augustine; the Jewish negative theology is mentioned only in passing, e.g., at 70–71), Derrida raises the obvious question: since God knows everything, what's the point of confessing to Him? Hence, Augustine's purpose is not to inform God. The confession does not belong on the plane of knowledge. Its concern is the address to God, for His love. The address is to a friend, an act of friendship and connection. "To turn into nothing is to turn into God," wrote Silesius, and Derrida responds: "turning yourself, as a turning yourself into God—or into nothing—here we have the impossible, more than the impossible, the most impossible possible. . . . Strangely, this thought is a familiar one from the experience that is called 'deconstruction' . . . 'Deconstruction' has not infrequently been defined as the experience of the possibility (impossibility) of the impossible. . . . The testimony, the secret, etc. Perhaps death" (31–32). "The Heideggerian concept of death, let us recall, is the possibility of the impossible for Being. Hence we may say that all the mysticisms of the theology of negation are contemplations of death" (34).

Absence, theology and deconstruction—these are Jacques Derrida's triple thread.

The encounter between *ruah*, religion, and Judaism in Derrida's philosophy is greatly indebted to Hegel's *Geist* (spirit) concept, on which Derrida elaborated in his *Glas* (1974). The spirit concept is defined here as a kind of circular movement of return, of the return to self after going astray in Otherness; in other words: as fulfillment of the negative process of self-negation. I know the world by means of my spirit and a process of self-recognition (I think the world no less than the thought thinks itself). This is the difference between man and beast. For the spirit that knows and internalizes the world is the spirit that knows itself in returning to itself. Self-negation, whose sequel is return to self, is in a synthesis of opposites and at a higher level of truth and self-awareness. The spirit's relationship with itself resembles the father-son relationship, writes Derrida (*Glas* [1974], 34). The spirit negating itself is thus the son negating his father. My freedom rests upon applying my spirit beyond itself (toward the world) so that the spirit shall return to itself, its self-awareness having undergone elevation (*Aufhebung*). In other words, the spirit requires matter that is alien to it, so as to fulfill itself as spirit.

Feeling, writes Derrida, interpreting Hegel, is still at the animal level; but the transition from immediate sensation to spirit, to comprehension of resolving contradictions (dialectic comprehension) reaffirms my humanity. The spirit has three levels: the subjective (psychology); the objective (moral); and the absolute (art, religion, philosophy). The absolute spirit— God—is infinite *Aufhebung,* above all else. Can God be embodied in the finite? Or take on flesh? Only in the form of Jesus, claims Hegel. Whereas Judaism leaves the spirit in abstraction (God as abstract spirit), in Christianity God is revealed as spirit negating and fulfilling itself (in the Son, Jesus), spirit returning to itself (at a higher level of truth) by means of the son. True, Judaism already revealed God as father, but a father without son is no father, says Hegel as quoted by Derrida (39). The infinite, absolute spirit fulfills itself in the movement of the dialectical relationship between the father (in heaven) and his only son, hence, according to Hegel, the secret of Christianity's superiority over other religions, and of its alliance with philosophy (as dialectical movement of pure truth). However, Derrida reminds us, the dialectics of the absolute spirit require that religion must die in order to be reborn as a higher and more abstract philosophical spirit—the death of religion as the birth of philosophy, the death of the father in the son. Is this Derrida's own story—The birth of his philosophy out of the negation of his Jewishness and expression of the death of the father in the son (see the chapter titled "Countenance Averted")?

Many years passed until Derrida published his *De l'esprit, Heidegger, et la question* (1987a), and in this time he managed to cultivate and develop his *ruah* (a *Geist*) which is the sum of his *ghosts:* Plato, Socrates, Nietzsche, Heidegger, Freud, Valery, Lacan, Lévinas, Benjamin, Artaud, Joyce—the list is a long one, as long as the length of Derrida's extensive and most interdisciplinary oeuvre, which is in the most part interpretative voyages to philosophical thinkings, poetry, painting, architecture, and more, as voyages to worlds of death and to encounters with *ruhot.*

Martin Heidegger is a kind of father-*ruah* (both *ghost* and *Geist*) for Jacques Derrida, and hence also the object of ambivalent attitudes. The father-*ruah* is a most heavy concept in Derrida's teaching. Throughout his books he does not cease dealing with the question of father-son relations: whether as the question of the origin and the copy (Socrates and Plato, the Hegelian Spirit and its materialization in matter, and more) or as a theological-Freudian question (God as the sanctification of a murdered father). Not infrequently, the thought occurs to the reader that the "primal" trauma that incessantly haunts Derrida, that of circumcision (the *Yom Kippur* of his existence, or in his words, "the day of the *coupure,*" the cutting, the day of the

Covenant), conceals at its basis castratee-castrator relations between son and father and between father and son. And the more that the figure of the mother arises and grows and even becomes sublime in Derrida's writings (reaching its peak in *Circonfession*, which is a son's transcendental love poem to his mother as she lies dying in Nice), the more conspicuous is the relative absence of the father figure, Derrida's father, as though, in his biography, he has actualized his philosophical thesis about the "Father" (God) being absent, or concealing himself, or turning his back (*La carte postale* is largely devoted to a clarification of Socrates' turning his back on Plato, based on an ancient illustration that Derrida found in a library in Oxford).

But we were on the subject of Heidegger as Derrida's spiritual father, or his father-as-a-spirit. Although Derrida began his path by translating and writing about Husserl, it would seem that Heidegger, Husserl's pupil, is the decisive figure (one of several key figures) in Derrida's spiritual world, and whose *ruah* is recurrently present in the numerous texts of the French philosopher.[1] In *De l'esprit, Heidegger, et la question,* he addressed himself to exploring the concept of spirit in Heidegger's thought. It would be better to say: the concepts of spirit. For there is the "spirit" from 1927 (*Being and Time*), there is the spirit from 1933–35 (the "Rector's Address," "The Self-Actualization of the German University," and *Introduction to Metaphysics*), there is the spiritual from 1942 (in the interpretation of Hölderlin's poetry), and there is the spirituality from 1953 (*Die Sprache* [Speech in Poetry], an introduction to the poetry of Georg Trakl). Heidegger indeed changed his position several times with regard to the concept of "spirit," and Derrida charts these changes meticulously in the light or the shadow of the miserable affair of Heidegger's association with Nazism.[2] It turns out, actually, that in the years 1933–35, some six years after he gave up the concept of "spirit," seeing it as a metaphysical "phantom," and only agreed to mention it in doubly doubled inverted commas (on the grounds that human *being* is not some spiritual interiority projected onto reality, but is the essence of the dynamic principle of asking questions about the meaning of *being*)—six years later, Heidegger removes the inverted commas from around the word and even crowns it with terrifyingly large wings: the "Rector's Address" from 1933 (and we all remember the significance of this year) becomes a speech of initiation for the German university as the torchbearer of the entire Western spirit. Yes, now the fire was already burning at the base of the concept of "*Geist*" (which, in the Hellenistic past, had been identified with the air, *pneuma*. The rector turned into a spiritual leader (*Führer*), a guide holding a torch. Although the reader does not read this literally, the image of thousands of Nazis holding torches at rallies in Nuremberg and elsewhere does not leave one. According to Heidegger, the spirit has to realize itself, and the movement of its realization is German! This is the German destiny!—"our destiny," Heidegger said. The spirit is the essence of *being* (Heidegger now identified with Hegel, as he never had before), and the spirit of a nation is the essence of its power and its greatness. The spirit "gives the tempo for the march that our nation has begun towards its historic future" (*L'auto-affirmation de l'université* [Paris: T.E.R., 1982], 14. More: a nation's spirit stores within it the deepest charge of the powers of the earth and of the blood! *Sic.*

Derrida, whose humane sensitivity, in both theory and practice, is a matter of record, does not hasten to take a univocal position on the difficult and embarrassing question of Heidegger. On the one hand, "one may say that he [Heidegger] perfumes National Socialism" (or, in our own blunt words, he perfumes the Nazi stench with a purifying perfume); and, "on the other hand, in taking the risk of perfuming Nazism, it is possible that he was seeking to rescue it when he imprinted upon it the principle of realization, realization as self-authentication, (spirituality, science, the question of questions, etc.)" (*De l'esprit, Heidegger, et la question,* 52). In any case, it is an undoubtable fact that in 1933 Heidegger defined the German nation as the most metaphysical of all nations (much later, in an interview published in *Der Spiegel* in 1976, he identified the German language as almost the only language worthy of philosophy. Here he also threw barbs at the French philosophers: "When they start to think, they speak German." Derrida has no choice but to take this sentence personally, and he responds: "In the *Spiegel* interview he spoke with an arrogant, perhaps slightly innocent, calm, . . . and I would even say, in 'our' language—without much *esprit*" (87). The Frenchman took from the German the monopoly on the word "*esprit.*"

For decades, spirit for Heidegger was a post-Hellenistic concept, spirit as *pneuma,* but during the forties and fifties, in his writings on Hölderlin and Trakl, the spirit turned into fire. This was the German language's contribution to the concept of "spirit," which in its Latin tradition, as *spiritus,* represented the theological idea of inspiration. Heidegger united the spirit with the soul that burns and is burned, with the flame, with burning. The spirit takes fire and gives fire (103); red fire and blue fire, which may darken in the night of the spirit, the darkness of the soul. The spirit as fire is its safety from the decay of the spirit that becomes rationalistic or intellectual or ideological. In other words: the spirit as fire means opposing spirit to its Platonic roots. The air—*pneuma*—of the spirit is now only a by-product of its being fire (which requires air). And, being fire, it contains the aspect of white ash, which is the white spiritual evil, the spiritual fire that burned (123). And Derrida adds, (in passing, as it were): "*Le Geist—le gaz*" (126)—the movement of the spirit, the movement of the *gaz,* which rises

while it piles the decomposing dead beneath it and interiorizes them in an
Aufhebung. Is it a coincidence that the moment of the "*Geist-gaz,*" which is
no longer pure *pneuma* but its smell, the smell of *Zyklon-B,* is also the
moment of Derrida's shift into Hebrew?

And indeed this is when the time for the Hebrew word *ruah* arrives.
Derrida writes *ruah* (still in Latin characters)—*ruah kodesh* [holy spirit/
spirit of holiness] and *ruah ra'ah* [evil spirit/ill wind] (129). For, in the face
of the Heideggerian pretension to appropriate the concept of spirit to
Greece and Germany, Derrida's question is presented: did the thinkers who
conceived the concept of spirit in Greek (*pneuma*) and in Latin (*spiritus*)
know the Hebrew concept of *ruah* (128)? And, Derrida adds, were not
Jewish thought as fiery thought (here he sends the reader to Franz Rosenzweig's *The Star of Redemption*) and/or the Jewish distinction between
ruah and *nefesh,* [soul] prior to the distinction between *pneuma* and *psyche*?

Although this is not the peak of Derrida's discussion of the Heideggerian concept of spirit (he will go on to examine the idea of the spirit's
wanderings, the affinity between the spirit and evil, including Heidegger's
important sentence "Evil is always spiritual"), it would appear that Derrida
has laid a large mine on the road of the Heideggerian spirit's wanderings
somewhere in the Rhine Valley—which is to say: as long as the road is a
"German" one, in the manner of the writings from 1933–35. A Jewish
mine. A typical Derridean mine, which seeks to remind Heidegger that before "the first origin," the Greek-German one, there may have been a prior
origin (which, too, is not the "first origin"), and that the human *ruah* has
no first origin, certainly not an origin that is a defined geographical place. A
Jewish deterritorialization?

14

Judaism and Death

The subtitle of Derrida's *Apories* (paradox? contradiction? no thorough-fare?) (1996a) summarizes its contents: "Dying—to await to 'the limits of truth'" The death theme, as we have already noted, is pivotal in all Derrida's books. It features in the "ash" signifiers (and their duality in "tomb" and "pyramid": *Marges de la philosophie* [1972b]) in deconstruction itself, in the subconscious (Derrida's fascination with the Freudian death wish). It is also present in all the versions of "writing" as abyss, ruins, traces, absence. And it is of course present in the Derridean concept of divinity divided, that is, in the self-concealing, absent aspect of the divinity. Thus, a Derrida book that addresses death directly is more than unsurprising, it is veritably self-evident.[1] Just as the concept of death is pivotal to the "authen-ticity" concept of Heidegger, with whom Derrida conducts an ongoing philosophical dialogue, it could be claimed to be equally central to Derrida's own philosophy. After all, in its unplumbed depths, Derrida's philosophy is the tragic thinking of a man imbuing his writings with the experience of eternal victim, to an extent that renders Derrida deserving of the title of philosopher of death.

Derrida does not deal with Judaism in *Apories,* where the topic is not even touched upon marginally. Nevertheless, on the penultimate page of *Apories,* he writes: "Neither language, nor the course of this analysis of death, are possible without the Christian (i.e., the Judeo-Christian-Moslem) experience of the death it witnesses. . . . One could say the same about the thoughts of Freud and Lévinas, *mutatis mutandis*" (139).

What is the connection between Judaism and death; or, better put: be-tween it and Derrida's analysis of the concept of death? A few lines ahead of the passage cited, Derrida hints at the link between the death concept and the religions of the Book of Books, and a certain connection between Hei-degger's *Being and Time* and the notion of the Fall—Original Sin and the expulsion from the Garden of Eden—(as the descent from the authentic to the nonauthentic). But in the context of Derrida's other works and his bonds (double, of course, like his binds) with Judaism, a scrutiny of *Apories* discovers the Judaism-death relationship to be far more complex. In the section to come, we shall indeed attempt to illuminate a profound if subliminal Derridean connection between the essence of Judaism and the essence of death.

This association commences with the notion of death as borderline. Right from the beginning of the book, Derrida devotes considerable attention to discussion of the borderline nature of death as transit point to that which lies beyond the border. The reference is to the line of demarcation between the possible and the impossible, between finite and infinite, between known and unknown. Just as death is unbounded, so does the encounter therewith take place at the "border-post" of the dying, of the departed: departure assumes the step (*pas*) and *passage,* or *trepas* (trespass) (*Apories,* 23). Death is thus so-far-and-no-farther, no transit, transit forbidden, transit impossible. It should be recalled that the French *pas* signifies both "step"/"pace" and the negative. Do these words not remind the reader of the experience of the refugee in flight from one country to another, reaching the border-post only to be stopped, denied entry? Do we not in effect confront Derrida's basic Jewish experience, which was to be extended to the refugee experience overall, and the dilemma of *hospitalité* or its denial (see above in the chapter titled "Shibboleth of Evil").

In Derrida's view, hospitality is the root and essence of civilization. Its recognition of the Other and lingual Otherness, and all they imply (*Apories,* 26. And see, of course, the definition of European culture in *L'autre cap,* as set out in the chapter titled "The Other *Kippa*"). But there is no hospitality without the experience of border crossing and standing the test of the code word, "Shibboleth" (as pointed out in Derrida's *Schibboleth* [1986c]): "The *shibboleth* effect operates *on the interior* . . . of the French language," writes Derrida in *Apories* (27), referring to the ban on entry of the Other, the one who does not share the lingual code. It will be recalled (see the chapter titled "Shibboleth of Evil," recalling the philosopher's analysis of Paul Celan's poem "Schibboleth") that, beyond its universal, hermeneutic context, Derrida regards the "Shibboleth" experience as a Jewish experience, associated with the Holocaust: expulsion, rejection, the sentence of annihilation passed on the Jew as Other, as one who is not of the tribe (like the members of the tribe of Ephraim), as one who does not stand the lingual test of the "slogan." We could even say: circumcision as "shibboleth." But as we have already observed, Derrida discovers the "shibboleth" effect in every language and all lingual diversity. The "Babelian" dimension of lingual diversity (as described in the chapter titled "Tower of Babel") presumes the impossibility of total translation. In other words: it presumes the negation of lingual "hospitality" and the supplanting of the *heimisch* (the cozy sense of home) by the *Unheimlich* (alien, weird, dejection). Present within language is the harsh experience of border-posts that deny transit; the experience of police, customs, visa, and so forth; in brief: the death experience. In language is the experience of the Jewish refugee denied permission to cross the border—like Walter Benjamin at the Franco-Spanish frontier in 1940, and the many thousands who came before and after—experiencing the barricade, the "no transit" of death; of the *arrivant* (arrival) who comes nameless, without identity, to whom the gates remain closed, who despite everything does not reach the Promised Land.

But according to Derrida, the borderline of death (as *Ableben*—"going beyond life") is also crossing over from here to there, it is the scene of an impossible encounter between the arrival and he who returns (*revenant*). The returnee is the ghost, the Other, the guest (= ghost) who makes hostages of the living (the guest is *hôte*, the hostage—*otage*). This is death that dwells within, whether as (Freudian) death wish imposing obsessive cycles of return, or internalization of the death of the Other as my moral responsibility (according to Lévinas). At both levels, the association between Judaism and death becomes plain. On the one hand, the Judaism of remembrance (the duty to "remember," of which Y. H. Yerushalmi wrote) and archive (from the seal of the circumcision, by way of the phylacteries, all the way to the Holy Scriptures); on the other hand, the Judaism of the principle of Otherness (the countenance of the Other appealing to the subject. Abraham forsaking his ancestral home for the other place) as alternative to the Greek principle of "the same" (according to Lévinas. See also the chapter titled "Facing Lévinas").

However, the assignation between *arrivant* and *revenant* is not so much an encounter between life and death, as a meeting of the possible with the impossible. Death as possibility is the essence of existence (*Dasein*), says Derrida, repeating Heidegger's statement (*Aporie*, 114)—death as borderline predictable for any person living an authentic life under the hallmark of "toward," the way (see Heidegger's concept of "*Weg*"): "The possibility most appropriate to *Dasein*, knowing death, is the possibility of the power of not-being-there, or of no-longer-able-to-be-there. . . . It [*Dasein*] can flee this truth nonauthentically (inappropriately), or approach it authentically, in awaiting it appropriately, in anguish and liberty" (*Aporie*, 122).

Death as possibility signifies the human experience as opening up to the future, being available (*zuhanden*) to the world, and to expectation. The dimension of Jewish messianism creeps into this onto-theological outlook, for it stresses life under the hallmark of hope of the Redeemer, without the possibility of meeting him. Elijah, the Messiah's harbinger, enters Jewish homes each year, in the course of the Passover *Seder*. Elijah represents the great messianic hospitality ("the coming of the Messiah," his entry, his transition from there to here), but concomitantly, as patron of the circumcised (on "Elijah's chair") he represents amputation, absence, and the Jewish "stamp" on the sex organ, as seal of pariah, the "shibboleth." In other words, Elijah signs the possibility, the "messianic," but Elijah is also a sign of the impossibility, the no-transit; the two aspects of death. Death is, in Heidegger's terms, adopted by Derrida, "as impossible possibility for existence (*Dasein*)."

It is "impossibility" because the encounter—between the living and death, between the here and the there, between he who arrives and he who returns—is out of the question. *Aporia*—diametrical contradiction, is and is not, the "no thoroughfare." Both possibility and impossibility are thus present in the peculiar cultural power of Judaism: in messianic futurism and death wish, the two opposing forces that Derrida had already identified in the depths of the archive (which, not fortuitously, prompts the question— posed by Yerushalmi in *Freud's Moses*: Is psychoanalysis—an "archival" concept, we should recall—a Jewish science?). And insofar as, according to Derrida, the "double bind" of possible and impossible characterizes the concept of death no less than the concept of truth (the deconstruction of the truth: its destruction by its revelation, the impossibility of its possibility, its concealment through its disclosure, its presence within its absence)—this renders the association between Judaism and death far closer: the self-concealment of the truth is embodied within the principle of divine self-concealment (see the chapter titled "Countenance Averted") denial of the image of god, which is the image of truth, its "presencing."

The Jew is thus the Other reaching the border-post only to be denied transit, arriving at death and sentenced to death by dint of the "shibboleth" seal, the absence imprinted with his identity. The Jew is one living in awareness of the possibility of the return of the transcendental Other from the other world, but also fulfilling the great contradiction between messianic expectation and divine absence. At each of these poles of his culture, the Jew is in dialogue with death, speaking the language of death, the language of trace, the *différance* and ashes, ashes as memory of a holocaust (holocaust = burning all). The Holocaust, both the onto-theological and the historical.

Messianism and death join hands. According to Derrida, the messianic is "desert within desert"—the infinitely open, arid vistas of boundless expectation of the arrival of the Redeemer who fails to arrive; but equally, it is the domain of the dead from which the Redeemer arrives as *revenant* and *arrivant*. On this subject, Derrida wrote in *Spectres de Marx* (1993d):

This desertlike messianism (without content and without identifiable messiah) of this also *abysmal* desert, "desert in the desert" . . . one desert signaling toward the other, abyssal and *chaotic* desert, if chaos describes first of all the immensity, excessiveness, disproportion in the gaping hole of the open mouth—in the waiting or calling for what we have nicknamed here without knowing the messianic: the coming of the Other, the absolute and unpredictable singularity of the *arrivant as justice.* We believe that this messianic remains an *ineffaceable* mark—a mark one neither can nor should effect—of Marx's legacy, and doubtless of inheriting, of the experience of inheriting in general. . . . If the messianic appeal belongs properly to a universal structure, to that irreducible movement of the historical opening to the future, therefore to experience itself and to its language (expectation, promise, commitment . . . how is one to *think* it *with* the figures of Abrahamic messianism? . . . Was not Abrahamic messsianism but an exemplary pre-figuration, the pre-name (*prénom*) given against the background of the possibility that we are attempting to name here? But then why keep the name, or at least the adjective (we prefer to say *messianic* rather than *messianism,* so as to designate a structure of experience rather than a religion) there where no figure of the *arrivant.* (*Spectres,* 68n)

The concept of sacrificial offering, as the essence of religiosity, further cements the alliance between Judaism and death—"the gift of death" (*donner la mort*) as supreme fulfillment of faith and morality (responsibility), the total surrender of oneself and giving of oneself to the transcendental Other in an act of infinite love (as set out by Derrida in the chapter "Donner la mort" in the anthology *L'éthique du don* [Paris: Metailie—Transition, 1992]; see above in the chapter titled "Derrida as Sacrificial Offering"). Granted, this act has been taken over in Christian theology, but it rests upon the experience of the biblical sacrifice of Isaac. Abraham's awful secret (not responding verbally to the divine command) was reincarnated as the Christian-Kierkegaardian *mysterium tremendum,* but is nothing if not Lévinas' dual *adieu* to his overall Jewish connections: *adieu* as farewell and *à dieu* as giving oneself to God. Internalizing Lévinas's concept of the Other into his own ethical and theological philosophy, Derrida has thus taken over the death dwelling between himself and the Other, be it the transcendental or the finite Other. Thus, when Derrida formulates his moral formula—*tout autre est tout autre*—he proffers a categorical command of moral responsibility that makes us confront the Other as though he were death, to face the possibility of the death of the Other and our duty to sacrifice ourselves for his sake, our death.

This chapter cannot be completed without drawing the reader's attention to the self-evident correspondence between the Derridean concept of *donner la mort* and a pivotal expression of Jewish theology: *mesirut nefesh* (self-sacrifice, self-abnegation), whose literal translation is "giving up the soul." *Mesirut nefesh* is an elevated level of sanctity in Hassidic thought (Rabbi Nachman of Breslau wrote in his *Book of Qualities:* "A miracle is not performed other than to one who has *mesirut nefesh* in sanctification of the Holy Name." In his *Book of Direct Counsels,* he added: "*mesirut nefesh* is the main principle of the desire for sanctity."). In a tradition that affirms that "the blood is the soul (life)" (Deut. 12:23), giving up the soul is surrendering life: the believer surrenders his life as a "gift" (a Hebrew term also denoting "sacrifice," he who offers up his life does so "on the altar of his faith"), that is, he offers his life as gift, a gift to the beloved. In Hegelian terms, the soul elects to surrender itself, that is, chooses to negate itself (to death) in an act of self-restoration (to its source in God) and self-elevation. We note a circularity: "He restoreth my soul: he leadeth me in the paths (circles) of righteousness" (Psalms 23:3); an act of restoration: he who unwittingly received his life (soul), consciously resolves to restore it—like repayment, or restoration, of a debt. This is the highest, Socratian, level of self-knowledge as knowledge of God. It is the highest ecstatic level (the Hebrew idiom "he did not know his soul" denotes enormous agitation). However, God being utterly concealed and mysterious, he who surrenders his soul restores it to the unknown. In another Hebrew idiom, the believer "bears his soul" (in yearning, as though conveying the soul from here to there) to his God: "Unto thee, O Lord, do I lift up my soul" (Psalms 25:1).

15

Jerusalem

Is it the Jerusalem of Jacques Derrida, or of Emanuel Lévinas? Derrida's studies of Lévinas's writings, marking the first anniversary of the latter's death (*Adieu* [1997a]), illustrates a blurring of boundaries between the two French Jewish philosophers. So great is the identification of the one thinker with the other who is the subject of his writing, that *hospitalité*—a basic Lévinasian term—features in *Adieu* and, in the latter nineties, became a key Derridean concept (and cornerstone of Derrida's political and social activity as deputy chairman of the European Writers' Parliament. Derrida makes no secret thereof; on the contrary: his debt to Lévinas's "trace" was already acknowledged in *De la grammatologie* [1967a]). In his attitude towards Lévinas's writings, and through the experience of Lévinas's death, Derrida seems to fulfill the Lévinasian principle of substitution—surrender of self in favor of the Other.

The book's final chapters shunt the discussion from Lévinas's ethics to politics and concepts like peace, war, nationalism, borders, and others, all considered in a universal context, but also in relation to the Middle East. The State of Israel makes a frequent appearance in these chapters as "state of David" (in contrast to the "Caesarian state"), Zionism is examined by the principles of "monotheistic politics," the Judgment Day, and messianism. The concept of hospitality or welcoming (*accueil*) now takes on a messianic hue that illuminates historical events, such as Egyptian President Anwar Sadat's 1977 visit to Jerusalem. Alternately, Lévinas's concept of responsibility (shared by Derrida) as response to the call of the "face of the Other" is also applied at the level of the relations between Israel and the Palestinians. And thus, as a kind of groundbreaking for his critical ethical and political studies, does Derrida conclude the first chapter: "Hospitality takes precedence over proprietorship, and that is not without consequence, we would conclude, for the location of the giving of the law [Torah - Au.], for the highly enigmatic relationship between the refugee and the Torah, the city of asylum, the land of asylum, Jerusalem, and Sinai" (*Adieu*, 85).

References to Jerusalem are not infrequent in Derrida's writings. As we have already observed, the philosopher touches upon the city's significance in his discussions of religion, sacrificial offering, and "gift of death." In this context, Jerusalem defined the location of the sacrifice, the site of the ultimate self-offering, the location of the sacrifice of the son, that is reiterated relentlessly throughout history. Elsewhere (in the chapter titled "Ruins") we have already mentioned Jerusalem as a city of "promise," like other cities of (utopian) "promise" such as Moscow, and we have quoted from the lecture Derrida delivered in Jerusalem in 1986:

> On what conditions is one in Jerusalem . . . and where lies the place so named? How to measure the distance that separates us, or brings us together? Here is the reply of Dionysius [Christian mystic of Roman times, the first bishop of Paris. Au.] who quotes Scripture in his *Ecclesiastic Hierarchy:* "Do not draw away from Jerusalem, rather await the promise of the Father that you have heard from my mouth, and by which you shall be baptized by the Holy Spirit." (512 c, 303). . . . [Jesus] spoke of Jerusalem as a place that has remained a place of expectation of fulfillment of the promise. (*Psyché* [1987c], 581)

Later, in *Spectres de Marx* (1993d), we find Jerusalem presented as essence of the war waged by messianic faiths in the Middle East:

> in the Middle East: three other messianic eschatologies mobilize there all the forces of the world and the whole "world order" in the ruthless war they are waging against each other, directly or indirectly; they mobilize simultaneously, in order to put them to work or to the test, the old concepts of state and nation-state, of international law, of tele-techno-medio-economic and scientifico-military forces, in other words, the most archaic and the most modern spectral forces. One would have to analyze, in the limitless breadth of their worldwide historical stakes, since the end of the Second World War, in particular since the founding of the State of Israel, the violence that preceded, constituted, accompanied, and followed it on every side *at the same time* in conformity with *and* in disregard of an international law. . . . Such an analysis can not longer avoid granting a determining role to this war of messianic eschatologies in what we will sum up with an ellipsis in the expression "appropriation of Jerusalem." The war for the "appropriation of Jerusalem" is today the world war. It is happening everywhere in the world, it is today the singular figure of its being "out of joint" [*Hamlet*, 1.5: "The time is out of joint." Au.]. (58)

In his aforementioned 1986 lecture in Jerusalem ("How Not to Speak?" *Psyché* [1987c]) Derrida delved into the depths of the theme of negative theology (whereby God is defined by negation) and, referring to his own presence in Jerusalem, stated:

> Does [a negative theology] exist? Is there [just] one? . . . Above all, I didn't know where or when I would [face up to it]. Next year in Jerusalem, I would tell myself, possibly to defer indefinitely the fulfillment of the promise. . . . Shall I do it [now]? Am I in Jerusalem? There's a question that should never be answered in the present tense, only in the future or the past. . . . In other words: am I in Jerusalem or elsewhere, very far from the Holy City? On what conditions is one in Jerusalem? Is it sufficient to be there, as they say, physically, and reside, as I do presently, in places which bear that name? What is it to reside in Jerusalem? There, it isn't easy to make up one's mind. Permit me to quote from the writings of Master Eckhart . . . "Yesterday I was in a place where I spoke a word that seemed veritably incredible. I said: Jerusalem is as close to my soul as the place where I am right now. Yes, in total verity, that which is more than a thousand leagues further than Jerusalem is as close to my soul as my own body." (546)

Derrida's Jerusalem is not so much a physical location as a text open to the varying interpretations of the monotheistic religions, which seek to interpret the city and appropriate it on different models of the sacrificial offering of Isaac. But Jerusalem undergoes what happens to numerous other texts that Derrida treated: deconstruction of the Jerusalem text. Although Jerusalem is acknowledged as the heart of the world (dwelling place of the Holy Spirit, the place of redemption, the capital city, etc.), it is also doomed (like any spiritual center) to entanglement in the "double bind": the father-son relationships of the various Jerusalem sacrifices entrap the Jerusalem reader in irresolvable contradictions. The "Jerusalem" route to the supreme and primal spiritual source is thus blocked by dual barricades of infinite love as against infinite sacrifice, the father-son barricades.

In 1986 it seemed that Derrida, reader and interpreter of the textual Jerusalem, remained and would remain remote from the city. Infinite loves demand infinite sacrifices, as Derrida has taught us. As long ago as 1967, in *L'écriture et la différence* (the chapter on Edmond Jabès), Derrida propounded that the place of the poet and the Jew (himself too, of course) is outside the center, in a nonterritorial "there," far beyond "the desert of promise": "this site, this land, calling to us from beyond memory, is always elsewhere. The site is not the empirical and national Here of a territory" (*Writing and difference* [Chicago: Univ. of Chicago Press, 1978], 66) It is thus evident that the Jerusalem of Derrida (and Lévinas) transcends any particular geographical location or historical event.

At the beginning of the sixth and final chapter of *Adieu* (1997a), Derrida writes: "Let us return momentarily to Jerusalem. 'We have come into thy gates, O Jerusalem.' What is this approach. And will this approach never end?" (177). Those lines reverberate like a mantra throughout the chapter, where Derrida (by means of Lévinas) ventures much further than ever before in expressing the transcendence of the concepts of Judaism and Zionist critique. Does the spirit of Lévinas serve him as ghost of a demanding father-figure? Be that as it may, Jerusalem resembles the notes of the lute whose echoes are theological, ethical, ontological: "Let us return momentarily to Jerusalem. . . . To Jerusalem, perhaps we are there. Is such a step of return possible? The possibility is measured here against the effectiveness of a promise" (182), an eschatological Jerusalem, a sublime Jerusalem, but equally, a mundane Jerusalem, between war and peace, engaged in "the peace process" (Derrida: "in that war which one calls from all quarters, without believing it . . . the 'peace process'" [183].). Being in Jerusalem is being between the present and the promise. To be precise: "We are within that menacing, or menaced, promise, within a present without present, in the proximity of a promised Jerusalem"(183). Jerusalem as *différance*: a hermeneutic time lag between present and future.

Jerusalem as promise is the Jerusalem of Judgment Day, but also of the humanism of the Torah (Lévinas thought likewise, as Derrida points out in this chapter). Jerusalem as promise is a place that opens its gates, the place of *hospitalité* and accordingly, a place where guests are made welcome, that is, a place where the host (*hôte*) is also the hostage (*otage*) of the guest. We have read much about this in the course of Derrida's study of Lévinas (in relation to *Totality and Infinity* [1980]). Jerusalem promises hospitality (for every promise is opening a door to a guest) just as the Torah is perceived as opening gates to its reader-guests.

This is the place for questions: Who are Jerusalem's guests and hostages? What is the meaning of "the humanism of the Torah" when Lévinas specifically refers to the earthly "mundane Jerusalem"? Will Jerusalem become a "city of sanctuary,"[1] one of the asylums that God commanded Moses to construct as place of exoneration and protection from blood vengeance? (Deut. Chap. 35. Derrida refers to this chapter both in *Adieu* and in the aforementioned booklet.)? Will Jerusalem fulfill its "femininity," in the ultimate hospitality of feminine being? (Femininity as Otherness and absence is the very essence of "the face of the Other." Acceptance [*accueillance*] within the house interior is acceptance in Otherness, directly denoting acceptance of the Other. Lévinas identifies this acceptance with woman [76–85].) In *Adieu*, Derrida reiterates the passage from Psalms 132: "For the Lord hath chosen Zion; he hath desired it for his residence" (verse 13). The wordplay between *désirer* and *resider* is applied to Zion.[2]

Jerusalem and Torah are a coupling of eschatological promise: the Torah itself becomes a "city of sanctuary" for those fleeing to the city and placing their trust in it (*Adieu* [1997a], 188). It is the Torah that defines Jerusalem. Any close reader of Derrida will of course recall that the Torah is doomed to a smashing of the Tablets.

The demand to interpret all these sublime matters in terms of "mundane" Jerusalem, the demand to establish the city of sanctuary beyond the "promise" of Jerusalem and the Torah, is imbued with the spectral nature in which Derrida envelops the hospitality principle. For the ego concepts of Lévinas's host, guest, and hostage have been stripped of any ontological title, of any proprietorship or property, to be transformed into spirit that is simultaneously *Geist* and ghost (192). Greater stress is now placed on the moral imperative of hospitality: receiving the Other to the full extent of his Otherness, without waiting for recognition of his real titles. Accepting the other as "phantom" (ibid.). Accordingly, the demand for a mundane Jerusalem cannot remain at the narrow physical level. Not fortuitously, Lévinas draws conclusions opposed to a merely political and national version of Zionism. A critique with a similar thrust having already featured in Derrida's writings, as we have observed in the various chapters of this work, Derrida quotes the following lines from Lévinas's *L'au-delà du verset* (1982):

> That which is promised Jerusalem, is the humanism of the Torah . . . a novel humanism, better than in the Temple. The text [from the Book of Psalms. Au.] . . . shows us that the longing for Zion, Zionism, is not nationalism, nor particularism; and it is not just a simple quest for asylum. That it is the *hope* of a science of society, and a society, that are fully humane. And that—in Jerusalem, the terrestial Jerusalem, and not beyond all places, in pious thought." (195)

But we have already learned that Derrida's philosophy presumes a disparity between promises and their fulfillment. The echo of any eschatology or messianism is mere silence: "a structural messianity, an irrefutable and threatening promise, an eschatology without teleology, of any well-defined messianism: a messianity preceding, or without, a messianism incorporated by such revelation at a determined place going by the name of Sinai or Mount Horev" (204).

Four years previously, in his *Spectres de Marx*, Derrida illuminated messianic expectation (of any sort) as the possibility of the impossible, Martin Heidegger's definition of death:

> It would be easy, too easy, to show that such a hospitality without reserve [expectation of the Messiah. Au.] which is nevertheless the condition of the event and thus of history . . . is the impossible itself, and that this *condition of possibility* of the event is also its *condition of impossibility*, like this strange concept of messianism without content, of the messianic without messianism." (65)

Silence, the silence of the self-concealed God, the silence of his Messiah, is the silence of the grave, the deathly silence that Lévinas had already defined as "no response" (Derrida: "all of Lévinas's thought, from beginning to end, is a meditation on death" [206]). It is also the silence that is cornerstone to all speech. For "That nonresponse conditions my responsibility, wherever I alone am bound to reply" (201). As Lévinas had defined the concept of "Chosen People" in terms of selection to bear responsibility, the Jerusalem of hospitality is stripped of national selection (which, in the manner of any nationalism, sets itself apart from the Other). Jerusalem has become the archetype of opening up to the Other, and responsibility for him. And as any response to the face of the Other is response to the possible death of the Other, hospitable Jerusalem is a city bearing the hallmark of deathly silence.

Jerusalem—capital of sundry religions, multinational center, arena of intercommunal strife, home to messiahs who were and messiahs who will return—has become a metaphor for any expectation of the revelation of truth. But the impossibility of fulfilling that expectation, as it is impossible to encounter the Messiah as *revenant* (returnee), lies at the root of the expectation, and it is death that dwells at the cornerstone of the city.[3]

16

Facing Lévinas

Emanuel Lévinas (1906–95) went to great lengths to expand upon his affinity with Judaism.[1] The tale is too long for inclusion in this chapter, but nevertheless, if only as brief and necessary introduction to Derrida's indebtedness to Lévinas, and his critique in relation thereof, we should note the Jewish aspect of the Other in Lévinas's concept of subjectivity,[2] coupled with the voice of Otherness (the face of the Other calling to the subject) to the Biblical prophets subject to the authority of the voice they were powerless to flee. Equally well known is the fact that Lévinas specifically defined his purpose as continuation of the Septuagint project. The Otherness principle that he identified in the foundations of Jewish thought offered Lévinas a philosophical alternative overlooked by the Hellenistic tradition throughout the ages. For example, here is an essential difference between the biblical Abraham and Homer's Ulysses: Abraham was summoned to leave his home and land, to launch out into the unknown; whereas Ulysses returned home, to Ithaca, reverting to his origins (thus symbolizing the Western philosophical tradition of return to primary unity, to the ideal, the original truth). Lévinas's Abraham is not the Abraham of Hegel or Kierkegaard who, knife in hand, offers up his son (see above, the chapter titled "Derrida's Sacrificial Offering"); he is the model of "hospitality," hosting strangers ("Others") in his tent and addressing them as "Lord," the name of God. For the overture to the Other is also an overture to the infinite, to God.

Derrida, intrigued by the tension between Hellenism and Judaism (was this a source of his fascination with the Bloom-Dedalus relationship in Joyce's *Ulysses?*) was obliged to resort to the broad expanses of Lévinas's thought for various reasons: ontological, ethical, linguistic (hermeneutic), etc. Thus, for example, in Lévinas's *Totality and Infinity* (which he had already hailed in his preliminary 1962 review as "a great work," see below), Derrida found passages whose importance to his own philosophy was incalculable: "The Other is liable to dispossess me of my work. . . . The work surrenders to this alien *Sinngebung* (endowing meaning) beyond its origin within me. . . . The work is always, in a certain sense, a missing act (*un acte manqué*)" (Derrida, "That Selfsame Moment," in *Psyché*, p. 192). Derrida adopts the notion, and even intensifies the wording: "The work . . . does not return—to the origin—to the same (*Même*). . . . Going to the Other, coming from the same never to return to it, thus it comes only from the Other that invents it" ("That Selfsame Moment," in *Psyché* [1987c], 192).

Here we have the Lévinasian track along which Derrida wheels his hermeneutics: the movement of a work's meaning, as movement from the level of the identical (*même*) to the level of its Otherness—a kind of necessary betrayal of the author, by virtue of the pursuit of the Other. We, who approach the work in gratitude to its author, are required to show ingratitude by seeking the Other (for seeking the author within his work constitutes a search for the similar). A work's meaning rests upon its Otherness, and it exists by virtue of the Other (the reader). For the text of the work is a field of traces of a nonpresent Otherness (*Psyché* [1987c], 170). To read a text is to dismantle it: to open up the similar to the dissimilar by way of the Other, the reader (172). "There, nearby albeit infinitely distant, is the dis-location; at the interior-without-inwardness of the language but open to an entirely different exterior"(187)[3] Derrida's conclusions are accordingly notable for their uncompromising abrasiveness. His adoption of Lévinas's principle of Otherness leaves the author with no claim to ownership of the meaning of his work: "He is not the subject-author-signatory-proprietor of the work. It is a 'he' lacking authority . . . . Without authority, he does not make the work, he is not the agent or creator of his work" (189).

Lévinas was among the thinkers who made Derrida and deconstruction possible, wrote Susan Handelman in 1994.[4] This was not merely because Lévinas was the first to introduce French philosophy to the notions of Husserl and Heidegger (with his first book, *The Theory of Intuition in Husserl's Phenomenology* [1930]), but mainly by virtue of the great debt Derrida's deconstruction owed to Lévinas's concept of "the Other." And indeed, according to Derrida, the critique of logocentrism is, above all else, a quest for the "Other" and the "Other" of language,[5] adding that deconstruction is not a withdrawal into nothingness, rather, it is opening up to the Other. (*Psyché* [1987c], 125). Indeed, when his critique of Lévinas identified the violence ("war") hidden within language, deconstruction was born.

Hence, Derrida's reservations in relation to Lévinas (see below) could not disguise Derrida's powerful—one could even say "deep-rooted"—affinity with him. What they hold in common far outweighed their differences, as is evident from the various chapters of this book. In effect, it is out of the question to comprehend Derrida's hermeneutics, his ethics, or his theology without Lévinas's concept of the Other.[6] Certainly, the Derrida of the past decade is highly influenced by Lévinas.

Who and what is the Other? Above all, what is the meaning of the curtain that divides me from the Other? These points would bring out the differences between Lévinas and Derrida. Thus, whereas Derrida regards the shattering of the Tablets of the Law as symbol of the violence of language (see above, the chapter titled "The Other *Kippa*") Lévinas regarded the smashing as signpost, or symbol, of an overstepping of the subject's egoistic expanse. To Lévinas, God is the infinite Other, whereas the negation within the Kabbalist formula of "reduction" (*tzimtzum*—God's withdrawal inward) is, in Derrida's writings, a cleavage within the Divinity. In other words: to Derrida, God's withdrawal and self-concealment are the cornerstone for the aspects of pretense and deceit acting at all levels of existence and consciousness, as divine deceit.[7]

In 1964, Derrida first published his critique of Lévinas's *Totality and Infinity* (1962) (the chapter titled "Violence and Metaphysics" in Derrida's *L'écriture and la différence* [1967b]). In fact, the motto of the chapter gives away the thrust of his appeal: Judaism versus Hellenism. Did Lévinas succeed in tearing his Jewish philosophy from the clutches of post-Platonic philosophy? If we assume that the two great philosophical voices of modern times, Husserl and Heidegger (both indebted to Lévinas for their introduction to French philosophical discourse) reflect the enormous debt Western philosophy owes to its Greek source—did Lévinas manage to make his way out of the Hellenic "domain" (the principles of similarity, being, and unity) to the non-Hellenic? Did he succeed in killing the Greek father?

Is Lévinas's prophetical biblical language (in offering this characterization, Derrida is careful to stress: despite the nonidentification of that language with Jewish mysticism and the absence of any indebtedness to Hebrew texts [*L'écriture et la différence,* 83]) indeed freed of the similarity principle by virtue of its advocacy of the Otherness principle? Right from this preliminary stage of framing the question, Derrida hints at his own point of view, as he adds in parentheses: "(but will the Other of the Greek be the non-Greek?)" (82).

As noted, Lévinas suggests the Otherness principle and the concept of the Other as alternative to the Greek similarity principle and as abandonment of the centrality of the concept of being. He set goodness above and beyond the "sunlight" of entities. The movement of the spirit is directed toward the Other, rather than toward "the essence of being." Yet again, Derrida hastens to pose the question: Can good indeed be separated from the essence? Is not the Platonic good the source ("father") of all light? (86). Affinity and remoteness are intertwined in the "double bind" relationship.

The solitude of the existing ego is the origin of the attitude toward the Other. The absolute distance from the Other also dwells within Lévinas's concept of Eros, which is the concept of duality. Erotic duality is extended as overall phenomenology, affirming the tension between being and nothingness. The Other is the one whose presence is absent, to use Derrida's term (91). Violence stems from imposition of similarity on the different, imposition of Greek "light" on the principle of the Other. In contrast with Hegelian dialectics, which recognizes negation (Otherness) for the sole purpose of drawing it into the unity of mutual assimilation (synthesis), Lévinas points to the craving for the Other from within Otherness, from the infinite departure. Thus, while Hegel analyzes the situations of separation, remoteness, and negation in Judaism as "unhappy" situations yearning for resolution by elevating the synthesis and completion of the dialectic process (as return and absolute knowledge), Lévinas does not seek to close the gap (these differences would not prevent Derrida, further into his critique, from specifying the proximity nevertheless to be found between the philosophies of Lévinas and Hegel).[8] Meaning and value rest upon recognition of Otherness, not its fusion. Conceptual thought (per se thought about the similar) is thus displaced from the domain of Otherness. The obvious conclusion is that language—as expression of Othernesses—is barred from the source and purpose of being language, that is, representation of the similar (95).

The Lévinasian source of Otherness is thus responsible for a further confluence between the two philosophers: language as wound, as infirmity, as fracture. The infinite Other will never be perceived as concept, nor will he ever be restricted by any "horizon" of similarity. The face of the Other, in speech and regard, is neither sign nor metaphor. It is expression itself, the speech that precedes sign (writing). Standing face-to-face with the Other thus signifies a posture of speech and regard that affirms the infinite separation. The presence of the Other is as his absence, his presence is as his departure from us. That is the religious dimension of existence (the infinite self-concealment of the ultimate Other and his evasion of any conscious representation). Derrida pinpoints this notion as the cornerstone of his creed, writing: "By definition, if the Other is the Other, and if all speech is for the Other, no *logos* as absolute knowledge can *comprehend* dialogue and the trajectory toward the other. This incomprehensibility, this rupture of *logos*, is not the beginning of irrationalism but the wound or inspiration that opens speech and then makes possible every *logos* or every rationalism" (*L'écriture et la différence*, 98).

True dialogue with the Other entails a refusal to accept the intimacy of the I-thou relationship as set out by Martin Buber. On the contrary: the I-thou relationship is fulfillment and experience of Otherness. Violence stems from denial of Otherness. Violence stems from any denial of Otherness in regard and in speech, from any imposition of uniform abstraction (similarity) on the countenance, and any attempt to phrase that which is concealed and infinitely distant. Violence stems from any intention of transforming the absence of the Other into presence. According to Lévinas, Judaism is a culture that defends the dread of confronting sanctity (the infinite Other) by means of writing, the Torah, the Book of Books. Writing, whether as Torah or literature, is the protective screen separating man from the primary source of speech. But without that source, writing is meaningless (*L'écriture et la différence*, 102).

In Lévinas's view, the utter *extériorité* of the Other (his existence forever totally outside of me) is not spatial, for every space is the place of the similar. As such, Otherness comprises the infinite Otherness of God, who, beyond any space or verbal description, conceals his countenance from us. So far, Derrida has depicted Lévinas as holding views almost identical with his own. But at this point, he specifies his reservation: Any discourse (whose substance is an address to the Other) is indebted to the space, and since, as already noted, space is indebted to the similar, and the similar is the source of violence, then violence is present in every discourse. In other words: the discourse of the Other as moral discourse enfolds within itself the immoral, by insinuating the similar. Thus is man condemned to the violence of language and place, and no address to the Other can purge man thereof. Wrestling with Lévinas's excessively sharp distinction between the similar and the Other, Derrida goes even further in his critique, demanding whether the similar is not the Otherness of the Other? (127). In greater detail: "That I am also essentially the Other's Other, and that I know I am, is the evidence of a strange symmetry whose trace appears nowhere in Lévinas's descriptions. Without this evidence, I could not desire (or) respect the Other in ethical asymmetry" (128).

Derrida follows that same path of reservation in examining the ontological-Heideggerian dimension of Lévinas's writings. But now, he seeks to point to the a priori nature of the being (*être*) as ontological condition from any ethics or epistemology of the Other. The significance of the being (*être*) precedes any observation of this or that Otherness. The existence of the Other is a condition for affirmation and acknowledgment of the Other as Other. This presumption of existence as preceding Otherness means assuming the similar as preceding the different, claims Derrida (140), thereby further locating violence within the heart of the ethics of nonviolence.

Indeed, similarity (if only at the underlying level of "being in the likeness," similarity of the face of the Other to the Lord's countenance) was not displaced from Lévinas's world, in disregard of his intentions. His task—

purging Hellenism by means of Jewish thought—was a failure, in view of Derrida's critique. The Platonic-Hellenistic concept of being must filter into Lévinas's domain: "There is no speech without the thought and statement *of* Being" (143). Language enfolds recognition of being, for every verb and noun presume the "is" (147). Thus, Derrida is free to conclude his preliminary excursion into Lévinas's significant work with the conclusion that Hellenism (of the principles of the "similar" and "being") is present within the notion of Otherness, that is, within Judaism (152). "Are we Jews? Are we Greeks? We live in the difference between the Jew and the Greek, which is perhaps the unity of what is called history. . . . Are we Greeks? Are we Jews? Are we . . . *first* Jews or *first* Greeks? . . . 'Jewgreek is greekjew. Extremes meet'" (153).

Derrida's conclusion is somewhat Hegelian: the unity of the opposites of Hellenism and Judaism. We could say it is a further revelation of Derrida's paradoxical Jewishness in terms of his non-Jewishness, in terms of the Other from the Jewish: it is Derrida the Jew who recognizes Derrida the Greek, and simultaneously, it is he that recognizes Judaism within Hellenism. But equally, it is Derrida as one who recognizes neither Jew nor Greek: in his opinion, the fruitful synthesis of Greek and Jew is what defines his thought paradoxically as neither Greek nor Jewish. He senses that, for the questions he formulates from without the tradition of Greek philosophy, there is an Other, and that Other is the Jewish model, that is, the Jew as Other.

Susan Handelman quotes this Derridean notion in her book, adding that it is Derrida's design to find a nonplace beyond the Jewish influences of his youth and beyond the Greek philosophical tradition of his studies in France.[9]

Thus, we find ourselves still immersed in the violence we have found stealing, with Derrida's assistance, into the very heart of Jewish ethics. Thus, in his discussion of the affinity between violence and law, Derrida refers to a further line from Lévinas's *Totality and Infinity:* "The link with the Other, that is, justice" ([The Hague: Nijhoff, 1969], 54). Now, working on his own *Force de loi* (Force of law [1994a]) Derrida seizes upon Lévinas's definition of justice as "Rectitude in relation to the face of the other." "Lévinas speaks of infinite justice," Derrida specifies. Infinite law means nonhuman law, "within what he calls 'Jewish humanism,' which at base is not 'the concept of man,' rather it is the Other; 'the expanse of the Other's rights' is that of 'practically infinite rights'" (*Force de loi,* [1994a], 49). Lévinas's concept of justice matches the Jewish concept of sanctity, Derrida adds, referring to Lévinas's "From the Sacred to the Saint: Five New Lessons in Talmud" (1977). In other words, Lévinas drew a distinction between human law and justice (the latter stemming from a source beyond human law)—a distinction Derrida does not accept. In his view, law and justice are intertwined (ibid.): the law claims to act in the name of justice, while justice requires application of the law. Deconstruction fulfills itself between those two polarities of law and justice and their eternal interdependence (and—their inevitable affinity with violence). An examination of the interdependency of law and justice turns up more and more contradictions (for example: to be just, I must be free, but my freedom requires the law so as to know itself as freedom. Or: a just judge requires the law, but simultaneously is expected to interpret the law in his novel and different way, i.e., by departing from the law. And so on.)

In his *Force de loi*, Derrida proves (to a large degree, with the aid of W. Benjamin) that violence dwells at the very heart of the law, that is, at the very heart of justice. Unlike Lévinas, Derrida declines to associate justice with messianism. Justice possesses a performativist dimension: justice is required to fulfill itself through pronouncement, which is a real act. In other words, justice is bound to implementation, and consequently contradicts the principle of messianic expectation of the arrival of justice at the end of time (60). On the one hand, we have violence; on the other, fraternity, responsibility, giving. The two polarities are interjoined like Siamese twins, or rather, in Derrida's terms, in a "double bind." The reader has already observed the profundity of this duality in Derrida's motley world.

One of Derrida's most important (and complex) studies of meaning focuses on Lévinas's "En ce moment même dans cet ouvrage me voici" (This very moment, in this work, I am here—an essay first published in 1980). Predictably, the article features Lévinas's concept of "the Other," not forgoing emphasis on the decisive role of the Other in language, meaning, in *réponse* and *réponsibilité*, in opening up to the Other, in conquest of the same within me by the Other, the voluntary subjugation to the command of the Other. As in a psychosis, Derrida notes after Lévinas, like a sickness, where the "I am here" is enfolded in the obsession of the Other (*Psyché* [1987c], 167). Giving as sickness: "for I am sick with love," declares the Song of Solomon (2:5). Derrida dwells on Lévinas's resort to that biblical book [and with unfailing virtuosity demands: Who is the speaker: the heroine, "*elle*," or Emmanuel Lévinas (E. L.)? Or is it *el*—God in Hebrew? (168)]—according to Lévinas, love as quest of the Other and surrender (giving oneself) to him, in the course of the surrender of the subjective. But Derrida's reading of the words of the Shulamite reveals that language "can't deliver the goods"; the negotiation between speech (*parole*) and saying (*le dire*) is condemned to hindrances and obstacles. "Love sickness" is an infinite search for the absent beloved:

> The negotiation formulates that which does not allow itself to be for-
> mulated: and on the same path of that transaction, it forces the language to
> enter into contract with the stranger, with the one which it can only blend,
> without assimilating. . . . [T]he Other signifies a false leap . . . the furtive
> eruption of speech which, no longer expressed in the language, nevertheless
> is not reduced to silence. The grammatical utterance is there, but it is dis-
> lodged to make place . . . to a kind of ungrammaticality of a gift intended
> for another: from self to the accusative. (169)

According to Derrida, this is the meaning of "I will seek him whom my soul loveth" in the Song of Solomon. This is the meaning of the hopeless, constant search for the vanished beloved: "I charge you, O daughters of Jerusalem, if ye find my beloved, that ye tell him, that I am sick with love" (5:8). Or: "Whither is thy beloved gone, O thou fairest among women? whither is thy beloved turned aside? that we may seek him with thee" (6:1). Alternatively: "A garden inclosed is my sister, my spouse" (4:12).

Derrida internalized the unity of opposites, of fraternity and the infinite remoteness from the Other, into his own complex and contradictory rela-tionship with fraternity as manifested within the Jewish community. His *Pol-itique de l'amitié* (Politics of friendship [1994b]) discusses, inter alia, the concept of fraternity, being drawn to the unclear relationship between friend and brother. Here (337) he quotes a letter published in *L'arche* (no. 373, 1988) with a declaration of generous fraternity addressed to Jews and Juda-ism: "It was evidently the Nazi persecution of the Jews . . . that made us feel that *the Jews are our brethren* and Judaism is more than a culture, and even more than a religion, rather it is the foundation of our relations with the Other." Quite perplexed by this (somewhat Lévinasian, we would say) definition of Judaism, he hastens to demand: "What is the meaning here of 'brethren'? And why is the other represented by the brother?" Further: ". . . I asked myself why could I never write the word 'communality,' if one can put it so, on my own account, in my own name? Where did I come upon such reticence? In view of this definition of Judaism, is this reserve insufficiently Jewish? Or on the contrary, Jewish to excess, more than Jew-ish?" (338).

Is this a confession of a rift? Of infinite remoteness from the Jewish Others, his brethren? But as soon as Derrida sets out his own vision of fraternity—a universal, democratic vision—we find him resorting to messi-anic concepts with which we have become highly familiar from the outspo-kenly Jewish contexts of his writing: "As democracy is yet to come, this is its essence . . . forever inadequate and of the future but, belonging as it does to the time of the promise, it will forever remain, in each of these future times, yet to come: even when there is democracy, it never exists, it is never present, it remains the theme of a concept that can never be present" (339).

All of which goes to show that aloofness from Judaism, and an affinity thereto, exist within one another in Derrida's world, even if the aloofness is professed, while the affinity comes to light as residue of concepts and values, as remnants, as traces. The association with Lévinas thus explains a philosophical opposition that is also a mental condition: intense attention to the voice of the Other, Jew and non-Jew alike, a total giving over of self to him, and simultaneously, remoteness from him.

"I cannot, and I wouldn't even try, to try to say a few words about the work of Emmanuel Lévinas. So great is it that one cannot even see its boundaries" (*Adieu* [1997a], 14). Derrida confessed (in both senses of the word) over the grave of Lévinas after his demise in the final days of 1995. Thus, in his moving leavetaking of the dead "Other," toward whom he adopts the intimacy of first name and sorrow, and resort to Lévinas's two-sided *adieu* ("goodbye" to the Other, and also "to God," the infinite Other), Derrida again gauges Lévinas's contribution in terms of the Jewish alternative to the Hellenist option:

> one of those powerful, singular, rare provocations which, throughout history, for more than two thousand years, have ineradicably marked the space and body of that which is more or less anything but a simple dialogue between Jewish thought and its counterparts, the philosophies of Greek origins or . . . the other Abrahamic monotheisms. This alteration came about *through him*, through Emmanuel Lévinas, who, out of that enormous responsibility, had, I believe, an awareness that was simultaneously clear, confident, calm, and modest, like that of a prophet. (25)

But even Derrida's words of farewell and admiration contain hints of his differences with Lévinas. Thus, Lévinas's words to him, "To tell the truth, what interests me isn't ethics, or not just ethics, but the sacred, the sanctity of the sacred," reminds Derrida of the *parochet* encasing the Torah scroll, "the 'vail' whereby God commanded Moses . . . to separate the Holy of Holies from the rest of the Sanctuary" (*Adieu*, 1997a, 15). It thus becomes possible to conclude this discussion with the conclusion that, over and above Derrida's indebtedness to Lévinas's philosophy, and in contrast with Lévinas's prime interest in sanctity (the sanctity of the Other), Derrida's principal interest lay in the screen, the *parochet*, which he identified with language, with dividing and violent writing.

17

Hospitality

On the first anniversary of the death of Lévinas, Derrida again undertook an intensive study of his writings, having grown particularly close to the philosopher, probably because of the central role he had conferred upon ethics in recent years. Derrida's new studies, largely resting upon his lecture to the convention on "Face and Sinai" (Sorbonne University, Paris, 7 December 1996) were collected in his *Adieu* (1997a), which commences with his eulogy to Lévinas. It is noteworthy that Derrida even took the title of his book from the heading of the eulogy. Indeed, Derrida was never so close to Lévinas as in this book, and consequently, Derrida's commentary is harder to distinguish from its subject than in his other works. Accordingly, as we shall see in this section, the reader of *Adieu* cannot avoid the impression that, in presenting Lévinas's fundamental ideas, Derrida is also presenting his own.

In view of Derrida's growing interest in ethical topics, it is natural that the subject of hospitality, to which his annual seminar was devoted in 1996, and which became a significant banner of his social and political endeavors, was discussed extensively in this book. The "being at home" (*être chez soi*) invites in and welcomes the guest, the Other. The concept of "hospitality" is avowedly attached to the concept of "acceptance (*accueil*) of the Other," and thus the two concepts, frequently featured in Lévinas's works—acceptance in particular—are bound up together. Commencing with characterization of Lévinas's personality as teacher (the teacher as welcoming "host") and the notion of study as acceptance—"hospitality"—of the Other, Derrida goes on to expand the "hospitality" at the root of all the meaning and roots of any language, and the universal moral code of "hospitality" as principle applicable to human relationships, and the relations between states and peoples. At this level, Derrida links Lévinas's concept of "peace" with Kant's concept of "eternal peace" (Kant, *The Eternal Peace*, 1795).

Derrida's "hospitality" concept arose out of his study of Lévinas's *Totality and Infinity* (1980), where the philosopher identifies hospitality as opening the gate, and opening oneself, to "the face of the Other." The face of the Other is a precondition of any welcome. The face of the Other precedes my existence. Furthermore, responsibility toward the Other precedes the essence. In other words, the nature of the principle of response is a priori: the promise of a response is the cornerstone of any call (*appel*) of the face of the Other to me. Any dialogue between host and guest commences with the response that precedes any discourse, the "Yes" response from the Other.

Into this intimate duality between me and the Other, the "third" is flung as bearer of the issue of justice. For while the relationship between me and the Other rests upon Otherness, the presence of the third now demands the question of similarity (*même*), equality, that is, justice. Derrida identifies here the "double bind," or even *aporia*, between my oath of responsibility (my responsibility vis à vis the Other, the "second one") and the violation of that oath through the very appearance of the "third" (bringing with him musings and queries in relation to justice). "Justice commences with the breaking of that oath" (*Adieu* [1997a], 69), writes Derrida, regarding the presence of the "third" as no less basic than the presence of the face-of-the-Other. The third is present in the eyes of the Other, regarding me through the eyes of the Other. Hence follows a characteristic Derridean conclusion: violation of the oath toward the Other underlies the oath to the face-of-the-Other. Or, in harsher terms, injustice lies at the very root of hospitality, which is the essence of morality: "it is necessary, that possible hospitality to the worst, or that the good hospitality gets its chance, the chance of letting the other come" (67).

Opening the door to the Other is linked with the concept of "dwelling" (*la demeure*), which Lévinas describes as the intimacy of the home, or *être chez soi* [being at home], in your own internal space that welcomes the Other. It will be recalled that Lévinas identified the principle of acceptance into internality with woman. For as Otherness (of distance and leave-taking, also evident in displacement and refugee status) is a condition for acceptance (*recueillement*) into the home, and woman is the expression par excellence of Otherness and absence, she is also the embodiment of hospitality.

The relationship between host and guest is dialetical. The host gives, but also receives. The guest receives the hospitality that he offers. The host is thus also guest. Furthermore, the ego is simultaneously the host and the hostage of the Other (in his total responsibility toward the Other). The substitution principle means: I set myself in place of the Other (as his hostage). The host's sojourn in his own hospitality redeems him from the alienness he senses in his own home. In the act of acceptance of opening the house door, he applies the principle of femininity. Equally, the act of acceptance opens the gate upon a total and infinite Otherness, reflected in every Other.

But again, here is the *aporia*: hospitality opens a gate from the finite to the infinite (total Otherness). It also widens the chasm of separation between me and the Other (and total Otherness). But now we come upon the most difficult paradox: the enigma of the face that is not revealed in the course of my responsibility toward the faceless face. The face-of-the-Other (transcendental) becomes comprehensible to me as mere trace. An act of breaking faith takes place. In welcoming the guest, I become aware of the "veil," the revelation of the truth through its very concealment. However, the power of this concealment is as the power of the promise to "visit," the revelation of the "face" as transcendental Otherness. In Lévinas's philosophy, the term "Sinai" (denoting the place of revelation and the granting of the Torah, but also the place of the shattering of the Tablets) is the place of the visitation—visitation as hospitality, opening the great gate to messianic Otherness. But to Lévinas, as to Derrida, transcendental hospitality is merely a signpost to mundane hospitality at the level of human fraternity. The command to love the stranger (Deut. 23:8) is an imperative demanding application in all places and at all times. And if we are on the subject of Sinai, then it includes the hospitality in Israeli-Egyptian relations there, on the border between the two states, close to Sinai—says Derrida (*Adieu* [1997a], 117). Monotheistic politics is thus that which expresses the "hospitality" principle, the "Sinai" principle, at the level of political and social practice.

18

The Sublime of the Jews

In his *La verité en peinture* (1978b), Derrida wrote: "[I]t is not then surprising that both [Kant and Hegel] consider a certain Judaism as the historical figure of the sublime irruption, the one, Kant, from the point of view of religion and morals, in the ban on iconic representation (neither *Bildnis* nor *Gleichnis*); the other, Hegel, in the Hebrew poetry he considered as the highest negative form of the sublime" (*The Truth in Painting* [La verité en peinture], [Chicago: Univ. of Chicago Press, 1987], 134).

This historical and cultural distinction comes as no surprise to those who recall that in "On the Spirit in Hebrew Poetry" (1782), Johann Gottfried Herder identified the sublime in the Book of Job, which he characterized as Oriental nature poetry relating the potency of God, hell, and heaven and the chaos blended into Creation, monsters and thunderbolts interwoven with infinite beauty, and so forth. Concluding his discussion of Psalm 26, Herder pronounced: "One way or the other, the picture terminates in such sublime tranquillity, whereas its commencement was such an awful hubbub."[1] There we have, in essence, the Kantian concept of the "sublime"—ten years prior to its formulation.

More important for the matter at hand is the question: How does Derrida connect the concept of "sublime," as evolved by Kant and Hegel, with Judaism? And what is this "sublime" we are talking about? In fact, Derrida leaves the work to his reader, who can only attempt to span the gap between Derrida's interpretation of Kant and Hegel, and his "perception" of Judaism as repeatedly indicated in his writings. In this context, the reader should bear in mind the (ambivalent) interest Derrida displayed in "Judaising" Kant: as in his interpretative analysis, in *"Kant, le juif, l'allemand"*; or in his analysis of Hermann Cohen's historical assessment that the Enlightenment overall, and Kant in particular, represent the supreme manifestation of the Jewish spirit (or in regarding Hegel as the man who "converted" Kant to Judaism: *Glas* [1974]).

It would be appropriate in this context to devote a few words to the

Kantian concept of beauty—of course, as read and interpreted by Derrida. True to his "dark" side, which pinpoints the darkness at the bottom of every metaphysical theory, Derrida identifies the "abyss" in Kant's concept of the beautiful. As he puts it, the "abyss" opens up owing to the setting of aesthetic judgment in the intermediary range between the judgments of truth and virtue, on the one hand, and on the other—of pleasure and utility. Kant's aesthetic doctrine is presented as an effort to bridge the gap between sensuality and intelligence, between necessity and freedom (*La verité en peinture* [1987 ed.], 35–36). Having forced his way into this dark "fissure," Derrida empties it, stressing the process of negation, distancing and vacuity of Kantian aesthetics: Kant's rules of beauty rest upon absences—absence of personal interest, absence of purpose, and absence of concept. In denying interest from the consciousness of the one who experiences beauty, the Kantian concept of beauty—at least, as read by Derrida—is "the burial of the existing subject": "It is an inexistent or anexistent subjectivity arising on the crypt of the empirical subject and its whole world" (46). At the same time, by virtue of the demanding nonconceptualism of the aesthetic consciousness, "the play of the powers of consciousness" (Kant: beauty as "free play of the powers of consciousness") is stripped of all knowledge or truth. Ultimately, Derrida presents the Kantian judgment of beauty as *parergon* (framing device), a kind of *passe-partout*, a loose interim domain located between the "external" and "internal," between the objective and subjective worlds; in other words, neither here nor there, or, succinctly, in the "abyss."

Predictably, Derrida sets the Kantian concept of the "sublime" over a bottomless pit, even if there are significant differences between the concepts of "sublime" and "beautiful." The "sublime" is not a *parergon*, if only because it surrounds no *ergon* (art work), for it does not apply to human objects, merely to raw nature, which is beyond physical or conscious framing. "The sublime" demolishes all concepts: an object is transformed into "Extraordinary!" "Way out!" or "Wow!" and so on (i.e., "sublime") through being perceived as exceeding (above and beyond) any measure, as it nullifies and reduces to nothing the purpose that constituted its concept (125). We are thus dealing with collapse of the form and/or the power of conscious formalization in view of the flow of infinity rising from the tempestuous waves of the sea, from the wilderness expanses, from myriad stars in the heavens, from the depths of the canyon, and so forth—collapse of consciousness as annihilation of the ego ("death") as foundation of the experience of the "sublime."

The Kantian experience of the "sublime," as understood by Derrida, focuses on what Kant terms "production of negative pleasure," which the philosopher from Koenigsberg depicted thus: "Deriving gratification from the sublime in nature is exclusively negative (whereas from the beautiful it is positive); that is to say, it is a sentiment of denial of freedom of the power of imagination per se, while the power of imagination is established as purposeful by a law other than the law of experimental usage. And thus the power of imagination derives extension and force which are greater than that sacrificed; but the reason remains concealed from the power of imagination, and in return, it senses the sacrifice or absence, and instantly, the reason it is enslaved thereto. Amazement verges upon alarm, horror, and holy trembling."[2] Accordingly, Derrida stresses that "the sublime" negates the vital play (of "the powers of consciousness") occurring in the experience of beauty, as it breaks through the floodgates of consciousness and floods the pretense of playing with a burst of violence. This is the duality of suffering and satisfaction, as he puts it, the "double bind" of pleasure and rejection, and the widening abyss: "Attraction/rejection of the same object. Double bind. There is an excess that widens the abyss. The imagination is fearful of losing itself in this chasm, and we pull back" (*La verité en peinture* [1987 ed.], 129). And a little further along: "[The colossal is condemned] to erect itself in the excessive movement of its own disappearance, of the unpresentable presentation. The obscenity of its abyss" (145).

Derrida's study of the Hegelian concept of the "sublime" is charged right from the outset by Ferdinand de Saussure's well-known semiotic distinction (*Course in General Linguistics* [1917]) between signifiers and signified, whereby the concept of "sublime" is connected with Derrida's concept of language and the great onto-theological tension between speech and writing. According to Hegel, the experience of "the sublime" enables the infinite spirit to demolish representation and symbol. In other words, the absolute content destroys the signifier (133). Equally, in the experience of the "sublime," the infinite content (the overall spirit, the spirit of absolute truth), which is the signified, undergoes elevation (*Aufhebung*) above form, that is, above the signifier. We are again in the domain of deconstruction: the signifier being form, that is, "writing," and the signified being the universal spirit, that is, the primal essence, "speech"—the Hegelian experience of "the sublime" proves the rupture between speech and writing, between signified and signifier. The signifier demolishes itself, being incapable of containing the infinity of the signified, of the content of absolute truth. This is the self-same Kantian collapse of the dams of consciousness and imagination under the mathematical force (i.e., the infinite quantity) of raw nature.

Here lies the gateway of the affinity of "the sublime" to Judaism of "Thou shalt not make thee any graven image, or any likeness" and to monotheism overall. Those who follow in Derrida's path know that the Jewish rejection of the representation of God, or His sensual signification, condemns the "writing" of God (His voice, "speech") to the shattering of the Tablets of the Law (upon which Derrida dwelled in *L'écriture et la différence* [1967b], in his commentary on Jabès's *Book of Questions*). The finality of the signifiers, their impermanence, their dispersion as fragments—we could even say, their status as "ashes," as tombstone of something that was and is no longer (i.e., dead)—leave no hope of representation of the abstract and infinite God. Beauty, as synthesis between finite and infinite, has no chance in the Jewish context, which does not recognize the representation of the infinite in the finite (the physical or sensual). Hegel's reference to the empty Holy of Holies (as interpreted in Derrida's *Glas* [1974]) set Judaism in the domain of refusal (or inability) to the sensual concretization of the general spirit. However, Jewish "infirmity" in the aesthetic domain, the infirmity toward beauty, is compensated—by both Kant and Hegel—through affirmation of the "sublime."

As we have seen, Derrida makes no more than oblique mention of Kant's reference to Judaism. Here is the original passage, as it appears in *Critique of Judgment*:

> There is no room for the worry that by the manner of such an abstract incarnation, that has become utterly negative in relation to the sensual, the sense of the sublime may lose. For the imaginative power, albeit it finds beyond the sensual nothing it can hold on to, at all events it senses itself, by this removal of its blockages, unrestricted. That removal is therefore fulfillment of the infinite, which can never be more than negative fulfillment, but nevertheless expands the soul. There may be nothing more sublime in the Jews' Torah than the commandment: Thou shalt not make thee any graven image, or any likeness of any thing that is in heaven above, or that is in the earth beneath, or that is in the waters beneath the earth, and so on. This commandment alone can explain the fervor the Jewish people sensed toward its religion in the period of its moral culture, when it compared itself to other nations.[3]

Hegel's claim regarding the "sublime" of the Jews appears in the chapter on the symbolism of the sublime, in his *Lectures in Aesthetics* (first published in 1835):

> The second manner of comprehension—that is, the negative praise to the power and glory of the one God—we encounter in Hebrew poetry as the sublime in its strict sense. This dismisses the positive immanence of the absolute in created phenomena, setting the single substance explicitly separate as God of the world, and in contrast thereto stand all His creatures, and these—in comparison with the Divinity—are presented as essentially transient and powerless.[4]

Hegel contrasts Hebrew poetry of antiquity (the Bible) with Indian and Moslem Persian poetry, although all are "sublime" poetry. He identified Indian and Persian poetry ("positive praise poetry" in his terms) as pantheistic art that proves a deity immanent in every detail of the Creation. In Judaism, by contrast, he identified the distance between God and His creatures. Stressing the sublime divine presence, which annihilates any formalism, Hegel noted: "This type of sublime, in its primary original character, can be identified particularly in the outlook of the Jews and their sacred poetry. As visual art may not appear here, where it is impossible to represent any matching picture of God; that can be done only by the poetry of ideas, expressed in words."[5]

The case argued by Kant and Hegel suggests that Jews, lacking the flair for beauty, have been compensated by a gift for the sublime. Visual art, representing the infinity in synthesis with sensual finity (of sight, hearing, touch), has been supplanted by the word. Jewish poetry of ideas represents the divine, reinforcing the elimination of sensual and formal representation. The second Commandment indirectly guarantees the negation of beauty, but also the affirmation of the sublime. But there is a substantive difference between the concept of negation as applied by Kant in relation to the Jewish sublime, and Hegel's negation. To the latter, the "negative praise" of the Lord rests upon the self-effacement of the one who renders adulation. God's remoteness from man (and from his people, the People of Israel) has robbed the adulating Jew of the infinite, which has been attributed in entirety to the Divinity. Man has been divested of infinity—not so for Kant: here the negation principle rests upon the inability of the power of imagination to embrace the infinite, in consequence of its liberation from its dependence upon sensuality. Imagination liberated from nature may not be capable of grasping whatsoever transcends nature, but its release from nature is per se an opening for consciousness to know itself as infinite. The "divine" has been revealed and confirmed in man.

The moment he identified the infinity of the sublime in the dark chasm gaping beneath the experience of the sublime according to Kant and Hegel, Derrida seems to have attained the ability to affirm both versions of the "negative sublime": the signifier demolished by the infinite signified has left the absolute spiritual content (absolute truth) incapable of representation by sign. The remoteness of God, who averts his visage, is exceedingly familiar from Derrida's onto-theology, which has banished "writing" from the original truth of primary "speech." The infinity dwelling within man survives only at the level of ashes (recalling the fire), ruin, mourning. Probably, Derrida could meet Kant and Hegel halfway by means of the sublime of the Book of Lamentations bewailing the destruction of the holy city, which he

characterized as the most sublime Hebrew poetry of all times. For verses
such as "He hath led me, and brought me into darkness, but not into light"
(Threni 3:2); "He hath set me in dark places, as they that be dead of old"
(3:6); "Mine eye runneth down with rivers of water for the destruction of
the daughter of my people" (3:48); "I called upon thy name, O Lord, out
of the low dungeon"(3:55); "and hath kindled a fire in Zion, and it hath
devoured the foundations thereof" (4:11); "They have wandered as blind
men in the streets"(4:14); "Our inheritance is turned to strangers, our
houses to aliens" (5:2); and many more—match the blindness that Derrida
detected beneath the regard, and the tear representing the victim of sightlessness (*Mémoires d'aveugle* [1990e]); the fire of a holocaust (that "burns
all") that leaves the consciousness with nothing but ashes (*Feu, la cendre*
[1987b]) as remembrance of the great light that promises but burns all; the
darkness lurking within all post-Platonic light (*Marges—de la philosophie*
[1972b]) and so on. Indeed, *Lignées* (1996d) with its drawings of destruction (destruction/deconstruction) by Micaëla Henich, accompanied by
fragments of Derrida's contemplative poetry, does indeed meet up with
Lamentations at several levels.

The notion of the regard (eye) that has withdrawn in favor of the spoken word (ear) is not alien to Derrida's philosophy, indeed lying at its very
foundations. His preference for the blinking beast (which lowers screens of
darkness over its eyes) over the beast condemned to constant vision (an
Aristotlean distinction to which Derrida resorts in an essay featured in *Du
droit à la philosophie* [1990a]) at least points out the weakness of the regard
(and concomitantly, the Western identification of sight and truth). In *Mémoires d'aveugle* Derrida pointed out that revelation of the divine light is
predicated upon sacrifice of the eye (i.e., the loss of sight). Derrida thus
takes up position halfway between regard and word, in the *parergon* (framework) between "pure work" and its external verbal contexts. His interpretative emphasis on visualization of writing and verbalization of the visual
propelled him toward the works of artists like Marcel Duchamp or Valerio
Adami, just as it enraptured him with structural writing of visual value (as
illustrated, for example, in his *Glas* [1974]). His verbal interpretations of
visual works such as photography (*Lecture de droit de regards* [1985a], a
commentary on the photographs of Marie-Francoise Plissart) or sketching
(*Lignées* [1996d]; commentary on the drawings of Micaëla Henich) rest
upon his assumption that photography and sketching are "writing."
Throughout his odyssey from the visual to the word, Derrida expressed his
critique of Western metaphysics concerning its aspiration to lucidity, white-
ness, light, and sun. The response is writing in black print. Writing is the
verdict of culture, and "there is nothing beyond the text." But that also

entails recognition of the darkness of the text, the darkness of writing and the darkness of signs. Writing condemns the reader to a labyrinth. Any soaring toward a Platonic sun ends up with a fall after the manner of Icarus.[6]

In his critique of the regard and his rejection of the Western alliance of contemplation with intelligence, Derrida pursues the tradition of the Jewish critique (all the way from Moses to Lévinas) of Hellenic culture. Having encompassed culture with the fence of writing and words (even if, as already noted, he did not liberate writing of the values of the regard!), Derrida trod his Jewish path. In the words of Geoffrey Hartman, Derrida is "Jewish rather than Hellenist; noniconic but with that, most graphic."[7]

The Kantian-Hegelian concept of the Sublime grew from man's facing an overwhelming nature. Being a cognitive image of an inconceivable quantity, it resulted from a sensual experience of the gaze. The Jew, so we are told, substituted the image of an infinite nature with a purely cognitive image of infinity, the image of God. But does not the Jew also have a physical, nonnatural image of infinity? This question does not aim at confirming a Jewish aesthetic sensibility (the Hegelian rejection of which cannot be too easily accepted, especially not today, considering the vast Jewish contribution to modern art). Rather, the aim of the above question is the confirmation of an image of an enormous quantity that is not connected to beauty or art, but to the memory of the mass extermination of Jews during the Holocaust. Is the Holocaust the Sublime of the Jews? Is the Holocaust's memory an experience of the "negative Sublime"?

In an interview given in January 1998 to Michal Ben-Naftali, Derrida said, "And there is also the fact of my being an Algerian Jew, of having a more distant connection to the European issue. . . . I know that I don't have the same relationship with the Holocaust as French Jews have."[8] Obviously, Algerian roots are no excuse for avoiding thinking about the Holocaust, especially for a philosopher, a humanist like Derrida. After all, was he not the one who criticized the analytic American philosophers for their indifference toward social-political issues, including the Holocaust? (13).

The word "holocaust," or "Holocaust," was woven into Derrida's conception of fire (in *The Postcard*); it reappeared in his interpretation of Paul Celan's poems (in *Schibboleth*) and in his tracking of Heidegger's short Nazi chapter (*Heidegger et la question*); the Holocaust stood at the background of Derrida's analysis of young Paul de Man's writings in Belgian newspapers that collaborated with the Nazis (*Memoirs pour Paul de Man*).

"Heidegger's approach is loaded with an endless guilt," Derrida told his interviewer at Yad Vashem. "According to this hypothesis, who has the right to say 'I forgive' or 'I do not forgive'? I don't know. At any rate, it is not me. My approach to this issue has never been that of a judge" (10). As to the de Man affair: "The only time in my life that I wrote or published the expression 'unforgivable' was in reference to de Man. . . . I wrote and said that in any case what de Man did at that moment was unforgivable" (11). But soon after: "I think it is unforgivable simply because, concerning any crime . . . man does not have the right to forgive unless he is the direct victim of that crime. . . . I myself cannot forgive de Man's or any other collaborator's sins, because this is up to the victims of these sins to forgive" (12).

Such quotations (one may add Derrida's use of the word "holocaust"—no capital H!—in "The Fire," together with his later reference during the 1998 interview, "I think that today nothing at all can be burnt, not even a love-letter, without thinking about the Holocaust" [15]) are enough to elucidate Derrida's complex and multidimensional position concerning the Holocaust. One may justifiably claim that the historical Holocaust and the onto-theological holocaust are inseparable in Derrida's thought. It was therefore natural that the philosopher who saved no efforts in defending persecutions in Prague, South Africa, and the Middle East would make a visit to Auschwitz (at the end of 1997) as it was no less natural for him (considering his tendency toward opposites and pluralism) to respond to his Auschwitz visit by saying, "It is terrible, Auschwitz, it is monstrous," but immediately rejecting the uniqueness of Auschwitz by saying, "But even during the extermination-experience it was but one place among many" (14). And at the same time, he called (together with other French intellectuals) for President Mitterand's recognition of France's guilt concerning the Vichy crimes.

One way or another, the spirit of the Holocaust or a holocaust hovers over Jacques Derrida's writing: the refugees who seek hospitality in his various books; the ghosts that frequent his thoughts; and above all, the verdict of "extermination" that awaits all redemptive metaphysical light—all prove and assure an intimate relationship between philosophy and that great trauma of the twentieth century. "The concept of survival occupies a very specific place in my work," admits Derrida (14), while reminding us of his central term, "trace," as another survival concept: "I insist that this word or this logic of survival refers to Auschwitz—but not only to Auschwitz" (ibid.). Therefore, it is no surprise that Derrida is ready to recognize a certain affinity between deconstruction (putting a question mark over the history of Western metaphysics) and "the traces of twentieth-century's totalitarianism, and more specifically any totalitarianism after the Holocaust" (5).

Thus one could argue that even Derrida's linguistic conception is somehow linked to the memory of the Holocaust. No doubt such a claim applies to the Derridean concept of the signature, being the effort of assuring the private name a presence. Derrida, who wished to bring the signature (and the date) back to the center of the philosophical discourse, is in a way responding to the Holocaust's acts of name erasure: "Speaking about signature, the Holocaust was in many cases an attempt to erase names, to erase the private names, not only to put to death [human beings] but to exterminate the archive. Yad Vashem is first of all a memorial of names. . . . As if the names were the very thing against which the extermination was intended" (9).

But simultaneously there is the inevitable Derridean pointing at the "archive-fever": an archival institute like Yad Vashem, which was meant to secure the names, the memory, is fated—like all archives—to forgetfulness and "death." Without resorting to the deadly archival principle of repetition, Derrida argues, "There is here a horrible duality: the very act of archiving contributes in a way to classification, to relativity and forgetfulness. Archiving conserves, but it is also the beginning of the forgetting. And it might be that one day—and this thought is shocking—Yad Vashem will be considered just another monument, no more; because it is kept enclosed within that enclosure that characterizes archives. . . . And thus, because it is guarded it can be lost, it can be forgotten" (ibid.).

Derrida's visit to Jerusalem at the dawn of 1998 was connected to two public lectures that he delivered, one in Jerusalem and the other in Tel Aviv. At the center of these lectures, especially of the first (at the Hebrew University) there stood the question of the forgiveness of Nazi crimes. Derrida was responding to two books written by the French philosopher (of Russian-Jewish origin) Vladimir Jankeléwitch, where this question of forgiveness was discussed.[9] Whereas in the 1967 book Jankeléwitch was defending the total imperative of forgiving, namely that forgiving must be stronger than evil, in his 1986 book he claimed that crimes against humanity are unforgivable. Shortly before Derrida lectured in Israel, the French church had issued a forgiveness petition for its behavior toward the Jews during World War II. Derrida wavered between yes and no: "'Should one forgive after Auschwitz?' I would say that in no case there is a right for anyone to argue that one must forgive or that one must not forgive. . . . A pure or unconditioned forgiveness must be an event or an act of grace which cannot be ordered. There should not be a duty to forgive or a duty not to forgive. . . . Everyone must reach the forgiveness in his own way, to take about it a responsibility without resorting to calculation of the judgment, the punishment, penalty, etc." (12).

Thus Derrida enveloped the question of forgiveness within the concept of responsibility (in its Lévinasian sense), considering forgiveness solely as the individual's moral determination. In terms of this chapter's subject one may conclude that according to Derrida, the dilemma of forgiving or not forgiving Nazi crimes can be solved only through the individual's facing of the negative Sublime. The individual's confrontation of the infinite evil united moral and religious commitments, and so it might be the opposite or the complimentary aspect of the individual's covenant with God (the secret shared by God and Abraham in the Sacrifice of Isaac).

19

Father's Talith

Late 1998. The tip of Jacques Derrida's Jewish iceberg is progressively revealed as a towering mountain; perhaps it is starting to melt a little. Increasingly, books of scholarly research address the Jewish aspect of Derrida's philosophy as something more than mere aspect. I refer to the following works: John D. Caputo, *The Prayers and Tears of Jacques Derrida* (Bloomington: Indiana Univ. Press, 1997); or Martin C. Srajek, *In the Margins of Deconstruction* (Dordrecht: Kluwer, 1998.)

Derrida himself contributes to this paradoxical trend (drawn into a vortex—*shibboleth* in Hebrew—of center and essence, amidst the flow of thought totally rejecting centers and true essence) as he reveals more autobiographical data to bind his philosophy, bandagelike, over his Jewish "wound." In September 1998, Derrida and Hélène Cixoux published the joint work *Voiles*, an amalgam of two works already published in 1977 in *Contretemps* (no. 2/3, winter-summer). Hélène Cixoux launches the slim volume with a literary-philosophical reflection entitled "*Savoir*," while Derrida, as is his wont, responds with "*Un ver à soie*" (silkworm), which also analyzes the work of his coauthor. The thread connecting the two weaves a fabric that is a *voile*—whether "veil" or "sail." The former term is masculine in French (albeit applied to a piece of female apparel); the latter is feminine. Male and female; one must draw the distinction, to avoid falling into *shaatnez* (a mixed fabric, proscribed by Jewish law).

But when Derrida writes "*Un ver à soie*"—and much more in concluding with a moving account of his cultivation of silkworms before his bar mitzvah—he wishes to say "*ver*," which is not merely the male-female/hermaphrodite worm undergoing its various metamorphoses until its demise; this is also the *ver* that is the basic syllable of *verité* (truth), *verdict*, and possibly even *verbe* (speech). In other words, Derrida's silkworm spins verbal thread (text-textile) into a fabric of truth that is a verdict. For the French *dévoiler* designates the opposite of *voile*, that is, unveiling, exposing-disclosing-stripping the truth concealed (behind "veil" or screen). Truth as pure fabrication . . .

It doesn't take Derrida long to splice the thread of exposure of truth with religious fabrics that conceal inaccessible divine truths. He recalls that "the Temple curtain will be torn on the death of the Messiah, the other Messiah, the ancient from Bethlehem, the one from the first or second resurrection, the false-true Messiah who cures the blind and introduces himself saying: 'I am the truth and the life'" (*Voiles* [1998b], 30).

Derrida resorts to the New Testament for a swift lunge at the veil beyond the veil, that is, the Jewish "curtain" (*parochet*) enveloping the Torah scroll, as Moses was commanded: "And thou shalt make a vail of blue, and purple, and scarlet, and fine twined linen of cunning work: with cherubims shall it be made: . . . that thou mayest bring in thither within the vail the ark of the testimony: and the vail shall divide unto you between the holy place and the most holy" (Exod. 26:31,33). Derrida somehow contrives to discover two different "vails" in this passage. Be that as it may, we have the fabric given-ordained (*donner, ordonner*) by God; the fabric that divides, the fabric as division from the absolute Otherness, or from the utterly Other (*tout autre*) (*Voiles*, 32). God's place is beyond the vail-veil-*voile*.

But the great surprise in store for readers of *Voiles* awaits at three of the book's most significant junctures, where Derrida goes into the significance of that other, more personal, Jewish fabric, the *talith*. Textile, tactile, *talith*, writes Derrida, regaling our ears with the similar ring of the terms: the weave, the textile, the prayer-shawl. If he writes, "it is neither veil nor sail" (62), that is merely to stress that veil and sail have become a kind of veil obscuring a supreme truth that is also highly personal and intimate: "A prayer-shawl I love to touch more than see, to caress each day, to kiss without even opening my eyes or even when it resides wrapped up in a paper bag where I plunge my hand during the night, with eyes closed" (44).

The *talith*, whether worn over the clothes or touching the body, that is, the skin ("There's another skin!" [44]); the *talith* that conceals nothing and promises nothing, merely seeking by its mere presence to recall a divine ordinance; Derrida again opens the Bible: "And it shall be unto you for a fringe, that ye may look upon it, and remember all the commandments of the Lord" (Num. 15:39). Here is seeing as memory, visual sign as memory—the ancient notion going back all the way to Plato's *Phaedrus;* the fringe as memory sign for anyone donning the *talith;* "The secret of a shawl enveloping a single body" (45). Here is the uniqueness of the *talith*, and its address to the transcendental Other; from father to Supreme Father; *Talith* and authority—an exclusively male matter; no mixing of male and female, we should remember: no *shaatnez*, heaven forbid. For above all else, the *talith* is enjoined to ensure the homogeneity of the fabric: a silk *talith* with cotton fringes brings no blessing, Derrida discovers in Scripture (66), whereas a silk *talith* with silk fringes certainly will! Worst of all is the mixture, the *shaatnez*, a blend of silk and cotton in the *talith*. Heterogenity is proscribed!

Derrida continues to draw nearer to himself, to his personal male secret. In *Voiles* he seems to display a daring he did not even show in *Circonfession* because it is only here that he dares at long last to confront the memory of his dead father ("This father, I still see him but I never saw him, by definition" [46].), or, to be precise, to confront the *talith* shrouding his father's body. Derrida writes of his private *talith*, Jacques's *talith* of pure white silk presented to him by his maternal grandfather, Moshe. The *talith*, meanwhile rather yellowed, he had left behind in El-Biar on his departure for France at the age of nineteen, relinquishing it for his father's use. It was this *talith* that reverted to him on his father's demise. "I almost never wear it . . . but I lay my fingers or lips on it almost every evening, except when I travel to the ends of the earth, for it awaits me like an animal well hidden in its cache, at home" (46).

Derrida has to touch the *talith* ("I touch it without knowing what I am doing" [ibid.]), comprehending the duality of the blessing and death involved in "the culture of the *talith*." The blessing is the blessing of the father, enfolded in his *talith* at the synagogue, laying the *talith* over his sons' heads as he blesses them. Again we stress: it is a matter for fathers and sons alone; the *talith* is a male preserve, like circumcision (79). The *talith* is prohibited to women, the ritual blessing is exclusively for sons. There are memories of the El-Biar synagogue, the former mosque; memories of the father extending his *talith* over his son like the Temple roof—simultaneously, as already noted, the *talith* as memory of death: the death of the father, his body enshrouded in his private *talith* ahead of interment.

Derrida's relationship with the *talith* thus transcends the attitude to a functional ritual article. Fetishism? That doesn't put him off (80). As he phrases it, he belongs to his *talith* no less than it belongs to him. He enfolds himself in it, without it covering him entirely. Part of his body remains exposed, vulnerable—the *talith* of benediction, like a roof; but equally, the *talith* as remembrance of the fatal, unhealed wound of Jacques Derrida, the (fore)skinless philosopher. The *talith* is thus a substitute skin.

We have noted: the sight of the fringe is a reminder of the divine law. six hundred thirteen commandments of the Torah (Derrida reminds us that the *gimatria* [numerical equivalent of the letters. Trans.] of *tzitzit* (fringe) is 600, add 8 strands and 5 knots = 613). But before ever revealing or concealing one sight or another, the *talith*—so Derrida writes—*touches;*

tactile-textile, as we have seen. Touch predates sight, as with the blind. We recall from *Mémoires d'aveugle* (1990e) the experience of blindness as an experience of knowing and creating. Here, in the catalogue for the Louvre Museum drawing exhibit of which he served as curator, Derrida presents a long list of representations of blindness, where he stresses the groping hand that replaces the eye. The truth of the work remains in the darkness of blindness. "The drawing is blind," Derrida declares: the line (*trait*) that seeks to move ahead to the por-trait, is condemned to retreat (*re-trait*) into darkness. Even a self-portrait is merely erasure and destruction of the visual likeness: *visage devisagé*. The visual line signifying is condemned to miss the concealed signified. Only the other, third, eye, the other vision, the vision of the blind—like that of the prophet Tiresias or of a "seer" like the blinded Oedipus—can penetrate. This is the other sight, like that of Paul (Saul of Tarsus) at his momentary blindness. Derrida's rich foray to the blind writers, the myths of blindness, the paintings of the blind, and so on, confronts us with the critique of *voir* (seeing) implied in *savoir* (knowing). The ancient Western sun symbol is condemned to eclipse. Now, in *Voiles*, Derrida reverts to this theme in the context of the blindness motif and its affinity with knowledge of the truth, as stressed in "Knowing" by Hélène Cixoux. The veil and the vail conceal, blocking the penetrating glance, but harboring the truth (physical truth at the level of touch, and/or spiritual-divine truth at the level of hearing). The *talith,* we recall, begins with touch, proceeding to sight (the fringe as reminder-sign) its hoped-for conclusion: hearing the divine pronouncement: "stretching the *talith* over the entire history of the eye" (44).

Derrida penetrates the secret of the *talith*. As never before, he permits himself to study Jewish Scriptures, a domain he hitherto left to Lévinas. Opening his black copy of *The Abbreviated Shulchan Aruch* bequeathed by his father, he sets off in quest of the regulations relating to the *talith:* it must be removed when answering the call of nature; it must not be trailed on the ground; the obligation of unraveling the knots of the threads, and so forth. But above all, the obligation of weaving the *talith* from white sheep's wool. What of Derrida's silk *talith* then? Is it capable of bringing blessing? Derrida does not really know what his *talith* is made of, whether the fabric is natural or synthetic. Wool or flax are natural materials, like hair or the living body. The extremity of the wool fringe has to be sewn into a strip of animal hide.

> The imperative—of the hair, the wool, the leather—seems to signify that, unlike the veil, the sail and the cloth, a *talith* is primarily animal. Like the *tefilin* (phylacteries): skin on the very skin. The skin that comes, not from any ordinary animal, but from the sheep, or the ewe, or the ram. It

somehow commemorates the experience that could be called "sacrificing"
. . . a living creature that envelops itself, even in death, in a living creature
that has been sacrificed. (66–67)

Here Derrida pinpoints "the truth of the *talith*" as he puts it: more
than concealment or revelation, the *talith* designates divine law (Torah) and
the sacrifice it requires. We recall Derrida's *Force de loi*.

Korban: "victim"; "proximity"—Derrida frequently refers to this lingual duality (the two Hebrew terms contain identical roots. Trans.); the
victim that brings near, like circumcision. Derrida does indeed reflect upon
the cloth bandage wrapped around the baby's member eight days after his
birth, immediately after excision of his foreskin. "The *talith* clings to the
body like a memento of circumcision" (68). Men's business, we reiterate for
the last time: that which distinguishes man from woman.

Thus, Jacques Derrida remains, wrapped in his private *talith*, oblivious
as to whether or not it brings benediction, the *talith* of which he knows
nothing, really. He is left with his *talith*, his undeciphered secret—like an
additional bandage on his wound, the wound of his sacrifice that is his last
way of drawing near to the absolute Otherness. Cutting is for the purpose
of reuniting. The *talith* enveloping a man, separating him from heaven, is
what brings him closer to heaven. Here is the *talith* that divides a man from
his Maker is that which also brings him nearer to his Maker, on earth and in
heaven. The fringe as additional visual sign, like language overall, whose
substance is a reminder of the truth while drawing away from it to an abysmal distance. At the same time, like the humans condemned to language
and blind acceptance of its promises (signified), here is the love of the *talith*
and the duality of blessing-and-death that it bears. For like language, the
talith equally is one feasible way (granted: infirm, lacking, injured) to con-
verse with the silent, invisible Father. Accordingly:

> I would sing of the singular softness of my *talith*, a softness softer than
> soft, utterly singular, simultaneously sensible and insensible, calm, acquies-
> cent, a stranger to sentimentality, to gushiness or pathos, in brief, to any
> "Passion." Compassion without limit, and simultaneously, compassion
> without idolatry, proximity and infinite distance. I love the peaceful pas-
> sion, the distracted love that my *talith* inspires in me, I get the impression
> that it accords to me this distraction because it is sure, so sure of me, so
> little disquieted by my infidelities. . . . I love it and bless it with a strange
> indifference, my *talith*, with a familiarity that is nameless and ageless. It is
> as if faith and knowledge, a different faith and a different knowledge, a
> knowledge without truth and without revelation, have woven themselves
> together. . . . My white *talith* belongs to the night, to absolute night. (79–
> 80)

Epilogue: Philosophy and Judaism

Derrida commences his *Marges de la philosophie* (1972b) with a quotation from Hegel about philosophy as an act of "throwing oneself into an abyss *à corps perdu*." The French idiom denotes "passionately" or "avidly," but Derrida is not the man to employ a metaphorical expression without taking full lingual responsibility. We shall say therefore that *à corps perdu* is, primarily, an expression that reduces him to victim (hurled into the chasm as scapegoat). It is the philosopher of the "circumcision" (see above, the chapter titled "Derrida's Yom *Coupure*") who elevates language, the word, while mutilating the body (the foreskin); at the onto-theological level, it is he who recognizes the truth of existence from its absence. The Yom Kippur experience of the scapegoat hurled into the chasm ("*à corps perdu*") is one of physical torment: fasting, accompanied by awareness of the body's deterioration and perdition (death): "Our days are as a passing shadow, and You, your years shall not end. . . . You know that our end is worm and maggot" (from the invocation terminating the Yom Kippur service). The dread of Isaac's sacrificial offering hangs over the Yom Kippur prayer, simultaneously the prayer of the exile whose city has been laid waste (see above, the chapter titled "Derrida as Sacrificial Offering"). There is the disregard for the body of the worshipper, who yearns for body (redemption of the Holy Land, construction of the city, the assurance of a long and good life) on the part of the transcendental, bodiless Other: God. From out of the darkness comes the prayer for light, from the mourning of ashes—for fire: "Your light shall bring dawn to the darkness. In great mercy shall you return to it" (from the Yom Kippur service).

Close to the beginning of *Marges de la philosophie*, the words "Philosophy has always insisted upon this: thinking its Other" (x) link philosophical creativity with the notion of Otherness, as variation on Hegelian *Aufhebung*, the intellectual uplifting as intelligence crosses its own borders—self-knowledge as knowledge of your Otherness and exceeding the boundaries of your concepts (though we should hasten to post a reservation: Hegelian

Aufhebung follows an upward path, but Derrida's movement of Otherness tumbles downward, toward the grave). What is the meaning of this philosophy's exceeding of self, this self-exile of the intellect (spirit), this wandering? Before ever giving expression to any echoes of "Jewish experience"[1] Derrida wrote of philosophy as pursuit of the nonphilosophical, the extraphilosophical, adding: "From philosophy—to separate oneself, in order to describe and decry its law, in the direction of the absolute exteriority of another place" (xiii). The principle of separation of self to another place, to the "absolute external"; do those words not define the Divinity, as we have come to know it throughout this book? Granted, the purpose of the divine self-exile (see above, the chapter titled "Countenance Averted") is to "describe and decry" the laws of the Divinity. With that, it is possible to span the gap between deconstruction and religious consciousness: man exits himself for his absolute and infinite Otherness (his God) as precondition for self-knowledge, but this knowledge also "decries," with harsh criticism, we might even say: destruction and collapse into nothingness. The plight of being condemned to rift, division, separation falls equally upon the Divinity, and on man's consciousness, which yearns incessantly for the lost unity (seeing the light, hearing the sound). This is a cosmic fate connected with the principle of the shattering of the Tablets. Gershom Scholem wrote:

> Thus is the experience of the Jewish Exile bound up with the crisis at the beginning of existence. . . . Exile is the most profound cosmic reality, that God Himself, at least from the viewpoint of the revelation of His essence, has been harmed hereby. . . . This Torah, sharply daring in its gnostic paradoxality, has introduced Exile into the Divinity itself. . . . The vessel spheres designated to contain the world delegated from the ancient Adam have been broken, and that breakage calls for repair. . . . The process of separation should go on, for there always remain residues of the forces of the harsh law in the system of spheres being constructed, and it is essential to exclude them and remove them, or change them by transforming them into forces of love and grace. [translated from the Hebrew][2]

Does Derrida's philosophy not follow the dual path of reparation and destruction? Does it not affirm the powers of division precisely as it adopts deconstruction, while yet simultaneously leaving an opening for "reparation" (construction) by means of concepts such as responsibility, friendship, love, and sacrifice? Does it not trace both of these paradoxical paths while tying the "double bind" of "*tout autre est tout autre*" (see above, the chapter titled "Derrida's Sacrificial Offering")?

Be that as it may, the way to the absolute Other is by way of the ear. Accordingly, the first chapter of *Marges de la philosophie* is entirely under the hallmark of the structure of the inner ear: the hammer bone, the eardrum (and their connection with the print drum). Philosophy in timpani, so as to hear with the eyes, Derrida quotes Nietzsche's *Zarathustra* (*Marges de la philosophie* [1972b], xii–xiii). Philosophy as utterance and hearing, with drum and hammer (likewise one of the bones of the inner ear) curving (like the curve of the eardrum, whose purpose is amplification of the vibrations) and the labyrinth (like the maze of canals of the inner ear) and forever in the margins—between inside and outside, or, to be precise, both inside and out. There we have the philosophical strategy. Substitution of ear for eye (a substitution resting upon a critique of vision as blindness, a recurrent motif in Derrida's writings, climaxing in *Mémoires d'aveugle* [1990e]) unwittingly echoes Jewish culture, which is mainly about hearing ("We will do, and we will hear," "*Shma Yisrael*" [Hear, O Israel]) while rejecting visual representation ("Thou shalt not make unto thee any graven image, or any likeness"). Substitution of the ear for the eye, as philosophical ground rule, could (obliquely) match up with something Martin Buber wrote in 1903:

> The fact of the absence of pictorial art in early Judaism can be explained by the traits of its race. . . . The Jews of antiquity were men of ear rather than men of eye, and more men of time than persons with a sense of space. The sense of hearing contributes more to creating a Jew's world picture than any other sense. Ancient Jewish writings stand out particularly in their acoustic character . . . leading to the inability of the Jew of antiquity to create visual art. In the place where the tangibility of the objects is not predominant, and where there is no sacrifice for the sake of existence, there will probably spring up a purely subjective art, an art of emotional expression unaccompanied by pictures, that is, poetry. . . . The Jew of the Exile . . . who is on the move to which he is often drawn against his will . . . picks up impressions that seem to dissipate on reaching the threshold of his awareness. . . . The unique money economy to which he is shackled does not permit him to leave his life resting upon relativity, to a life where real objects exist. . . . Man's body becomes contemptible. Beauty is an unfamiliar value. Seeing is sin. Art is sin.[3]

No, Derrida would be the first to reject this depiction of the Jew banished from the worlds of art and beauty. This Buberian-Wagnerian fantasy (whose "cure" Buber himself registered in his preoccupation with Zionist art) was unlikely to be acceptable to Derrida, who was curator of the exhibition "Mémoires d'aveugle" held at the Louvre in 1990, as well as collaborating with artists (*Lignées* [1996d]) and architects ("Music Centre," La Villette, Paris, 1986). All the same, the philosophy of the ear as Jewish philosophy. What of the eyes then? Derrida would compromise on blinking (see the appendix, "The Black Academy").

Philosophy, according to Derrida (doubly so—his own philosophy), is oblique thinking twisting through mazes and forever in the margins, so it seems, in relation to Judaism. Derrida comes to, and from, Judaism (Judaism? A different Judaism, we would suggest, a Judaism from without) by the tunnels of the labyrinth, of the pits and pyramids, the numerous, dark onto-theological catacombs, and forever on the margins of Judaism: both inside and out. From his point of view, his is a non-Jewish, universal philosophy. To us, it is a universal philosophy that is also a different Jewish philosophy, the fire of its Judaism having turned to ashes and mourning, but it is entirely afire. But between the universality of the philosophy and the relatively constricted national sense of the term "philosophy on the subject of Judaism," there could exist a tension of opposites, of which Derrida is not oblivious.

In his 1992 essay, "The Onto-theology of National Humanism," Derrida posed the question of nationalism as against the question of philosophy. To him, nationalism is not merely one more topic resembling all other subjects of philosophical discussion, because it sets philosophy a challenge that could contain a "prospect" (an examination of the concept of nationalism) just as it could constitute a "scandal" (offering a stage to narrow, imperialist, nationalism). In his view, nationalism is not a fortuitous value, neither is it extraneous to philosophy. On the contrary, it is an essential value to philosophy. Perforce philosophy even has its particular "local dialect," even if it is bound, by its very nature, to attempt to overcome it. Philosophy is thus condemned to tension between nationalism and universality. Philosophy's universal aspirations seek to transcend the particular (certainly its chauvinist version). This opens up the rift between legitimate philosophical nationalism and nonlegitimate philosophical chauvinism.

True, chauvinism, too, is philosophical: according to Derrida, nationalism never presents itself as particularism, rather as universal philosophical model, as philosophical *telos*. Therefore, it is always philosophical in essence, even in its most corrupt manifestations ("Onto-Theology of National Humanism," *Oxford Literary Review* 14, no. 1–2 (1992): 11). As to legitimate national philosophical discourse, where preoccupation with "the Jew" is one of the revelations, it is characteristic—claims Derrida—that it should present a particular nation as representative of humanity as a whole. As such, national philosophical discourse establishes an "exemplary" philosophy—the paragon of the nation as model for the entire world. This takes us back to the paradox of "Chosen People"[4] which, it will be recalled, led Derrida to conclude that the more Jewish one is, the less Jewish one is.

And at this point, which closes a circle and opens up a paradox—we take our leave.

Appendix

Notes

Selected Works by Jacques Derrida

Index

APPENDIX

The Black Academy

In April 1983, Jacques Derrida gave a lecture at Cornell University in Ithaca, New York, entitled, "The Principle of Intelligence and the Idea of the University," later published in *Du droit à la philosophie* ([1990a], 461–98). The lecture seemed to grow out of the question: "*L'université en vue de quoi?*" (The university in view of what?). Once again we encounter presence, appearance, aspect. Indeed, as Derrida reminds us in all his writings, right from the outset, Western metaphysics has connected knowing, and presencing of the truth, with seeing. Ever since the rise of the Platonic sun, and the identification of light with idea, the West has relentlessly trudged the well-lit avenues that reached their summit with the *Aufklärung, Lumières*—the Enlightenment, that jubilant eighteenth-century emergence from darkness into light that was channeled into language with expressions like: "*Ich sehe*" ("I see") to signify "I got it." Hebrew likewise, with terms like *hashkafa* (outlook), *histaklut* (observation), *he'ara* (elucidation), and so on, has drawn a connection between contemplation and rationality; aligning outlook as sensual glance with outlook as spiritual viewpoint, characterizing the wise man as *bar-orian* (enlightened, i.e., man of light), and adopting elucidation as supreme knowledge, and observation as pure regard, inward and spiritual.

Let us emulate Derrida and open Aristotle's *Metaphysics* (bk. 1, chap. 1) to read: "All men by nature desire to know. An indication of this is the delight we take in our senses; for even apart from their usefulness, they are loved for themselves, and above all others the sense of sight. For not only with a view to action but even when we are not going to do anything, we prefer seeing to everything else."[1]

To Aristotle's mind, the eyes, the regard, are the proof of pleasure from sheer knowledge, and confirmation of the substantive connection between knowing and observation. We should stress: what is self-evident in an art academy, which by very nature trains to observation and the values of the regard, is extended by the foregoing argument to the foundations of all academy, any university. However, at the end of the twentieth century, it is not the connection between sun and truth that fascinates us; on the contrary, it is the eclipse concealing the flame, darkness. In the

"The Black Academy" is the title of a lecture delivered at a colloquium on the subject of "the academy," at the Bezalel Academy of Art and Design, Jerusalem, March 1997.

167

declining days of this century, at this hour of dusk, and against the setting sun, a new concept of academy "dawns." This new concept resorts to the argument that observation is inadequate for learning. Acquiring knowledge also calls for closing eyes and opening ears, or in Derrida's terms: "Laughingly, I would say that one must know how to shut the eyes so as to listen better" (*Du droit à la philosophie* [1990a], 464).

Derrida remembers well Aristotle's words about the animals: "[T]hose which are incapable of hearing sounds are intelligent though they cannot be taught, e.g., the bee and any other race of animals that may be like it; and those which besides memory have this sense of hearing can be taught."[2] In other words, the bee sees and therefore knows. But the bee cannot learn because it does not hear. Derrida reiterates: "Opening the eye to know, shutting the eye, or at least listening so as to be able to learn, and learn to know, there we have the primary outline of the rational creature" (466).

In other words, we cannot speak solely of the light of intellect, but also must speak of the voice of intellect. In other words, we must blend "We shall do and we shall hear" into "The Lord make his face shine upon thee" (Num. 6:25) so as to achieve "And all the people saw the thunderings" (Exod. 20:18). Another concealed aspect of intelligence would have to wait hundreds of years for its rescue from the darkness of oblivion, for intelligence, *logos*, is "speech" in Greek, and the voice of the intellect is the divine voice. In time, Martin Heidegger, in his *Principle of Reason* (1956) saw (saw? we should rather say: interpreted) intelligence as demand in speech, *Anspruch*, demand or command. In other words, the principle of intelligence is as commanding speech. For our purposes, the principle of intelligence is a principle, not of sight, but rather, of listening. We must obey the intelligence principle as one obeys a voice. Derrida attached great importance to this essay of Heidegger's, recruiting it to his vision of the new academy (here, too, the word "vision" betrays the message; for vision, like apparition, has to do with sight, i.e., it connects truth with seeing). Is the academy then required to block the regard? Heaven forbid! Derrida is still a man of the "En-lightenment," and knowledge remains lucidity. But the concept of the Platonic sun is banished from his thought in favor of a different understanding of the great ball of fire, which is indebted (without his acknowledgment, we should remember) to pre-Socratic fire notions, that is, to the Heraclitean fire, that destroys itself by burning itself out, burning and dying out at the same time, the sun sinking even as it rises, the night within day.

With the reader's indulgence, I will revert to a short passage from my chapter on "Fire":

> How is the fire to be doused? How is the destructive fire of holocaust to be contained? How is the sun of *brûle tout* to realize its decline and fall? How is it to bring forth from within itself the fire, the dynamics of the worst of all, any stable body, a monument to preserve the traces of death? [Derrida] cast around after the body to preserve both living and extinguished fire . . . the *brûle tout* is required to fulfill its contradictions: to be preserved in the movement of its self-destruction, to appear in its disap-

pearance. For that is the secret of fire: survival within its own perdition. This internal contradiction is the source of the movement of time—from sunrise to sunset. Sunrise enfolds sunset, east enfolds west—the movement of history. . . . [I]n other words: if you wish to burn everything, you must burn the conflagration, to prevent its continued existence as presence. It is vital to extinguish the fire, to preserve it for the sake of its annulment, or its annulment for the sake of its preservation. They are mutually dependent. The movement of history, the sun's progress from east to west, the dialectic . . .

A black sun, to adopt the metaphor of Derrida and Julia Kristeva. Again with the reader's indulgence, we shall open with Aristotle's "On the Soul" (bk. 2, chap. 9): "[Man's eyes have a certain superiority] over those of hard-eyed animals. Man's eyes have in the eyelids a kind of shelter or envelope, which must be drawn back in order that we may see, whereas hard-eyed animals have nothing of the kind, but at once see whatever presents itself in the transparent medium."[3]

In other words, the distinction is between blinking animals (those that close their eyes to achieve the inner darkness of thought, Derrida would say) and non-blinking animals (that see, do nothing but see, see constantly). Man is a blinking animal, and therefore learns. Man is a seeing animal but one that also closes its eyes to hearken to the voice of the intellect.

Here is a question: Do people blink in Bezalel? Does the art academy also offer lessons in closing the eyes? Do people learn to listen at Bezalel? Asking such questions on Mount Scopus ("the mount of the observers"), in the area engulfed by the Hebrew University, means not overlooking what university is: *università, université*—the place of the universe. Okay, let's assume that that is indeed what a university is. But what is the most basic root in Latin etymology of the word "university"—denoting the temple of learning that grew in the Middle Ages and flourished during the Enlightenment? Well: *unus* is "one," *versus* is "against"/"opposite"/"vis à vis"; in other words, unification of the stance taken up against the world, or the one facing the world. According to Heidegger, the principle of reason (upon which the university was founded right from the outset) is linked with the notion of the essence of being as an object present, present before (*versus*) a subject. Object, too, means "ob-ject"—being before the ego. Knowing is the transition from "*présence*" to "*représence*"—re-presentation of the object (in the consciousness). An object present is a visible object. The man of representation, the man of the ob-ject, is one who does not blink, argues Heidegger (according to Derrida): his eyes are incessantly open upon the world, for the purpose of dominating it. Knowledge means mastery, for knowledge means archival representation resting upon man's stance against, in the pose of master. According to Heidegger, this stance is the source of man's antiecological exploitation of nature and the world (*Du droit à la philosophie* [1990a], 485). And this, we would say, is *unus-versus,* the individual against the world, in other words: the university.

Hence, too, comes the architectural and panopticonal perception of universities as observers from above and beyond. At his Cornell lecture, Derrida delved into the archives to elicit the intentions of Ezra Cornell, founder of the Ithaca campus, to build it on a hill overlooking the town. But to Derrida's reading, "overlooking" in both senses enfolds a dark seed, pinpointed by the following quotation from the archives:

> for Ezra Cornell the association of the view with the university had something to do with death. Indeed, Cornell's plan seems to have been shaped by the thematics of the Romantic sublime, which practically guaranteed that a cultivated man on the presence of certain landscapes would find his thoughts drifting metonymically through a series of topics—solitude, ambition, melancholy, death. (468)

The university (we would add: the academy) here is as observer above and beyond ensuring the regard, the representative stance, the ob-ject, and it fulfills death and resurrection in the experience of the sublime: the collapse of consciousness vis à vis infinite Nature (of peaks, canyons, wilderness, tempest, etc.) and the rebirth of the infinite idea in man.

Before plunging into the innards of this perception, let us recall the tireless efforts of Bezalel's founder, Boris Schatz, to locate the academy opposite *the Temple*, or as he put it: "the place of the Temple." Numerous letters to David Wolfsohn (President of the World Zionist Organization, residing in Cologne) in 1907, sought to ensure that the art academy would overlook "the site of the Temple" (now, the rock of the Rockefeller Museum) as fulfillment of the spiritual and messianic regard—the regard of redemption out of desolation—of the teachers and students of Bezalel. And how can we avoid recalling the unblinking panopticonal regard that Bezalel now projects from Mount Scopus, the regard at the "sublime" of the occupied territories and villages and the desert? It has the blend of height and abyss.

"Abyss" is a decisive Derridean term, which we will not expand upon again just now. We shall settle for the affirmation that Derrida was taken with the dimension of death in the university's regard to the "sublime," and yet again, he sought to complement the regard-sight-light-knowledge with the deadly darkness of sightlessness. For the purpose of this abyss of the shadow of death, Derrida again calls upon Heidegger's "principle of reason" (the 1955–56 lectures). The German philosopher argues that the principle of reason reveals nothing as to the substance of reason itself. Accordingly, the principle of reason is incapable of elucidating itself. Within the principle of intelligence there is thus an abyss (*Abgrund*). To enlighten those who stand perplexed over this knotty but nevertheless pivotal point of Heidegger's philosophy (a point that is most decisive for Derrida) we should draw upon George Steiner's interpretation: The presence of the present (that which is present before us) is rendered possible by means of enlightenment, of "being enlightened"; but the light itself remains concealed. In itself it is neither "is" nor "idea" nor "energy." Being is not revealed outside that wherein it resides and that which it illuminates. In Steiner's view, that is the main paradox and source-spring of Heidegger's thought; from 1929 onward, Heidegger stressed increasingly that the concealment of being must entail the reality of "nothingness." Being is, in the final resort, merely an appearance, a revelation out of nothingness (*Nicht*).[4]

The university, the temple of the knowledge principle, is built and hangs over an abyss (*abîme*), an empty black hole (*Du droit à la philosophie* [1990a], 473), as is also affirmed by the testimony of Charles Pierce, the American philosopher of language, who wrote in 1900: "experience of life has taught me that the only thing that is really desirable *without a reason for being so, is to render ideas and things reasonable*. One cannot well demand a reason for reasonableness itself" (quoted at 474).

Derrida's conclusion is clear; and as ever in his philosophy, it is a contradiction in terms. The academic imperative is the imperative of a dual metaphorical vista of heights and abyss, observation and blindness, light and dark, on the one hand, imparting knowledge, information, and professionalism (the principle of lucidity, representation of the world, the ob-ject); on the other hand, groping through the dark and forbidden passages, of the rejected, the unknown, and the nonprofessional. The imperative is light that turns upon itself and is therefore extinguished, and the academy that sets upon itself.

Furthermore, Derrida's philosophy connects the duality of heights and abyss to link academy with art. For if we study his *Marges de la philosophie* (1972b) we will find his signs theory resting upon movement from the dark pit to the pyramid. Derrida's post-Hegelian interpretation of the concepts of "imagination" and "sign" commences in the dark pits of the fantasy (the storage where consciousness preserves the images, before hauling them out for the purpose of their intellectual elevation— *Aufhebung*) to end up at the pyramid, which is the sign (*Margins of Philosophy* [Chicago: Univ. of Chicago Press, 1982], 76). This is the movement from darkness into light, from within to the outside, from sensual image to intellectual concept, from intuition to intellect, the movement of the sign as the movement of art. We shall note that the dual movement between the dark pit and the pyramid retains the hue of the grave (82); this shows that even the heights (academic heights included) guard a secret, the secret of the dead.

The duality of the metaphorical vista of the academy—the high view and the fall into the abyss—is, of course, also the duality of high and low; a hierarchy. Academy and university merely affirm the tradition of the Platonic sun; they set the thinking head at the apex of the academic ladder, while at the bottom of the academic hierarchy is the working hand. Head and hand, philosophy and art. From Plato to Kant, and even later, the study of philosophy has been set at the head of the metaphysical ladder. Derrida reminds us that Aristotle's *Metaphysics* (981b and further) distinguishes the manager—the man of the head, the man of theoretical knowledge, knowledge of reasons and primal principle (the *arche*)—from the man situated below him, the worker, the practical man, the manual laborer, the man of the hand, who does not use knowledge and awareness in his creativity, who instead is employed-activated-operated. It should be recalled in this context that even a philosopher like

Heidegger was still required to "purge" the hand when he singled out the human hand as maker of signs ("writes"). In other words, he transformed the hand into head, eye, brain.

Denial of the distinction between pure knowledge and practical knowledge, of which Derrida speaks, will probably not surprise an audience like the Bezalelians present here, long accustomed to the pairing of practical instruction with theoretical studies (although Israel, like all other Western countries, is particular to draw a distinction between university and academy: arts are studied at an academy—of dance, music, art—whereas pure knowledge is acquired at university). We shall accordingly skip Derrida's arguments proving that the distinction between applied and pure research is artificial, false, and ineffective. Instead, we shall consider the sought-after duality of *archon* and *an-archon:* the *archon* (Greek: "ruler") is guided by the Heideggerian principle of reason and the quest for primal principles. The *archon* is also architect and archivist: the man of knowledge and systematic theoretical representation. By contrast, the *an-archon,* or the man of anarchy, is the one who opposes the ruler's way, the possibility of returning to basics, to primal grounds: the *an-archon* rebels against the ruler, raising the banner of deconstruction, querying the revelation of the secret reasons; he is also the man of the abyss, blindness, and listening, even if the voice is unheard, for God appears in silence.

No, let us make no mistake: we have not reverted to Camus's "rebel." We have returned to the man who blinks, to the duality of regard and blindness, light and dark; two that are one: "[I]n the blink of an eye, I would go further: 'in the twilight of an eye, for the murkiest of situations . . . increase the chances of this twinkling' of thought" (*Du droit à la philosophie* [1990a], 497). We are therefore speaking of an academy that fulfills itself in the tension between the states of tranquillity and of crisis, between awakening of the intellect and knowledge, and the admission of the nocturnal blackness of the unknown.

In these contexts, we must refer—however fleetingly—to Heidegger's lightning. In his two works on pre-Socratic Greek philosophy, Heidegger dwelled on the lightning image in the fragments of Heraclitus. Lightning is the fiery light that flashes from the night, Zeus's light illuminating existence. This is the light that resorts to darkness, to the tempest and the dread of the thunderbolt. Knowledge and awareness are entirely unlike the daylight of the Platonic sun, which at most dazzles whosoever looks directly at it for any length of time. Heidegger, dissatisfied with modernism and modern man, denounced them as "lightning conductors" which, in their great fear, have lost the flavor and depth of the authentic knowledge that comes from the tempest and the night.

Derrida's "black academy" takes us back to the fire and the lightning. Equally, it takes us back to father and son (i.e., to the relationship of castration of the son and patricide) of the annals of academy, to Athens of the fourth century B.C. It takes us back to two woods: the wood of Academus and the wood of Apollo Lyceus. The former has bequeathed us Plato's "academy", the latter—Aristotle's "lyceum," the first two academies in history. I would like to conclude with a personal study of the two copses and the two academies, while seeking the way to the third wood.

When Plato founded his "academy" in 387 B.C., he elected to locate it in a certain wood close to his home, where he was in the habit of going to meditate: the Academus wood, an amusement park on the outskirts of Ceramikus, a suburb one mile northwest of Athens, dedicated to the memory of Academus, Attica's hero of antiquity. Hundreds of years previously, when the Dioscuri invaded Attica to rescue their sister Helena who had been kidnapped by Zeus, it was Academus who discovered her place of concealment, in that wood. In time, the Lacedaemonians, who honored the memory of the Dioscuri, took care to spare the wood during their forays into Attica. A wall was built around the wood, paths of bushes wound their way through it, and splendid fountains were installed. It was the perfect place for contemplation, thinking, or meeting. No wonder, then, that this was where Plato elected to locate his academy, which perpetuates Academus's heroic name. It is equally not to be wondered that Plato stayed there to teach for the remaining forty years of his life; it was here that he developed the dialogues expounding his idealist philosophy to his pupils (including one answering to the name "Aristotle," who attended the classes for nineteen years!).

Aristotle's copse is entirely different. After three years of voluntary exile in Assos in Asia Minor, a few years more of research into marine biology far from Athens, and a further three years of intensive tutoring of the boy who was to grow up to be Alexander the Great—Aristotle founded his academy northeast of Athens, in a garden still retaining its original paths, close to the temple of Apollo Lyceus. It was 335 B.C., thirteen years after the death of his mentor, Plato, and thirteen years after his own bitter disappointment at failing to be appointed to head Plato's academy. Aristotle taught at the "Lyceum" for twelve years; here he founded the first library in Greece (and the Western world) resting upon a collection of manuscripts, maps, and a nature museum—all the fruit of his empirical research. He was in the habit of strolling among the trees and columns in the morning hours, voicing his thoughts out loud to his entourage. On the death of his pupil and patron, Alexander of Macedon, and in consequence of the growing Athenian mistrust and hostility toward the Macedonians and their supporters, Aristotle was again forced into exile from Athens, up to the time of his death.

We commenced with the American Ithaca of Cornell University, and we conclude with the Greek Ithaca of Plato and Aristotle: two academies, two woods; one to the west of Athens, the other to the east. The first bore the hallmark of the hiding place of beauty (Helena) discovered by the hero, that is, the dark place of concealment. The second was in the garden of Apollo Lyceus, the sun god, source of light. The first academy was that of the teacher, the father; the second—that of the pupil, the rejected son, the exile who returns to rebel against his father (Plato's name is mentioned very sparingly in Aristotle's numerous writings). From copse A to copse B; from academy A to academy B; from the gloom of concealment to emergence into the light—this is the historic movement of the spirit where speech (Platonic dialogue, featuring Socrates, who never wrote a word) is replaced by writing (Aristotle's library), mystic ideas are transformed into the empiricism of matter and senses, a mathematical ideal is converted into an ideal of physics. For we have not forgotten the inscription on the gate of the Platonic academy: "No entry to the nongeometrican!"); by contrast, the study of medicine at the academy of the doctor's son, Aristotle, was central. And of course, we have not forgotten the hostility: for example, the libel apparently originating at the Lyceum, denouncing Plato's *Timaeus* and portions of his *Republic* as plagiaries from the Pythagoreans.

Between the Academus wood and the wood of Lyceus, the truth of the academy came into the world, the truth of castrating father and patricide son. The answer to the question of the academy is to be found neither in the copse of the father nor in that of the son; rather, in the tension between the two and in a third copse that will spring up from the Oedipal tension. The story of Plato and Aristotle teaches that perfection of the academy requires leaving its domain, for voluntary or forced exile; in returning to oppose it; in the progression from the *arche* to an-archism, the eternal movement from light to darkness and from darkness to light; the movement of fire.

Fire of the spirit, the *Geist*. Beware of this fire, it burns everything, *brûle-tout*, *holos-caustos*, this holocaust-like fire is liable to bring on a holocaust. We have not forgotten Heidegger's rector's address of 1933, the year Hitler took office and Heidegger was appointed rector of Freiburg University. In his commencement speech (that Derrida analyzed, it will be recalled, in *De l'esprit, Heidegger, et la question* [1987a]) he referred to the university as leader of the torch of the German spirit. He spoke of the *Geist* as flame; and the *Selbstbehauptung* (self-affirmation) of the German university as a trait of the spirit. The fire-spirit was sustained by a spiritual imperative: the imperative of leadership, the imperative of mission, the leadership undertaken by the leader, the rector, over his staff of teachers, his students, the German people. To Heidegger, the movement of the spirit fulfilling itself at the university (or academy) is an authenticating movement whose purpose is to grant the German people "its true historic character," as he put it. For the fire-spirit is German to its roots.

Heidegger's fire-spirit is accompanied by an excess of ashes and crematoria. Accordingly, in relating to his words about the nation's spiritual world, about the reason's penetration of the essence of being as the penetration of "the forces of soil and blood," Derrida writes: "One could say that he spiritualized National Socialism" (*De l'esprit, Heidegger, et la question* [1987a], 52). We should beware of spirit that is transformed into fire, even if we incessantly seek the spirit as fiery lightning at nighttime. Differentiation between the two is difficult, the borderlines are perilous, but they may convey the flavor of the spirit. Let us also beware of the equation spirit-nation-academy ("national," "Hebrew"). Unless we understand and internalize the fire in Derrida's terms (approximating to those of the later Heidegger of the Heraclitus seminar, 1966–67, where he depicted fire as comprising self-revelation and concealment): the fire of light and darkness, the flame and its extinguishing, the darkness within the light.

Let us return to the woods: national forests tend to burn (not merely in the prophecy of A. B. Yehoshua's story "Facing the Forests" and its fulfillment in the forests near Jerusalem in 1995–96, and all over Israel in 1998). They burn of themselves. For if we revert, however briefly, to another copse, in David Shim'oni's idyllic poem "Hedera Forest," dating from the days of the Second Aliya [the Zionist wave of immigration to Palestine, 1904–14], what do we encounter? We discover Rabbi Pinhas and the group of pioneers felling—felling!—the eucalyptus trees of the Hedera Forest "in joy, in the joy of strength and labor. Wood chips turned white in the air, axes gleamed at their work and the saws shrieked with joy . . . and long life to every young man who has an arm to raise and lower the ax! And long life to unsullied Galilee and its hills, long life to proud Judea . . ."[5] You heard: ecological sin at the very root of mythical national revelry, destruction at the heart of the construction project.

We will thus locate our academy neither in the "Hedera Forest," nor in the "Euculyptus Wood" [Title of a popular Israeli song relating to bygone generations of pioneers. Trans.]. The third wood belongs elsewhere. True to the nocturnal fire, but careful of its torches, we may return to the sacred wood on the banks of the Lake of Nemi ("Diana's mirror" as the ancients called it). Here is the wood, here the temple of Diana, goddess of the forest. Here, as we learn from James George Frazer's *Golden Bough* (1890), is the root of all myth and all culture. Here, into the heart of this wood, creeps the murderer at the dead of night, avid to kill the priest of Diana's temple and succeed him, so as to become the priest, the "king of the wood." Here, in the wood, grows the Golden Bough tree. None but fugitive slaves are permitted to break off one of its branches, and, having broken it, to fight the priest; if the slave kills him, the slave becomes "king of the wood," and the dead man is a sacrificial offering to Diana. Is this the third copse—the copse of the slave rising up against the king, son against father, pupil against teacher, academy against academy, in other words: against itself? Equally, does the copse's challenge lie in its penetration from without, the penetration of the "Other"? Is this the Jewish sage Elisha ben Avoya, nicknamed "the Other," who glanced into the *pardess* (trees again!) of mystical wisdom and was injured thereby?

The third academy. If you so wish it, Plato himself dropped a hint about it, even before his own "academy" adopted wine-drinking banquets. I refer to the commencement and conclusion of the amazing dialogue *Lysis,* devoted in entirety to the unresolved question of friendship. Here we find Socrates strolling between the academy and Lukeion—which was the Lyceum (in fact, many years would pass before the Lukeion became Aristotle's academy; all the same, the location is familiar as Socrates' favorite spot for meditation. See the conclusion of *The Symposium*): "I was walking straight from the Academy to the Lyceum, by the road which skirts the outside of the walls." And then, close to the small gate in the wall, Socrates runs into a group of young men who ask him as to his destination. "'From the Academy,' I replied, 'and I am going straight to the Lyceum.'" (*Plato: The Collected Dialogues* eds. Edith Hamilton and Huntingdon Cairns [Princeton: Princeton Univ. Press, 1961], 146). The young men invite Socrates, "Won't you turn in? It will be worth your while," and point to the *palaestra,* a building set aside for training in wrestling, although "we are passing our time principally in conversation." This, then, is another "academy," where sturdy young men mix wrestling with philosophical discussion. Socrates does indeed turn to the *palaestra*, where he engages the young men in a long conversation on the essence of friendship. It is significant that the discussion—the whole of the *Lysis* dialogue—is not just a brilliant exercise in deconstruction, consisting as it does of building arguments that demolish themselves one after another, until the final admission of an absence of any answer as to the question of friendship, but also in the termination of the dialogue through the entry into the hall of the drunken pedagogues. It was the feast of Hermes that day, and the inebriated teachers driving the pupils and the old man away from their discussion in the hall endow this "third academy" with a unique character: it is a different academy, an academy of "wrestling," an academy without solutions.

I wish to conclude. Shall I entrance you with the magic pipe of Pan, or the magic flute of Mozart, according to the libretto of Immanuel Schikaneder? Hearken to Tamino, arriving at the temple of Wisdom, between the temple of Reason and the temple of Nature (i.e., Tamino reaches academy):

> TAMINO: Where am I now? What will happen to me?
> Is this the domain of the Gods?
> These portals, these columns prove
> That skill, industry, art reside here;
> Where action rules and idleness is banished
> Vice cannot easily gain control.
> I will boldly pass through that portal;
> Its design is noble, straightforward, pure . . .
> CHORUS OF PRIESTS: O Isis and Osiris, what bliss!
> Dark night retreats from the rays of sun.
> Soon the noble youth will feel a new life,
> Soon he will be wholly dedicated to our order.
> His spirit is bold, his heart is pure,
> Soon he will be worthy of us.[6]

Two hundred years after Mozart's hymn to Enlightenment, while we continue to lick the unhealed wounds of the Holocaust, while we continue to be plagued by walls and curtains that separate and divide even after they have been smashed to dust, it is evident to us that any Giving of the Law (of Moses) is also the right to shatter the Tablets; that revelation is simultaneously blindness (St. Peter); that it is the nature of truth to conceal itself behind the fissure separating it from us. No academy will show, or prove, or set before us, the utter truth. And when we listen, the divine voice speaks from the flames: if you are not burned—you will never know.

Notes

Pre-face

1. Apart from texts mentioned in this work, see Martin Jay, *Downcast Eyes* (Berkeley and Los Angeles: Univ. of California Press, 1993), 499 n. 18, listing additional sources dealing with Derrida's Jewish aspect.

2. Robert Smith, *Derrida and Autobiography* (Cambridge: Cambridge Univ. Press, 1995), 42.

3. Ibid., 43.

4. Gideon Ofrat, *Three Darknesses* (Jerusalem: Ha-Academia, 1997).

5. *Bamidbar Raba,* Parasha 4, sec. 20, 5.

6. Judah David Eisenstein, *Otzar Midrashim* (1915), 104.

7. Martin Buber, *Pnei-adam* (Human face) (Jerusalem: Mosad Bialik, 1962), 319–320.

1. The Last Jew

1. Elisabeth Weber, *Questions au judaïsme* (Paris: Desclee de Brouwer, 1996), 78.

2. Weber, *Questions au judaïsme,* 87.

3. The conversation took place in Paris, 17 May 1996.

4. Geoffrey Bennington, *Jacques Derrida* (Paris: 1991), 303.

5. Weber, *Questions au judaïsme,* 79.

6. On this point we agree entirely with the observation of Geoffrey Bennington. See Bennington, *Jacques Derrida,* 300.

7. Consider his marriage in 1956 to Marguerite Aucouturier, a non-Jew; or his refusal to circumcise his sons, Pierre and Jean.

8. Weber, *Questions au judaïsme,* 77.

9. Weber, *Questions au judaïsme,* 103.

10. For Susan A. Handelman (*The Slayers of Moses* [Albany: State Univ. of New York Press, 1982]), Derrida's thought is a Jewish heresy, a slaying of Moses by displacing origin and dispossessing the father (174). According to Handelman, Derrida is a prodigal son, but unrepentant, enjoying his escapade (175). In a chapter titled "Reb Derrida's Scripture," Handelman is prepared to admit that "he is more at home in Scripture than nature, as are the Rabbis" (176), but she argues that, at its bottom, Derrida's thought reflects a Christian conception more than a Jewish one, once it adopted the duality of speech/writing with the former's precedence over the latter. Whereas Paul, and later Christian thought, assumed the precedence of soul-writing and the Book of Nature, Judaism conceived writing as precedent to speech and

even to the world! (186). For Handelman, the Jewish Derrida is Reb Derrisa (no spelling mistake!), as he signed the end of his book *Writing and Difference*. Reb Derrisa is the laughing Derrida (*risée* is French for laughing or laughable).

11. Gershom Scholem, *Major Trends in Jewish Mysticism* (New York: Schocken, 1973).

12. Moshe Idel, "Infinities of Torah in Kabbalah," in *Midrash and Literature,* edited by G. H. Hartman and S. Budick, (New Haven: Yale Univ. Press, 1986), 149. According to Harold Bloom (*A Map of Misreading* [New York: Oxford Univ. Press, 1975]) Derrida performs Rabbinic revisions of Western philosophy: "Though he nowhere says so, it may be that Derrida is substituting *davhar* (thing; speech) for *logos,* thus correcting Plato by a Hebraic equating of the writing-act and the mark-of-articulation with the word itself. Much of Derrida is in the spirit of the great Kabbalistic interpreters of Torah, interpreters who create baroque mythologies out of those elements in Scripture that appear least homogeneous in the sacred text" (43).

Thus, according to Bloom, Derrida has more in common with Isaac Luria that it might appear: "One can believe in a magical theory of all language as the Kabbalists, many poets, and Walter Benjamin did, or else one must yield to the thoroughgoing linguistic nihilism, which in its most refined form is the mode now called deconstruction. But these two ways turn into one another at their outward limits. . . . Is there a difference between an absolute randomness of language and the Kabbalistic magical absolute, in which language is totally over-determined?" (Bloom, "The Breaking of Form," in Harold Bloom et al., *Deconstruction and Criticism* [New York: Seabury, 1979], 4).

2. The Mono-identity of the Other

1. Derrida extends the notion of Judaism as "injury" from the autobiographical to an onto-theological, hermeneutic level of cleavage between man and meaning (as absolute truth). The notion of Judaism as "injury" was expanded by Jean-Francois Lyotard in *Heidegger and the Jews* (Paris: 1988) to present the Jew as the "injury" of Western culture. The "injury" originates in the Jew's divided identity resting, all the way back to the days of Abraham, upon suffering and dissatisfaction: obeying the voice of a God unseen and utterly remote, Abraham sets out on a plunge into the unknown, that would be transformed into the "wilderness" destiny of a people. The Jewish people are condemned to an absence of any permanent relationship with land or history; being a nation that roams the desert, seizing upon a Covenant and a promise that are eternally incomprehensible and unattainable, in obedience to a concealed God whose justification is beyond the conscious grasp but who demands utter fidelity and is pitiless in his retribution. The Jewish people are a nation deprived of the visual, a people condemned to narration and attention, divorced from reality, "psychotic" in their refusal of compromise between pleasure principle and reality principle; a nation beset with feelings of guilt and indebtedness that have not found their psychic or cultural resolution (unlike the repressive solution of Christianity). Is it to be wondered that Jewish memory has always been associated with misery and dissatisfaction? Such a Jewish identity, argues Lyotard, is an open wound reminding Western culture of its repression, that is, the limits of its conscious control of reality. The presence of the "Jew" undermines the delicate psychic *modus vivendi* whereby the West beset itself with its repression. Persecution of the "Jew"—reaching its extreme in Nazism—sought to reduce that "wound" to utter oblivion. The West's eternal confrontation with the "Jew" denotes forgetfulness; his banishment is the dismissal of primordial dread, its transferal by means of objectivization, creating an image amenable to control, and therefore also to

annihilation. Anti-Semitism thus can be seen as aggressive defense mechanism against the Jewish "wound" or "malaise." The patient is Western culture, the sickness (wound)—the "Jew." We should stress again that Derrida sees Judaism primarily as the "wound" (infirmity) of the Jew; it is not by chance that he focuses upon the circumcision scar as open wound that will never heal.

3. Shibboleth of Evil

1. I do not know whether Derrida is aware of the midrash depicting the appearance of Elijah in a brothel, going so far as to depict him in the form of a prostitute! See *The Book of the Prophet Elijah,* ed. Yehuda Yudel, son of Rabbi Yisrael Yitzchak, (Piotrkow, 1911), 25. I am grateful to Dr. Elhanan Reiner for drawing my attention thereto.

2. Into the etymological foundation of the "archive" concept, Derrida injects the *arkhon* (ruler) and *arkhe* (primordial).

3. Hamlet, Freud, Oedipal father-son relations, and Jewish identity were discussed by Jean Francois Lyotard in his notable essay "Jewish Oedipus", 1970. On Hamlet conversing with his father's ghost, see Derrida's *Spectres de Marx* (1993d).

4. See above, note 2.

5. Inter alia, *Schibboleth* considers Judaism (according to Paul Celan) as a form of "accepting the memory of a vocation you did not choose." Interpreting Celan's "Conversation on a Mountain," which represents the Jew as one who has nothing that truly belongs to him, Derrida concludes: "The Jew is also the Other, I and the Other" (90–91).

6. In his *De l'esprit, Heidegger, et la question* (Paris: Flammarion, 1987a) Derrida noted that Nazism "was not born in the wilderness"; rather, it grew mushroomlike "in the shade of the tall trees, under cover of their silence or indifference," trees joining in Europe into one great black forest (Paris: 1990, 139). Was Derrida enlarging the German "Schwartzwald" into the forests of Europe?

7. Published in the anthology *Phénoménologie et politique,* ed. Jacques Taminiaux (Paris: 1989).

8. In his various books and seminars, Derrida reverted repeatedly to German Jewish philosophers—Hermann Cohen, Franz Rosenzweig, Walter Benjamin, Gershom Scholem, Martin Buber, Hannah Arendt, Theodor Adorno. "Certainly I'm not only a Jew, but I am a Jew; and even though I am not German, I was brought up in a culture and philosophical tradition in which the German heritage is incontrovertible, and above all, in a century or half-century when that which happened to that [German-Jewish] coupling or by way of that coupling engaged, not only the world, but me too. . . . [I]t is a duty to try to comprehend how all that was possible, without resting content with images and conventional concepts current on the issue of the *Shoah* [Holocaust]" (*Questions au judaïsme,* ed. E. Weber [Paris: Desclée de Brouwer, 1996], 83). According to Derrida, the Jew and Germany "are fascinated with one another, attracted to one another, internalize one another; but simultaneously, the Jew remains utterly strange, infinitely strange, to Germany" (84). In discussing an essay by Walter Benjamin in his *Force de loi* (1994a) (where he confessed, "I have taken a great interest in what I have called the Judeo-German 'psyche'" [72]), Derrida went so far as to remark that the close affinity between German thought and Jewish thought—mainly in the era of the Weimar Republic—is liable to induce people to lay some of the blame for what happened in Germany on the Jews (*Questions au judaïsme,* 85).

4. L'autre *Kippa*

1. The principle of pluralism of heterogeneity also guides the cosmopolitanism Derrida himself professes in the title of his 1997 pamphlet *Cosmopolites de tous les pays, encore un effort*. The pamphlet's origin was an address Derrida delivered to the European Writers' Parliament (where he officiates as deputy speaker) on the topic of "cities of asylum." Being involved in the creation of cities of asylum for persecuted writers (twenty-four such refuges were established in Europe and the United States), Derrida analyzed the concept of *hospitalité* (hospitality), probably in relation to Europe's growing rejection of outsiders. He overtly expounded his notions in the light of Hannah Arendt's research (c. 1950) on the growing hostility of Western countries toward the homeless (refugees, D.P.'s), and of Lévinas's philosophy (see below, the chapter "Facing Lévinas"), and of Kant's appeal for "hospitality" (opening borders) in his *Eternal Peace* (1795). Derrida called for a reconsideration of the concept of "city," with the aim of its conversion into "city of asylum." He also called for reconsideration of the power of the police (to a considerable degree, in the light of W. Benjamin's study of the violence of the law, which Derrida had already considered in his *Force de loi* [1994a]). Toward the end of his address, Derrida attributed the ethical value of hospitality—which he depicted as the essence of all ethics—to biblical origins and Jewish tradition (43–44).

2. Jabès's concept of desert is connected with the wandering principle, which he translated into the overall cultural and spiritual essence of the Jewish people, as an existence that rejects territorialism or soil. The Jew is condemned to wander. We can find a distant echo of this principle in Derrida's concept of representation: in his article "Consignments: On Representation," (*Social Research* 49, no. 2 (summer 1982): 32) he defends the analogy between consignments that fail to reach their final destination and representation. The latter likewise condemns the subject or idea represented to "wandering" (analogous to the wanderings of the Jewish people), for the representers will never achieve the pure presence of the represented. The idea was developed further in *La carte postale* (1980).

3. Derrida's commentary on *The Right to Control* (1985), a photographic anthology by Marie-Francoise Plissart, referred, inter alia, to a photograph representing a girl smashing a framed photograph, which he perceived as an analogy of iconoclasm: momentarily, she resembles Moses grasping the Tablets of the Law—the law of the regard—holding them up over her head on display before flinging them to earth. But what the photograph exhibits is more or less indescribable in the normal processes of objective representation. Derrida was referring to extension of the interpretative domain from the visible to the invisible and the verbal. From this viewpoint, his words affirm the visual and verbal equally, an interim stage between Hellenism and Judaism.

4. We should point out the distinction between Derrida's attitude toward desert and wandering, and that of Lévinas: according to the latter, Judaism is committed to one place, the Holy Land. The Jewish desert does not condemn those who roam it to eternal wandering. Abraham planted the tamarisk tree (*eshel*) in the desert, the Jewish sages interpreting *eshel* as acronym for the Hebrew phrase "food, drink, sojourn," that is, home. To Derrida (and Jabès) desert denotes eternal wandering. And see Susan Handelman's *Fragments of Redemption* [Bloomington: Indiana Univ. Press, 1991] 296).

5. Derrida himself relates to Kant in "*La religion*" (18–19).

6. In July 1995, a convention was held at Luton University, England, under the title: "Applying: To Derrida." One of the lecturers dealt with application of Derrida's ideas in the domains of Judaism and Israel (Gary Banham, "The Terror of the Law: Judaism and International Institutions," in *Applying to Derrida*, ed. J. Brannigan, R. Robbins, and J. Wolfreys [London: St. Martin's Press, 1996], 96–106). Banham's point of departure was Jean-Francois

Lyotard's *Heidegger et 'les Juifs,'* and his apparently paradoxical arguments relating to society and memories of the Holocaust: In Lyotard's view, "the 'politics' of extermination cannot be represented on the political scene. It must be forgotten. The term fixed to the interminable must itself be forgotten, exterminated. For the nightmare would continue in the memory even of its end. . . . The forgotten is always there, for it has never been there in any other way than forgotten, and its forgetting forgotten" (Jean-Francois Lyotard, *Heidegger and 'the Jews'* [Minneapolis: Univ. of Minnesota Press, 1990], 29).

In view of the trend toward denial of the Holocaust, the question should be posed: What is the attitude of society and others residing within it? Is it feasible that an effort be made to constitute a social memory that will erase any substance whose content is society's relationship with the others? According to Banham, Lyotard drew from Derrida the notion that a concept repressed within a system itself possesses a capacity for organizing the system. Accordingly, any social inclination to relegate genocide to oblivion would merely testify to the presence of the annihilation principle in the functioning of the social system.

Already in *Glas* (1974), Derrida studies the relationship between state and Jews, in the context of his reading of Hegel's historical-religious writings in response to Moses Mendelssohn ("Jerusalem," 1783). According to Mendelssohn, Judaism is more fitting as "religion of law" than Christianity, being freed of the revelation principle (which he identifies as superstition) and accordingly more rational. Hegel believed otherwise: Judaism remains materialist and objective in its relationship with God, for it had yet to internalize the love principle. Christianity, being based on love, is more perfected ("higher") in its spirituality; accordingly, the Jews are slaves of the law (slaves of God) whereas Christianity fulfills the true law that unites man and God. Inter alia, it does so in the political system, with which the Jews cannot cope. Judaism is a religion of separation, of alienation between man and God, and among men; a religion of death. Derrida sums up Hegel's notions: The Jewish regime is a regime of death; it annihilates the existence of other national families, radiating its domination out of its own kernel of death, which is marked by subjugation to a transcendental God, jealous, exclusive, cruel and nonpresent (*Glas*, 1974).

Derrida's consideration of the relationship between social ideology and (an unrealizable) messianism (in *Spectres de Marx* [1993d]) is thus a response to the Hegelian divorce of Judaism from the wished-for social and political law. Unlike the Christian, who regards the state as incarnation of the relationship between God and man, Jewish thought presents the God-man relationship as existing in an utterly open domain whose hallmark is infinite expectation. However, like Hegel, Derrida understands this "messianism" as expectation of death, of the impossible advent of the *arrivant* or *spectre*. What is to be made of the state of Israel? In Banham's view, "Israel is founded upon messianic hope"—the hope of clothing the testimony of separation of God and man in political dress. This testimony also exists in Jewish secular life, derived from the Marxist effort to create a godless messianism. Zionist messianism claims divinity, but a divinity that is Jewish as distinct from human. In other words, the very idea of a Jewish state is a philosophical scandal, open to interpretation by Hegelians exclusively as a general politics of death. "The Jewish *polis* thus appears as response to the imperative of genocide, and will be required to ingest an expectation of death, that will testify to the total non-presence of God" (Banham,"Terror of the Law," 100).

In that case, the state is seen as messianic expression, as hope, but a hopeless hope, bearing within it the kernel of death. This is the supreme Jewish law, the law of laws. As such, it lays the foundation for the aforementioned analysis by J-P Lyotard, adopting the oblivion principle, the fire that burns itself out, "the holocaust of holocausts" (as expounded below in the chapter "Fire"): the law that bids memory to forget.

5. Derrida's "Yom Coupure"

1. For Derrida's discussion of Lacan's doctrine, see the chapter "The Postman of Truth" in *La carte postale* (1980). Here the reader encounters a broad analogy between the Derridean absence principle and the principle of the missing phallus in Lacan's doctrine. Nevertheless, when Elisabeth Weber (*Questions au judaisme* [Paris: Desclée de Brouwer, 1996]) proffers Lacan's psychoanalysis as a relevant category to elucidate the concept of "circumcision" in Derrida's own philosophy, Derrida declines a categorical commitment. He argues that if psychoanalysis is a metalingual discipline, the concept of "circumcision" eludes this category and any other system of knowledge (82). At this level, circumcision resists the logic of sign and castration (ibid.).

2. In *La carte postale* (1980), Derrida recalls Jewish rites in Algeria, where the mother chews a scrap of foreskin at the termination of the circumcision ceremony (237). Derrida may be confusing the mother with the *mohel*, for in various traditions, it is the latter who raises the foreskin to his mouth. As for the matter of the seventh day, we should note another possible inaccuracy of Derrida's: he read in Y. H. Yerushalmi's *Freud's Moses* that Freud's father gave his son a Bible inscribed: "On the seventh of the days of the years of your life" taking it to mean seven days (instead of seven years, the age when the child learns to read, and is therefore given the Bible), as Derrida specifies in his *Mal d'archive*. It should be noted further: Derrida knew that the correct translation was "seven years" but insisted on reading it as seven days in the circumcision context, both in *Mal d'archive* and in *Circonfession*. That is the advantage allegorical interpretation (*Drash*) holds over a simple reading (*Pshat*).

3. Hegel of course erred on this point. Isaac specifically commanded his son: "Thou shalt not take a wife of the daughters of Canaan" (Gen. 28:1).

6. Countenance Averted

1. In this context, we should recall the Rambam's perception of God's negative appellations, whereby God can be described exclusively by negation of his appellations: "Know that description of the Lord, may He be glorified and elevated, is the correct description. We have no way to describe Him but by negativism, nothing else" (*Guide to the Perplexed*, pt. 1, chap. 58). The limited range of the human intellect, along with the contradiction between the abstraction and simplicity of the God concept on the one hand, and the sensual impressions, on the other hand, lead Maimonedes to a negative theology, even if his Aristotlean rationality is far removed from the mystical path of the negative theologians with whom Derrida is preoccupied. After all, Maimonides upholds the possibility of speaking of divine truth, whereas the latter is utterly absent according to Derrida. Be that as it may, Derrida's indifference to Maimonides may offer additional evidence that Judaism constitutes a "black hole" in the philosophy of the French Jewish thinker. Needless to recall, the basic property of a "black hole" is the attraction it exercises upon various bodies.

2. Derrida's path to Heidegger runs by way of Plato, for he is well aware of the Platonic roots of negative theology (*Sauf le nom*, 88). Indeed, as far back as 1986, in his lecture-essay "How Not to Speak?" Derrida noted the early Platonic strata in negative theological thought. One such layer, originating in the dialogue on *The Republic*, deals with the notion of goodness dwelling beyond existence and substance: goodness like a spiritual sun above and beyond the visual sun. The second layer, arising out of *Timaeus*, deals with the concept of "*khôra*": the principle of the total inclusion that cannot be characterized and/or reconciled with any *logos*, or any form. The sole way of relating to *khôra* is by way of the lingual mold that endows it with existence. The God concept of negative theology amalgamates these two Platonic concepts.

Derrida expands upon these distinctions in *Sauf le nom*, pointing to the concept of hyperbole that functions in Plato's writings as the transcendental movement beyond the being, as the gateway to grasping the Heideggerian *logos*. Platonic openness toward the beyond exercised a fascination upon Heidegger, who defined *Dasein* in terms of openness and emergence from yourself toward the beyond-yourself. Accordingly, Heidegger defined negative theology as paradoxical hyperbole. A "Jewish" reading of the Heideggerian concept of "being" ("being" is the nameless) would stress the time dimension, perpetual motion of being (as perpetual Creation) and its attachment to the future tense (to be translated into the dimension of expectation).

3. When Derrida raised the issue of Jewish and Arab negative theology, he remarked in passing that he was risking the most autobiographical discussion he had ever undertaken. A little later (584) he had already resolved to avoid Jewish and Arab territory. An unsurprising decision on the part of a man who elects to define identity by means of Otherness.

4. The forbidden subconscious secret, to which there is no return, is just one side of the coin of the dual secret. For the therapist, the psychoanalyst, likewise keeps his distance and protects the "secret" from his patient. Now that the concepts are derived from the domain of Michel Foucault, Derrida discusses the physician's secret as the secret of authority: the doctor applying treatment is a mystic (once again, we encounter the *pharmakon,* Derrida's Platonic pharmacist). He preserves an esoteric secret (in Foucault's terms, the patient's subservience to the doctor is as though to a demon, or devil, or divinity [Résistances, 119]). The psychoanalyst, simultaneously absent (distant, declining to intervene) and present, remaining silent throughout the treatment, is the father, the ruler, God.

7. The Place of *Makom*

1. For Derrida's study of Lacan's interpretation of the aforementioned Poe story, see "The Postman of Truth," *Dissémination* [1972d]. See also below, the chapter on "The Scroll of Eros and Death."

2. On this subject, see the chapter "*Force et Signification*" in Derrida's *L'écriture et la différence* [1967b].

3. For my observations on the concept of place in the teachings of the Jewish sages, I am indebted to the lecture of Dr. Menaham Hirschman on this subject at the Alma Forum, a departmental seminar on the subject of "place," held at Alma College, Tel Aviv, in 1997.

4. These observations on the concept of the divine place in neo-Platonic thought are indebted to the lecture delivered by Dr. Yosef Schwartz at the Alma Forum (see note 3) on the concept of place in the philosophies of Maimonides and Eckhart.

5. I go into detail regarding the concept of home and its connection with Kafka's story "The Den" in the chapter "The Mole's Home" in my book *Shama* (Yonder) (in Hebrew) (Tel Aviv: 1998).

8. Tower of Babel

1. A different Babel makes an appearance, albeit fleetingly, in Derrida's *D'un ton apocalyptique adopté naguère en philosophie* (1984a). Here a study of (apocalyptic) vision brings Derrida to the vision of a single race, a single God, a single tongue. "The Babelic scene" he recalls. But this time, it is the Babel of the "Vision of John," and the topic is not diversity of language; rather it is the Great Whore, mother of all whores.

2. It is scarcely necessary to point out that we have already encountered a similar *motif* in discussing Derrida's circumcision trauma, which constitutes imposition of "a name" (incising the seal of identity into the skin) by father on son.

3. Geoffrey Bennington, *Jacques Derrida* (see *Circonfession* [1991a], 164.

4. In an article entitled "The Theology of Translation" (in *Du droit à la philosophie* [1990a], 371–93) Derrida delved into Schelling's perception of translation as the spirit's emergence from itself into itself. Schelling drew a distinction between sensual and intellectual intuition, with imagination (the domain of poetry and translation) spanning the gap. In his view, both rest upon the primary unity of truth. Translating the original unity into the duality of sensual intuition and intellectual intuition (the duality of the real and the ideal) requires a symbol (which is the imaginary reconstruction). Hence the importance of poetry (the sphere of imagination) to philosophy. As power spanning two worlds, imagination is the force behind translation. The pinnacle of the translation of the ideal one is the translation of absolute (divine) knowledge. Here, probably, is the cornerstone of Derrida's observations regarding "the theology of translation." In Derrida's terms, Schelling tells us that art is total translation, which guarantees the true objectivity of philosophy. Each and everyone offers a translation, an image, of absolute truth. That holds true whether it is a matter of knowing or action (when knowledge is translated into action). The concept of translation, applicable also to a process that is not necessarily lingual, rests upon a notion of Schelling's, following in the footsteps of Goethe, whereby nature is the author of a book that must be translated. Be that as it may, there is no separating philosophy from poetry. One can only translate one into the other. Philosophy as art denotes philosophy in novel and fresh forms of expression. This does not correspond with total translation, particularly as philosophy demands translation into art. The task of translation shall be carried out at university which is, according to Schelling, the institute of translation whose primary function is translation of original (divine) absolute knowledge into the intuitions of human consciousness. Certainly Derrida fulfilled this principle of translation along a trail winding between philosophy and poetry.

5. Derrida is of course referring to Benjamin's "Arcade project," his uncompleted study of the development of the urban arcade as expression of early capitalism.

6. In *Schibboleth* (1986c) we again encounter Babel, this time by means of an analysis of the poems of Paul Celan: "And the sight of earth, ours / Is / And none of us is sent / Down / To you / Babel." Derrida reads Babel as propagation and migration of languages, multiplicity and wandering, even within language (52). Babel is the last word in the poem, its address and destination; simultaneously, it is the place to which nothing is sent ("none of us is sent"). This is a reference to the duality of lingual connection and disconnection arising out of the myth of the Tower of Babel.

7. Bennington, *Jacques Derrida*, 157.

8. Ibid., 158.

10. Ruins

1. It should be noted that Derrida even depicted the structure of the book in terms of a vista of desolation: "52 very uneven sections, like crypts scattered over an unidentified field . . . being like a wilderness . . . or like a field of ruins and mines and pits and caverns and tombstones and scattered seeds; but the field is unidentified, not even like a world" (54).

2. Walter Benjamin, *Reflections*, pt. 2, trans. David Singer (Tel Aviv: 1996), 15, 22–24. Retranslated here from the Hebrew.

3. In his analysis of the American Bill of Rights (*Otobiographies* [1984b]) Derrida sought the authority for the proclamation, ultimately locating it (after Jefferson, the people's elected representatives, the people, and Nature) in God.

4. See Irene Harvey, "Derrida and the Issues of Exemplarity," in *Derrida, A Critical Reader*, ed. D. Wood (Oxford: Blackwell, 1992), 201.

5. Ibid., 266

11. The Fire

1. The French *feu* denotes a person's demise, like the English phrase "the late." The title *Feu, la cendre* thus stresses the dimension of death contained within the concept of fire, along with ashes as sign of death.

2. In his *De l'esprit, Heidegger, et la question* (1987a) Derrida cites Heidegger's study of a Georg Trakl poem whose theme, inter alia, is "the burning flame of spirit." Trakl comprehends the spirit as fire, not as "air" (*pneuma*). The nature of the spirit is its autoeffective spontaneity, which requires nothing extraneous to enter into the fiery flames. The spirit endows and takes fire, for better or for worse. The spirit-fire extends beyond itself so as to illuminate, while simultaneously consuming everything into white ashes (124).

3. Granted, at the end of his *Politique de l'amitié* (1994b), Derrida would refer to Heidegger's Heraclitus Seminar, but with the stress on the concept of "debate" and its relationship with the concept of "war."

4. See M. Heidegger, *Early Greek Thinking* [New York: Harper and Row, 1975], 90.

5. This is how we would read the following: "[T]he Torah that the Almighty granted to Moses gave him white fire embossed in black fire, that is the fire enclosed in fire hewn from fire and engulfed in fire, as it is written: 'from his right hand went a fiery law for them.'" ("Jerusalem Talmud," Shekalim, chap. 6); "The Torah was given in flames of fire, and everything in it is fire and written in white fire upon black fire, and the letters float and rise into the air" ("Zohar," Pikudei, 226, B).

6. "Likutey Moharan," pt. 1, 82.

7. For a discussion of fire and Judaism, see below in the chapter titled "Derrida's *Ruah*."

12. Derrida's Sacrificial Offering

1. See "The Sacrifice of Isaac in Israeli Art," catalogue, Museum of Israeli Art, Ramat Gan, 1987; reprinted in my *Hanging Gardens* (Jerusalem: Omanut-Israel, 1991).

13. Derrida's *Ruah*

1. Still, much of Derrida's thought can be traced in his readings of Husserl (e.g., his 1967 *La voix et la phénomène*) where concepts of representation and absence are discussed with all their future Derridean significance. Thus Husserl's claim that the unity of being and presence could be preserved in speech only, and thus Husserl's statement: "Only when communication is suspended can pure expression appear" (*Speech and Phenomena,* trans. David B. Allison [Evanston, Ill.: Northwestern Univ. Press, 1973], 38). Tracking Derrida's philosophical roots in Husserl, while admitting Derrida's stronger affinities with Heidegger, means tracing another parricidal father-son relationship in Derrida's work. The "father" (Husserl) is relatively hiding,

whereas the "son" (Heidegger) comes forth. At the same time, the Jewishness of Husserl precedes (and nourishes) Heidegger's non-Jewishness, thus securing a hidden Jewish root of Derridean thought. After all, much of our Jewish interpretation of Derrida's writings can be applied to Husserl's ideas as set forth by Derrida.

2. Derrida's interest in the subject appears to have been whetted by Victor Farías's *Heidegger et le Nazism,* (Paris: Verdier, 1987).

14. Judaism and Death

1. See, for example, the chapter titled "The Gift of Death" in the anthology *L'éthique du don* (The ethics of giving), eds. Jean-Michel Rabbaté and Michael Wetzel (Paris: Metailie-Transition, 1992). In this chapter, Derrida draws deductions from the concept of death to an ethical outlook.

15. Jerusalem

1. The concept, originating in chapter 3 ("Beyond the Verse") in Lévinas's book *L'au-delà du verset* (1982), is applied by Derrida in philosophical and practical terms to the city-of-sanctuary project established for writers in Europe and the United States. See also his address in the booklet *Cosmopolites de tous les pays, encore un effort!* [Paris: Galilee, 1997).

2. In respect of this insight, Derrida concedes his debt to Michal Govrin's *Chant d'outre tombe (Adieu,* 185, n. 1).

3. These insights are well expressed in the passage already quoted in the chapter on "Judaism and Death": "At stake first of all is that which takes the original form of a return of the religious, whether fundamentalist or not, and which overdetermines all questions of nation, state, international law, human rights, Bill of Rights—in short, everything that concentrates its habitat in the at least symptomatic figure of Jerusalem. . . . One may deem strange, strangely familiar and inhospitable at the same time (*unheimlich* [uncanny]) this figure of absolute hospitality whose promise one would choose to entrust to an experience that is so impossible. . . . Some, and I do not exclude myself, will find this despairing 'messianism' has a curious taste, a taste of death" (*Spectres de Marx* [1993d], 167–69).

16. Facing Lévinas

1. See, for example, his lectures at the Jewish teachers' college in Paris, "Essay on Judaism" (1963); "Four lessons in Talmud" (1968); "Five New Lessons in Talmud" (1977), etc. (Lévinas, *Nine Talmudic Readings,* tr. Annette Aronowitz [Bloomington: Indiana Univ. Press, 1990]).

2. See Zeev Levy, *The Other and Responsibility* (Jerusalem: Magness Press, 1997). Here the reader will find an extensive and instructive chapter on the Lévinas-Derrida relationship. With that, it should be stressed that the present chapter was written prior to publication of Prof. Z. Levy's contribution to the subject.

3. Similarly, a few pages later Derrida wrote: "Here we have his dislocation. . . . It remarks with each atom of his Utterance a remarkable outburst of uttering, of an uttering which is no longer an infinite present but already a past of trace, a performance (of) something utterly different" (191).

4. See Susan A. Handelman, *Fragments of Redemption* (Bloomington: Univ. of Indiana Press, 1994), 179.

5. See R. Kearny, *Dialogues with Contemporary Continental Thinkers* (Manchester: Univ. of Manchester Press, 1984), 123.

6. Likewise, Derrida's critique of Hegel, published in *Glas* (1974), and his identification of dialectics as the tyranny of the identical, of the similar, of the narcissism of one who, locked within himself, forever returns to himself—are all guided by the Otherness principle.

7. Handelman, *Fragments of Redemption,* 340.

8. Derrida's consideration of the concept of love depicts it in Lévinasian terms as follows: awareness of my unity with the Other to a degree that I am no longer by myself, rather bringing myself to my self-knowledge, elevating my being unto myself by my unity with the Other and the unity of the Other with me. Love rests upon my reluctance to persist in being an autonomous being unto itself; and love fulfills itself in the Other, through whom I know myself. "I find in the Other that which I lose in myself" (*Glas* [1974], 25). But, paradoxically, love eliminates Otherness, leaving only unity (ibid., 76).

9. Handelman, *Fragments of Redemption,* 264.

18. The Sublime of the Jews

1. Johann Gottfried Herder, "On the spirit in Hebrew Poetry"; this passage translated from the Hebrew, trans. Yosef Hauben-Nevo, (Tel Aviv, 1994), 50.

2. *Critique of Judgment* [re-translated from the Hebrew], trans. S. H. Bergman and N. Rotenstreich (Jerusalem: Mosad Bialik, 1960), 93.

3. Ibid., 97–98.

4. Re-translated from the Hebrew, from the chapter on "Symbolism of the sublime" in Hegel's *Lectures in Aesthetics.*

5. Ibid.

6. For more on the visual regard in Derrida's philosophy, see Martin Jay, *Downcast Eyes* (Berkeley and Los Angeles: Univ. of California Press, 1993), 493–523.

7. Re-translated from the Hebrew. Geoffrey H. Hartman, *Saving the Text* (Baltimore: Johns Hopkins Univ. Press, 1981), 17.

8. The interview was part of a special project of Yad Vashem (Jerusalem's Holocaust memorial institute). It was published in Hebrew in *Teoria Vebikoret* (Theory and Criticism), no. 15 (winter 1999): 5–17.

9. *Faut-il pardonner?* (Paris: Edition Aubier-Montaigne, 1967) and *L'impreciptible: Pardonner?; dans L'honneur et la dignite* (Paris: Editions de Seuil, 1986).

Epilogue: Philosophy and Judaism

1. On the aspect of the trek in the desert, which Edmond Jabès specified in detail, see the chapter titled "The Other *Kippa*"; and/or the aspect of refugee, crossing borders, the chapter titled "Shibboleth of Evil."

2. Gershom Scholem, *Elements of the Kabbalah and Its Symbols,* (Jerusalem: Mosad Bialik, 1977), 108. [translated from the Hebrew].

3. Introduction to "Jewish Artists," ed. M. Buber (Berlin: Jüdischer Verlag, 1903) [translated from the Hebrew].

4. See above, the chapter titled "L'autre *Kippa*."

Appendix: The Black Academy

1. Aristotle, "Metaphysics," in *The Basic Works of Aristotle,* ed. Richard McKeon, (New York: Random House, 1941), 689.

2. Ibid.

3. Aristotle, "On the Soul," in *Basic Works,* 575.

4. George Steiner, *Martin Heidegger* (London, 1978).

5. David Shimoni, *The Book of Idylls* (Hebrew) (Tel Aviv: Masada, 1956), 21–22.

6. *The Portable Enlightenment Reader,* ed. Isaac Kramnick (New York: Penguin, 1995), 25.

Selected Works by Jacques Derrida

1962   Husserl, Edmund. *L'origine de la géometrie,* translated with an introduction by Jacques Derrida. Paris: PUF.

1967a   *De la grammatologie.* Paris: Éditions de Minuit.

1967b   *L'écriture et la différence.* Paris: Seuil.

1967c   *La voix et le phénomène.* Paris: PUF.

1972a   *La dissémination.* Paris: Seuil.

1972b   *Marges de la philosophie.* Paris: Éditions de Minuit.

1972c   *Positions.* Paris: Éditions de Minuit.

1974   *Glas.* Paris: Éditions Galilée.

1975   *Économimesis: Mimesis des articulations.* Paris: Aubier-Flammarion.

1976   *L'archéologie du frivole.* Paris: Denoël/Gonthier.

1978a   *Éperons: Les styles de Nietzsche.* Paris: Flammarion.

1978b   *La verité en peinture.* Paris: Flammarion.

1980   *La carte postale.* Paris: Flammarion.

1982   *L'oreille de l'autre: Textes et débats.* Edited by C. Levesque and C. McDonald. Montreal: VLB.

1984a   *D'un ton apocalyptique adopté naguère en philosophie.* Paris: Éditions Galilée.

1984b   *Otobiographies: L'enseignement de Nietzsche et la politique du nom propre.* Paris: Éditions Galilée.

1985a   *Lecture de droit de regards,* de M. F. Plissart, photographer. Paris: Éditions de Minuit.

1985b   "Préjugées: Devant la loi." In *Faculté de juger.* Paris: Éditions de Minuit.

1986a   *Forcener le subjectile: Étude pour les dessins et portraits d'Antonin Artaud.* Paris: Gallimard.

1986b   *Parages.* Paris: Éditions Galilée.

1986c   *Schibboleth pour Paul Celan.* Paris: Éditions Galilée.

1987a   *De l'esprit, Heidegger. et la question.* Paris: Éditions Galilée.

1987b   *Feu, la cendre.* Paris: Des Femmes.

1987c   *Psyché: Inventions de l'autre.* Paris: Éditions Galilée.

1987d   *Ulysse gramophone.* Paris: Éditions Galilée.

1987e   "Des Tours de Babel," in *Psyché* (Paris: Galilée, 1987), 203–35.

1988a   *Mémoires: Pour Paul de Man*. Paris: Éditions Galilée.
1988b   *Signéponge*. Paris: Seuil.
1990a   *Du droit à la philosophie*. Paris: Éditions Galilée.
1990b   *Le problème de la genèse dans la philosophie de Husserl*. Paris: PUF.
1990c   *Limited, Inc*. Paris: Éditions Galilée.
1990d   "Kant, le juif, l'allemand." In *Phénomènologie et politique*. Brussels: Ousia.
1990e   *Mémoires d'aveugle*. Paris: Louvre.
1991a   *Circonfession: Jacques Derrida par Geoffrey Bennington*. Paris: Seuil.
1991b   *Donner le temps: La fausse monnaie*. Paris: Éditions Galilée.
1991c   *L'autre cap*. Paris: Éditions de Minuit.
1992   "Donner la mort." In *L'ethique du don* (Colloque). Paris: Metailie-Transition.
1993a   *Khôra*. Paris: Éditions Galilée.
1993b   *Passions*. Paris: Éditions Galilée.
1993c   *Sauf le nom*. Paris: Éditions Galilée.
1993d   *Spectres de Marx*. Paris: Éditions Galilée.
1994a   *Force de loi*. Paris: Éditions Galilée.
1994b   *Politique de l'amitié*. Paris: Éditions Galilée.
1995a   *Mal d'archive*. Paris: Éditions Galilée.
1995b   *Moscou aller-retour*. Paris: Éditions de l'Aube.
1996a   *Apories*. Paris: Éditions Galilée.
1996b   *La religion* (avec Gianni Vattimo). Paris: Seuil.
1996c   *Le monolinguisme de l'autre*. Paris: Éditions Galilée.
1996d   *Lignées*. William Blake.
1996e   *Résistances de la psychanalyse*. Paris: Éditions Galilée.
1997a   *Adieu*. Paris: Éditions Galilée.
1997b   *De l'hospitalité* (avec Anne Dufourmantelle). Paris: Calman-Lévy.
1998a   *Demeure*. Paris: Éditions Galilée.
1998b   *Voiles*. Paris: Éditions Galilée.
1999   "L'animal que done je suis." In *L'animal autobiographique: Autour de Jacques Derrida*. Paris: Éditions Galilée.
2000   *La contre-allé*, in collaboration with Catherine Malebou. Paris: La Quinzaine Littéraire-Louis Vuitton.
2000   *Le toucher: Jean-Luc Nancy*. Paris: Éditions Galilée.

Index

Page numbers with the form 178n. 3.1 indicate notes where 178 is the page, 3 represents the chapter, and 1 is the end note number.

114; language of, 73; lingual essence
of, 69; morality and, 109; as name
giver, 100; names of, 56–58, 70–71;
Otherness of, 137; place of, 63–67;
prayer and, 57; as principle of inclusion, 64; representation of, 148;
revealed in fire, 100–101; ruins and,
82–83; rupture within, 81, 135; self-
concealment of, 37, 80, 104, 108, 118,
124, 132, 135, 149; self-definition of,
27; separation from, 156, 159; Tower
of Babel and, 68; as writer, 114–15
Golden Bough (Frazer), 175
goodness, 52, 107, 135, 182–83n. 6.2
Guide for the Perplexed (Maimonedes), 64, 70
Gulf War, 109

Habermas, Jürgen, 62
Haezrachi, Pepita, 65
Handelman, Susan, 62, 134, 138, 177–
78n. 1.10
Hartman, Geoffrey, 151
Hassidim, 7
Hebrew language, 17
Hebron massacre, 110
Hegel, Georg Wilhelm Frederich: circular
course concept of, 3, 10; concept of
God, 88–89; concept of sublime of,
147; dialectic of, 10, 136; on Holy of
Holies, 148; on inauguration of society,
47–48; on Judaism, 61; Judaization of
Kant, 114; on natural religion, 96;
Nietzsche's Jew and, 50; notion of
God, 106–7; on philosophy, 160–61;
spirit concept of, 116–17; on the sublime, 145, 148–49, 151; on truth/
light, 53; on unity of opposites, 138;
view of self-sacrifice, 125
Heidegger, Martin: death theme and, 30,
55, 121–24; duality of earth/world,
34; on existence-death relationship, 22;
as father *ruah,* 118; fire theme and,
99–100; on Greek sources, 135; and
the Holocaust, 151–52; on homelessness, 67; influence on Derrida, 2; on
intelligence, 168; on last god, 38; on
logos, 55–59; nationalism and, 27–28;

on philosophy/theology, 35–36, 115;
on reason, 169, 170–71; on university,
174; wandering and, 35; on writing, 172
Hellenism: founded on Judaism, 26;
Heidegger and, 27; Judaism vs., 133,
135, 137–38, 141
Henich, Micaëla, 82–83, 149
Heraclitus, 99–100
Herder, Johann Gottfried, 145
here-there relationship, 90–91
heterogeneity, 31, 155, 156–57, 180n. 4.1
history: vs. fiction, 74; place of, 90; purpose
of, 40; in ruins, 85; violence and, 87
holocaust, 151–52; of the academy, 174;
ashes as memory of, 124; of Book of
Esther, 73, 75, 78–80; dates and, 25;
God and, 88–89; in Jewish poetry, 150;
truth in, 93; writing and, 94–95. *See
also* ashes; fire
Holocaust, 151–52; denial of, 180–81n.
4.6; effect on fraternity, 140; Germany
psyche during, 179n. 3.8; God and,
88–89; *shibboleth* and, 122; as the Sublime of the Jews, 151; universalization
of, 25; witnesses to, 29
Holy of Holies, 61, 148
hospitality: Abraham and, 133; Derridian
concept of, 122–23, 127, 142–44; ethical value of, 180n. 4.1; Jerusalem and,
186n. 15.3; Judaism and, 50; messianism and, 41–42, 125; place of, 130;
political asylum and, 19–20
"How Not to Speak" (Derrida), 56, 84–
85, 128–29
human spirit, 10
Husserl, Edmund, 135

iconoclasm, 180n. 4.3
Idel, Moshe, 14
identity: circumcision and, 22; of Derrida,
4–5, 31–32; fulfillment of, 37; of Jews,
33, 124, 179n. 3.3; language and, 16–
17; of original, 51; self-denial and, 30–
31; as source of Derrida's work, 3; of
Yerushalmi, 22
imagination, 147, 171, 184n. 8.4
injury. *See* wound

place: of beauty, 173; of Bezalel Academy, 170; of dreams, 59; of eternity, 57; of God, 156; of hospitality, 130; of Jews, 129; of Judaism, 180n. 4.4; *khôra* as, 105; of law, 60; of poet, 129; as promise, 35; of religious experience, 34; of sacrifice, 109; of secret, 56–57; of truth, 60, 63–67; of visitation, 144; of worship, 83. *See also* desert; *khôra*

Plato: dispute with, 7; on memory, 156; on mystics, 58; on place, 64; on writing/logos, 52

Plato's "academy", 172–73

pneuma, 118–20. *See also* ghost; *ruah*

Poe, Edgar Allan, 63, 75, 78

poetry, 31–32, 111, 148–50, 184n. 8.4

poets, 24, 35, 81

Politique de l'amitié (Derrida), 140–41

"Postman of Truth, The" (Derrida), 63

prayer, 57

Prayers and Tears of Jacques Derrida, The (Caputo), 155

prayer shawl. *See talith*

principle of general reason, 4. *See also* reason

principle of inclusion, 64, 66–67

principle of negation, 57

Principle of Reason (Heidegger), 168

principle of self-destruction, 57

principle of subjective individual, 4

prostitution, 20

Pseudo-Dionysius, 56

Psyché (Derrida), 55, 68

psychoanalysis, 21–22, 182n. 5.1, 183n. 6.4

"Purloined Letter, The" (Poe), 63, 75, 78

pyramid, 96–97, 171

Question au judaïsme (Weber), 33

reason: imagination and, 147; principle of, 169, 170, 172; religion and, 35–36; unification by, 47–48

regard, 150

religion: authority and, 77–78; in Book of Esther, 80; death and, 106; death/

rebirth of, 117; development of, 96; duality of, 106–7; essence of, 110; place of, 34; reason and, 35–36; sacrifice and, 107–10, 125–26; writing and, 77

Religion, La (Derrida), 34

religion as, 129

Résistances de la psychanalyse (Derrida): on dreams, 59; on duality, 106; on father figure, 103; on Otherness, 51; on traits of deconstruction, 55

responsibility: hospitality and, 143; sacrifice as, 107, 125; speech and, 108; violence and, 139

Return of the Book (Jabès), 92–102

Revelation of St. John, 56

Righteous, The (Lyotard), 60–61

romanticism, 84

Rosenzweig, Franz, 25, 26

ruah, 112–20. *See also* spirit

ruins: death theme and, 121; identified, 81; Jerusalem as, 84–85; in the path to God, 81–91; sketches as, 82–83. *See also* abyss; death; desert; holocaust; *khôra*

sacrifice, 107–10, 125–26, 158–59

sanctity, 36, 126

Sartre, Jean-Paul, 22

Sauf le nom (Derrida), 28, 55, 115–16

Saussure, Ferdinand de, 147

Savior (Cixoux), 155

Schatz, Boris, 170

Schibboleth (Derrida), 20, 23

Scholem, Gershom, 14, 66, 161

seal ring, 77–78

secret: of absent foreskin, 46; ash as, 94–95; centrality of, 112; of Derrida, 157; duality of, 108, 183n. 6.4; of father figure, 105–6; of fire, 168–69; as Kabbalist term, 13; *khôra* as, 67, 104–5; mystics and, 58; in negative theology, 56–59; of psychoanalysis/Judaism, 38; of *talith,* 158; university and, 171

Sefer Ha-Bahir, 66

self-concealment: as deceit, 135; of God, 37, 80, 104, 108, 118, 132, 135; oblivion and, 99–100